Memoirs of a Keeper: Angels & Demons

Copyright © November 30, 2020 by Erin Marie Harrison

ISBN Print: 9798574306932

Memoirs of a Keeper may be purchased at special quantity discounts. Resale opportunities are available for Bible Studies, Sunday School, Churches, gifts, fund raising, book clubs, and premiums.
Visit http://www.keeperofthehomestead.com/ for information on this and other products produced by Homesteading Productions LLC

Requests for special discounts or general information can be emailed to Mark Harrison homesteadproductions@gmail.com. Written requests to:

Mark Harrison
Homesteading Productions LLC
Primm Springs, TN

All scripture quotations are taken from the King James Holy Bible.

ALL RIGHTS RESERVED. This book contains material protected under International and Federal Copyright Laws and Treaties. Any unauthorized reprint or use of this material is prohibited. No part of this book may be reproduced or transmitted in any form or by any means, electronic or mechanical, including photocopying, recording, or by any information storage and retrieval system without express written permission from the contributing writer or the publisher except in the case of brief quotations embodied in critical articles and reviews.

This publication is designed to provide accurate and authoritative information in regard to the subject matter covered. It is sold with the understanding that the author, contributing writers or the publisher is not engaged in rendering counseling, or any other type of professional services. If counseling or other expert assistance is required, the services of a competent professional should be sought. All names have been changed to protect the characters within the book.

I. Harrison, Erin II. Memoirs of a Keeper: Angels & Demons

Cover design by Erin Harrison
Interior design and layout by Erin Harrison
Edited by Jessica Heck Faidley
Printed in the United States of America

MEMOIRS
of a Keeper

ERIN MARIE HARRISON

INTRODUCTION

About ten years ago, I felt an urgency to write my story, my whole life story. Many times I would start typing it out, and I would stop because I didn't want to write the bad parts. I desired the chronicle to be fun and happy. It seemed to me that I needed to write it down if it could help others out there who were struggling to find their way in the same ways I did. My life was nothing of the ordinary. It was always a test for me to see if I could get back up every time I was knocked down. There were times I thought I would kill myself with forces so evil that seemed to get into my very soul to destroy me. Some stories along the journey were hard to tell because they seemed so unbelievable that anyone reading it would think I made it up. But I didn't. You see, I have had a crazy life, and it is a story that I ran away from because I cared more about what people thought about me than what God did.

I ran away because I was scared to tell stories that might offend people or estrange my loved ones. After all, sadly, the truth is that no matter who you are, you will let someone down. My goal in writing this book is to reveal the REALITY of God and show that no matter who you are, what you have done, what others have done to you, God remains the same. I changed all names of all people in the story to protect the reputations and privacy of others. I kept little records of dealings with people along the way to illustrate the way that it frequently is the little foxes that spoil the vine. People can't always relate to the crazy stories I have to share, but they can relate to having a hard time dealing with people. Those little misunderstandings can be the very things that destroy relationships, marriages, and life itself. Navigating through rejection, hurt, and betrayal are things all people must face one time or another this side of heaven, and I aim to show you how, through the grace of God and humility, there are ways to restore peace among those for whom you care.

I decided that I would be made a fool for His sake. My life is not mine anyway, and if God wants to use these stories to show people that they are not alone, that He is always listening and working even when we don't tune into it, I have to be willing to lay my own life before His throne. I can't keep my story for myself because it has the power to set others free. There is power in our testimony.

"And they overcame him by the blood of the Lamb,
and by the word of their testimony;
and they loved not their lives unto the death."
Revelation 12:11

He takes all of the things that happen in our lives, and he gives us opportunities to learn and grow from them and then show others the way. It took me too many years wandering around in life, making some of the same mistakes, playing the fool, and putting too much value on what others thought of me to find out who I was in Christ and what my purpose was. This book is the reality of life; the ins and outs, the raw stories of failing, finding joy in all of life's crazy ordeals, while learning to relate to God in a world that seems so unfriendly at times.

It has been many years of me chasing dreams to watch those same dreams crumble before my eyes and still NEVER GIVE UP. It is incredible to live long enough to understand that people will let you down no matter who they are, yet God NEVER WILL.

I don't write this book to have a pity party because what would be the point? We hear enough tragedy and despair in the world to know terrible things happen. The sad part is that often we are left there. We don't get to know the people behind the stories we hear. What happened next? Did the pain cause the person to drink or commit suicide? Did their struggle end in divorce or quitting? People want to know how to get out of the pit, and they are sick of feeling worthless or ashamed. Many suppress pain by distraction, while others just go around numb. They want to find purpose but do not know where to start or how to achieve real joy. Life is a series of choices. The same is true for all—we all want to be happy and find inner peace.

People hurt people. I have hurt people. None of us are perfect. We all do what is within our strength to the best of our ability. We all have our journey and our way of perceiving things. What is hurtful to one is humorous to another. As we journey through life, we will have breaches in communication and relationships. There are things we will regret and things that are done to us by others that can affect us for a lifetime. Parents have children and never know all the best things to do. My parents did the best they could at the time, and they loved me in a way that I did not always understand nor appreciate. I was self-destructive, and no matter how much my parents tried or anyone tried to reach me, I was lost.

There is hope. My relationship with my parents is so precious to me today. I hate writing about some of the stories that estranged me from them, but I write them for you. I don't write because I am mad or hurting to get my feelings out on paper. No. I write because if you can read through to the end, you will see a picture of redemption. You will find that God redeems me from everything that was meant to destroy me. Instead of burning bridges, God healed relationships and made them beautiful. My joy is so overflowing. I have found inner peace. I may have gotten lost along the way, as you will read, but I charted a course that not many dare to travel. I found real joy and genuine faith that nothing this life can throw at me will take away. It is unshakable.

I spent my life striving for ways to redefine myself; to find where I fit. I discovered through the course of life that I could not belong anywhere but to heaven itself. I never could, nor ever will, understand how people can be so exclusive and so cruel. The ability to find joy in unfortunate circumstances, finding beauty in a sea of ugliness, finding hope in moments of utter despair and love in reproach is something I have chosen. There is a great deal of pain to be told to realize the beauty that came out of it. Understanding the depth, the breadth, the height of God's love, and how I fit into His picture has come piece by piece. It is nothing that could be learned in one moment, for it takes many trips into the valley to realize the depth, many challenging climbs up the mountain to know the height and a lifetime of stretching one to their breaking point to grasp the breadth of this mysterious love: the love of God.

Memoirs of a Keeper: Angels & Demons

Chapter One
THE BIRTH & THE AWAKENING

*O*ne cold November morning in the year of 1976, birth pains came to a young mother. Be it, boy or girl; the name would be the same—Erin. The sweaty brown curls stuck to her face as she heaved, and her hands gripped the metal bars of the hospital bed. The doctor came in to check with a cigarette hanging off the side of his mouth; he tells her that it won't be long until she meets her baby.

Barely twenty-two, Mom lay in wait of her second child. In actuality, this would be her third child. My brother, Ian, was born two years before in Southern California, where Mom and Dad got married. Dad had his first teaching job out there.

Six years before, Mom gave birth to a baby out of wedlock. She was just a child herself. The baby girl she had only ten days after her 16th birthday was ripped from her. It was like something from her very soul was torn away that day, something that could never be redeemed. Having a baby so young was a shame in those days. She was forbidden to go to church or school, and her family felt it was a disgrace. I can see it all now in my mind as I try to imagine the moment she birthed my sister, whom I barely know today.

Mom wanted the baby. Everything in her mind told her that she was too young, too inexperienced, and too bad to be a mother. Her long life of self-loathing started the moment she signed off her rights to that child on the adoption papers. It was final. Weeks before the birth, she had made her mind up. There was no turning back. She loved the unborn child so much that she felt true love was to let go and allow the child to be raised by someone in a better situation. It was the most unselfish thing she ever did. She wanted the best for the child growing in her womb. Just a girl herself, she couldn't possibly understand the magnitude of this decision that would impact the rest of her life.

A long-winded, gnashing grunt pressed against the urge to push and the urge to hold on, for fear of losing something sacred. The sound of life's first breath, and then a cry that would haunt Mom for a lifetime. Melissa. Melissa was what Mom called her. Mom watched as the nurses grabbed the slippery girl, muffling the cries for her mother as they wrapped her gently in cloth to keep her warm. Mom never got to hold her sweet baby girl. There she sat with a broken, tear-stained face and eyes staring into the deep corners of the room as they marched out with the swaddled child.

While they waited for the adoptive mother to come to whisk the child into a loving family, Mom just peered through the glass of the nursery. Tears streamed down her face as her breasts filled with milk, begging to feed her baby. It took the strength of a thousand men to keep her behind the glass, to keep her from changing her mind. She knew the fight in her heart to take the baby would disappoint everyone. She had to be firm against what nature was urging her to do. All-day and all night, she stood there, like a person who was stripped of everything and left to die, just cold and waiting for a miracle, a miracle for facts to change like age, position, and acceptance, which were as immovable as the glass.

Some days Dad gazed through the glass with her, longing to raise her with his childhood sweetheart, but in those times, adoption was something they felt forced to choose. Putting his arm around Mom could not ease her pain. The day came when she was asked to go back to her room. When she returned to the glass, the baby was gone. Like a shooting star that you gaze and marvel at, just glittering across the sky for a moment and then gone, the glory of new life disappeared. The sight of that empty baby bed shuts out the light of a young mother's heart. It was the pain of this moment that drew my parents closer. They ended up getting married some years later when they were both finished

The Birth & The Awakening

with school. They welcomed my brother nearly a year after.

Time passed, and Mom's heart longed for that little girl, an ache that nothing could fill. Well, that cold November morning in '76, a small cry broke the silence of her heart, and the doctor proclaimed, "It's a girl!" Dad sat there in awe, tears streaming down his face, for God had given them another baby girl.

Dad was a band director for the high school. Mom was a nurse. We lived in a very humble home, nothing fancy. My childhood was challenging in a lot of ways. I remember so many things from a very early age. My parents were both born and raised in Wisconsin; each was the youngest of five children. I am sure they did not have an easy life either, so it gives me some perspective on why they allowed things into my life that really should not have been. Drinking was a big thing in their families. It was a way that the hard farm-working people would unwind and feel a sense of community. Going to the tavern was just what the family would do after "church." It was a part of the culture and the times that my parents grew up in. My great-grandfather owned two saloons downtown, and the other great-grandfather owned a small tavern. One family was the "high-class drinkers," and the other was considered the "trash," a cultural divide.

They were hard-working farmers and tradesmen. My aunt Tess remembers fetching beer by the pail-full. Raising kids, making ends meet, and even as poor as they were, the beer would flow like a river. All the people would drown themselves in it, and, in like manner, my parents carried the torch; the tradition. All holidays and birthdays were grand parties, loud with laughter and bursting at the gills with as much beer as any could ever need, often graced with beer by the kegs.

At these "get-togethers," the kids would run wild while the parents would wildly indulge. We would play in a torrential river for fun. It is a wonder how we all survived with no adult supervision on a raging river. It was the Fox River, and it reeked down there where we played from the paper mills that employed a good portion of our community. It smelled strongly of Sulphur as I recall. When we weren't trying to cross the river on the rocks that poked through the current, we were begging parents for sleepovers with the cousins. Smoke-filled basements, cussing, and laughter was all a part of the scene. I could part the thick clouds of smoke with my hands, and every breath felt nauseatingly heavy—a suffocating feeling. Just thinking of it makes me want to run outside and breathe the fresh air in. I still hate the smell of smoke.

When you are a kid, you do not have a choice. If your parents smoke, well, you have to smoke, too, secondhand. Your parents shape you into their life; you go along for the ride. A parent could be religious and pious and could take their children to hell with that, too. My parents boycotted the church thing because it was just an empty religious activity for them growing up. None of the God stuff was real to them, so they did not see the point in going through the empty motions of sitting in the big Catholic churches rubbing the beads on a cheap ten-cent rosary. The church folks were into partying, heavy partying, so what was the point? I can't blame them for that kind of reasoning. Many paths lead to hell, and few people find the path that leads to life. Hell is colored in so many different packages. It can be wrapped up in a pretty-looking package with the cookie-cutter family dressed in their finest, or it looks like plain old trash. My family must have fit in there somewhere in between.

My parents grew up in the same town through that cultural divide. Dad was nineteen, and mom only fifteen. He was a lifeguard at the local swimming pool, and when he saw my cute little mother swimming, he was very attracted to her. Mom was about five feet, one and full of vigor. He was a budding music man. Mom finally fell for him when she heard him playing a romantic song on the piano. They were star-crossed lovers, young and striving for what we all are after—a happy life together. It's sad because Dad's mom rejected the girl he loved. She called her "Bouleau Hill Trash." When Grandma found out she was pregnant, she told mom, "If you keep that baby, you will ruin my son's life!" Mom didn't want to ruin anyone's life. People-pleasing became one of Mom's greatest talents after that day. She owned her label nearly her entire life, feeling like she didn't deserve happiness. Giving up that baby was the most selfless act she ever did, seeking to help save everyone but herself. The rest of her life would be Mom just trying to keep from drowning in her sea of pain.

After years of Mom trying to prove herself, she was known by my pious grandmother as a "Rose among thorns." As I sit here and try to wonder what Mom had to go through being pregnant and shamed, I grieve. I can understand why having another girl was a double-edged sword. I could never replace what she felt forced to relinquish.

My earliest memories are of living in a small rural town. Mom worked, so she sent us kids off to the babysitter. She tells me horror stories of when she would pick me up, and how I would scream in pain. It was unusual for me to cry. Mom said I was the most well-natured baby, but I was the most homely-looking baby she ever saw. She recalls moments after my birth talking to the other mothers saying how beautiful their babies were, and she would just laugh and say her baby was so homely and "a face only a mother could love." I sometimes wondered if my sister was born pretty.

The babysitter spanked me for wetting my diaper at only two years old. Mom said I was black and blue from my neck to my legs. When she would set me down, I would cry. Somehow, she brought me back there. I am sure it was because she had no other option, and I can't remember it anyhow. The babysitter must have had a screw loose because who would beat a baby for peeing their diaper? It's madness. I am glad I can't remember that. Mom did tell me she didn't want to keep bringing me there. I guess she figured out a different lady to watch us. I think her name was Darla. She was so kind. I still remember Darla. She was a farm girl, big and strapping.

Mom said I was a fat baby, a fat and happy baby who loved to eat. I would wave my little chubby hands when I saw a spoon coming in my direction like a baby bird waiting for a worm. Dad called me "Lumpy" because I was like a little lump on a log. Mom once brought me into the doctor because she thought I was mentally handicapped. The doctor looked at her while my brother was pulling all the cups out of the holder in the office and said, "Just be glad she is not as hyper as your son! There is nothing wrong with your daughter; she is just contented."

It wasn't long before I found my voice. I used to scream at the top of my lungs and learned how to use my voice to get my brother in trouble at a very early age. Mom or Dad would run to my rescue, and eventually, I wore out my ability to get their attention like the old story about the little boy who cried wolf. Soon, my cries were just another manipulation, and my voice was silenced, another mountain out of a molehill and an exaggerated truth. My words were of no consequence.

Mom and Dad say that we were "dirt poor." Mom would wrap little cheap things like a small box of crayons and a coloring book, among other things, and put them under our little Christmas tree. She wanted us to have a lovely Christmas, and they could only afford a few items. When you break up those few items into different packages, it makes it look like you have a lot of presents to open. Mom never wanted us to feel inferior. There is a difference in knowing you are poor, and feeling like you are poor. You can know you don't have money but still feel rich.

Christmas was a massive deal for Mom and her "Ma." She called her mother, Ma, and her dad was Pa. I called her Grandma Reichel. Her name was Julia, and she was a full-blooded Hollander. They called her "Blackie" because she had the blackest hair for a Dutch girl. She was the oldest of fourteen kids, and her dad was a drunk who was very physically abusive to her mother. She told me how she had to hide the small children when her dad was drunk and violent. I think Christmas was everyone's way to brush the past away with glitter and magic. Christmas was like magic for me. It was that one day out of the entire year to see miracles happen. Getting dolls each year was like a miracle for me. I could have my little doll to carry around and dress. My dolls always slept in bed with me. As a Christmas gift, Grandma would sometimes sew my little doll a dress. That was so special.

The only scary part I remember about Christmas was when Mom would tell us that St. Nick would get angry and pound on our window at night if we did not clean up our rooms. When I was four years old, Mom told me, "You better watch out, better not pout, 'cause St. Nick is coming, and he knows your room is a mess. You both might be getting coal this year!" I quickly ran to my room and started picking up when I heard a pound on the window. I didn't want to look up. I was so scared as I darted for my closet. The light was on in my room, but I laid as low as my closet would allow. I was hoping and praying that St. Nick was not at my window, yet something inside me had to know. The pounding proceeded for a long time until I peeked through the crack in my sliding closet door.

There he was, St. Nick with an angry face hitting his fist on the window. I heard him say in a gruff voice, "Clean your room!" I never cleaned my room so fast after he left my window, and the coast was clear. Later I found out Mom put a creepy mask on one of the neighbors to scare me. It worked. Afterward, she told us it was a family tradition to scare the little children when it came to Christmas to get them to behave. Her Ma and Pa did it to her. They all loved the thrill of seeing children screaming or hiding from fear. I never left cookies for

The Birth & The Awakening

Santa because I was afraid he might stay too long and come after me.

Grandma would decorate her home for several weeks, and not one shelf was missing tinsel and little elves or angels. All the relatives would gather at Grandma and Grandpa Reichel's house. It was something we all looked forward to. Kids sported their new gifts, and shreds of paper would litter the floors. Beer bottles and ashtrays were all around the room. As the night rolled on, the party would get louder, and the drunk fools would slop around until they figured it was time to drive home. Yes, they would drive home drunk! That was normal in our family.

I have some cozy memories of my parents in our tiny home. We took special nature walks together. My parents did not bring us to church; instead, they brought us to nature. We would pack a picnic and be gone most of the day. It was important to Mom and Dad that we had a "family" day, and those memories are very precious to me. Those were some of the "on the top of the mountain" moments in my life. I would drink in those moments like freshwater.

Every mountain has its peaks and plateaus and also their dark caverns. One of the darkest caverns in my life I walked into was when I was at the tender age of four. Camping in the wilderness was a big deal for us. Grandma and Grandpa had a cottage in the Northwoods of Wisconsin. My parents grew up making the trek up north each year, and it was a part of the cycle of life in our family. We all stayed in the same cottage with our relatives. We had everyone stacked in there somehow. Grandma Reichel, Mom, and my aunties made sure the place remained clean, and everyone was fed. We would go to the beach and swim all day long. Grandpa Cyril would always lather his body with a soap on a rope until he looked like a white ghost. We would all giggle as that big white ghost would run to the water and dive under as it left a white cloud from all the soap. Grandpa always rose out of the cloud with a big smile on his face when he saw how excited the onlookers were. It was such a fun time for everyone as long as they were good at pretending everything was normal.

I was young and naive as all little girls are. I trusted all adults. Mom and Dad taught me to respect my elders and believe everything they said. Grandpa would read the paper and tell me that there was an article about me in the news. He would get this surprised look upon his face every time he would announce, "It says right here, a young girl by the name of Erin Mereness sh*t her pants last Saturday." I always believed him, and I wondered how the people who wrote the paper knew my name. Even though I knew the part about me messing my pants wasn't true, I somehow always tried to steal the paper away from his fat little hands and read it for myself. He was jolly with a deep chuckle and perfectly round at his waist. When he laughed, his belly would shake up to the loose skin that hung around his neck and under his chin. He looked like the cartoon character Fred Flintstone, except with grey hair. Grandma continued to dye her hair as black as night until she was too old to care. Grandpa always snuck up on me when I was coloring pictures to squeeze the muscles around my neck and cry out, "Holland Biscuits!" I would thrash back and forth with laughter until he let go. He was a good grandfather, but a prankster. Even though I should have been wiser to his tricks, others in the family were lurking around corners and who did mean harm. Grandpa never hurt me. He was a gentle soul.

One day, when I was about four years old, something changed me. The pages of my book were blank, and the darkest chapters were about to unfold before my innocent eyes. I played on the grass in the front of the cottage, with sticks and pine needles in the bright sunshine. My white-blond hair was hot with the reflection of the sun. All at once, I heard the crunching of pine needles, and the light became shaded by the outline of a man. It was my creepy uncle-in-law. He extended his twisted hand in my direction. I did not realize that the faith I put into following him into the dark parts of the forest that day would forever change my future. My eyes were darkened by new perversions that a child should never have to witness. It was like I walked right into the lion's den.

What happened that day stole my innocence, and I was driven mad for a great many years as a result. What happened to me can't be repeated. Why did I go with him so many times? Why did I trust him and listen to his lies? When I think of what a tiny girl I was and what was done to me, I cannot imagine how this could happen, and it was all done while I was with my family. Oftentimes, in sexual abuse cases, it is done while the children are in family gatherings or with trusted individuals. While I was young, I felt that I was left unprotected. I know that if it was in plain sight, someone would have rescued me. But preditors never do these things in plain sight and they sneak around to grab their prey when everyone else is distracted. It was common knowledge in the family that the creepy uncle would do inappropriate things in front of children. Many years later, when I had my children, I found out that this sort of thing was going on when Mom was a little girl. Her sister married him when Mom was very young herself, about five years old. A family's big dark secret had been brushed under the rug. I feel terrible that Mom also had to endure this disgusting man.

Beer breath and smoky hands, dark corners, and depravity of the devil's prison was a place I called home. It truly was a prison of my own making from my perspective, but the fears and shame I bore felt like a suffocating place to me. Mom and Dad truly tried to make our home a nice place for us. My own set of demons infiltrated every area of my mind until it was my reality.

I would wake early in the morning after a big party to find my parents hungover in bed. The smell was strong. It reminded me of a fog. It lingered and felt moist with beer breath. My parents would go out at night to the bars and leave us with babysitters I am sure they thought were respectable. In contrast, they proved to be ridiculously perverted souls who would plug in the pornography. I had to view the vilest of affections on a giant television screen. It was one of those old television sets that were big as a box. Most days, Dad would tell us that the "T.V. will rot our brains." How could he know that my mind was already rotting from each time they paid a babysitter to "watch" us, even worse, the times that the babysitter would enjoy role-playing some of the twisted scenes we were watching? Dad was so much against things that would harm our minds, and if he would have known these babysitters were making us watch such things, I am sure he would have put a stop to it. I guess I must have been too afraid to tell him at the time. Some things cannot be unseen. Years later, he was shocked and horrified that we had to see such things.

We were not allowed to watch television except for Saturday mornings or Sunday evenings. Occasionally, there was a special program airing in which we would excitedly tune in. I distinctly remember our Sundays. They stick out like a ray of sunlight that bursts through the clouds. Sometimes you see a rare anomaly of light streaming through a cloud, and you feel heaven is peaking through to give you a signal of hope in the blackness of a depraved world. Sundays were my ray of hope. Somehow, Dad had an urgency to use that day to gather his little family and make the most treasured memories. No, we did not attend church. Dad was fed up with religion, and he felt the churches were full of hypocrites trying to shove their God down his throat. We simply had a family day. Those family days were heaven to me.

Some Sundays were spent hiking on forgotten railways. We would walk on the tracks. I remember trying to balance on the tall rails with my arms stretched out to keep my body from falling to the left or the right. Mom always packed lunches. We would often sit in a field of tall grasses and make a nice picnic area. All you could hear was the rustling of the grasses slipping past each other with each gentle push of the breeze.

At times we would hike on a big hill called Mosquito Hill. It was a vast nature preserve. Dad would teach how to identify the various trees by their bark, the leaves, or other characteristics. He would simply teach us about everything; the animals, the birds, the clouds, the ponds or streams, all the way down to a little bug that you could see skipping across the surface of the water. I always loved learning about nature.

We would climb the mountain, and I would stand on, what seemed to me, the edge of the world. I could see clear across the land and hold my small arms out as if I were a bird. All I wanted, at that moment, were wings to fly and strong winds to carry me soaring high like an eagle. If only I could have flown away and found a different world than the one I lived in. It was those days of hope, those precious family days, that kept me from falling apart. I am thankful that my parents found it necessary to spend those days with us kids.

My brother and I would run down the biggest hill with our mouths wide open uttering a loud cry. The sound still echoes in my mind. With every vibration of the foot, the vocal cords would fluctuate to make a trill. All kids do it. It is a rite of passage for a kid. When you run down a hill, you feel so wild and free. You open up your mouth, and the voice comes like that.

If it wasn't playing on forgotten railways, it was cliff-jumping into the rock quarries. Mom and Dad were adventure seekers. Dad would dive from 20-50 foot cliffs into the clean, clear blue waters that laid completely still below. Not only did he dive, but he would also do several tucks and turns that would impress the drunks that gathered by to watch. It seemed like everywhere we went, there were lots of drunks. For all I knew at the time, there were two kinds of people—drunks and

The Birth & The Awakening

kids that would grow up to be drunks.

We spent a lot of time in the summer at a particular quarry. The water was breathtaking when you looked down into it. When you were swimming, it was so clear that you could open your eyes and see twenty feet in front of you. I got brave at an early age, and I would jump off the cliffs to the still waters below. Dad showed me how to point my feet so that I would safely enter the water without hurting my feet. I had seen people rip the skin off their feet when they jumped 100 feet down, landing flat-footed.

When you had your head under the water, you could hear nothing, and nothing was better than the loud rock and roll music blaring above the water. The quiet of the water was an escape for as long as the lungs could hold breath. As my head would emerge, I would see the rowdy souls on top of the cliffs littered with vile graffiti and profane words written in bright colors. It was a trashy contrast from the beauty of the world beneath the surface of the water.

Hortonville was the town we lived in. The house was a small, ranch-style home with a muted green siding. My dad refinished the basement with old barn boards and stones around an old wood stove. He built a bar for the drinking parties on one side, and the other side was meant to make music. He had a fish tank set into the wall like a painting filled with exotic fish. The tank was above the old black piano. Dad said, kept perfect pitch. He never had to have that piano tuned. You could sit there and play the piano while watching the fish gracefully swim.

Behind the wall was a room filled with tanks. Dad had critter collections; he had long snakes, big hairy spiders, gerbils, fish, turtles, and other small creatures. I remember a particular fight between Mom and Dad. One of the snakes got out, and Mom freaked out. She found a snake coiled up in among her towels in a laundry basket. That was not the last of these types of exotic animal escapes.

A few years later, Dad bought a giant hairy tarantula and claimed that it would not climb up the glass on a fish tank, so there was no need for a cover. Mom was worried it might escape, so Dad asked me if I could keep the aquarium with the spider inside in my room. I thought it would be okay since he said it would not climb the glass. Well, the next morning, when the creature went missing, Mom threw a gasket. I was scared to sleep in my bed for fear of that giant spider crawling over my face in the night, and Dad said it had to have gone down the ductwork to find heat. I think we all had the heebie-jeebies for a while after that one.

The last straw came soon after this episode when another snake escaped. Mom was dusting around the TV when out slithered one member of the snake collection. Mom rose the stakes and drew her line in the sand; it was her or the snakes, as I remember. She stayed, so it was safe to say that the snakes never returned.

We had loads of gerbils. You start with a male and a female, and you end up with literally hundreds in a short period. They are very prolific. I recall dusting under the piano to find a few gerbil skeletons. Besides the little mammals that scurried around and around in their habitats, we also had plenty of birds.

Beaker was one such bird. He was our parakeet with a teal-blue body and a yellow head. Dad trained his little bird to mimic all the bird calls you heard outside each day. Beaker did the goldfinch, Nellie call, the oriole, the red-winged blackbird, and even the lonely calls of the mourning dove. This bird would push things off our kitchen table. If you had a fork next to your plate, Beaker would tip-toe over and take his beak to shove it off the table. As the fork would drop to the floor, he would cock his little yellow head over the table to watch it hit with the one eye on the side of his head. Most days, Beaker was perched on Dad's shoulder. Dad could call any bird to him from outside with his whistles. He would chirp, and soon, he would be conversing with a finch who would nearly land on his other shoulder. The best was his squirrel call. Dad was in touch with nature. One time the bird and the mice in the basement all died because the pet food was poisoned. Dad said he heard lots of people had dead animals from it. We were all pretty sad to bury Beaker, our unforgettable parakeet.

The animal side of the basement not only had lots of tanks and cages; it had all of Dad's wine-making supplies. He was always making some kind of wine. There were lots of parties down in that basement where people would drink his homemade wine. He grew the grapes that he pressed and fermented into wine.

He had a grand garden. It was connected to the cornfield and about the length of half of our backyard. We had grapevines, strawberries, red raspberries, sweet corn, cabbage, green beans, broccoli, lettuce, and many other vegetables. He was a very skilled gardener, and he put his heart into every inch of that soil. I used to be entrusted with the red raspberry picking, and it was all I could do to stop myself from eating every single berry as they were picked. My hands would be stained red, and my little bucket always came in the back door, full. Mom made jam, freezer jam. It was pretty amazing. If you have had strawberry freezer jam and liked it, raspberry is that much better. That slight tartness against the sweet will get you every time.

After carrying something up from the basement, Mom asked, "How would you like to look like a princess? I think we should get you the Princess Diana haircut." My eyes gleamed with the thought. Because I did not know who Diana was, I pictured stories of Sleeping Beauty with her golden locks of hair cascading down her back with long dresses. Mom brought me into the salon, and when I turned around to get my first look at my new "princess haircut," I nearly fell out of my seat in sheer horror. It was a mullet! I had the business in the front and party in the back look. It was so horrible that I never trusted Mom with her suggestions again. Not only did I look like Diana, but it was also the new style of the time. However, it was not what I thought a princess looked like.

When Mom and Dad went on big trips, they always left my brother and me with Grandma Isla, Dad's mom. He called her Mumma. His Daddy died when I was born, so I never did get to meet him. Even though Grandma Isla had her favorites, I never noticed because I was one of her favorites. She treated me like I was a princess. I remember the throne she would make for me right beside her armchair. She would prop one pillow behind my back and one for me to sit on. We would watch her favorite T.V. shows which included, Murder She Wrote, Golden Girls, David Hammer, and Wheel of Fortune.

Grandma Isla taught us how to gamble pennies at her favorite card game called "Spite and Malice." She even made me a hand-crocheted penny pouch for my winnings. She always smoked and drank hard liquor when we were with her. Her ashes would stretch the length of the cigarette before she would flick them off. I saw her ashes fall on the carpet a lot. I don't know why she always waited so long. Every time she would act surprised when they would fall, and her magnified eyes would blink under her coke-bottle glasses that sat on her face. She was a high-class drinker. Her daddy owned the saloon, and the upper-class people of that day would drink liquor instead of beer. She always said her daddy made three fortunes and lost two of them. She only drank booze and a lot of it. She would tell us stories of how her mother died in childbirth when she was only four. She told me that she saw her mother make the sign of the cross in her living room window after the funeral. It was her one spiritual experience that she could remember where she felt the presence of God. Every day, Grandma Isla prayed to her Rosary.

I would sit there beside her, listening to all of her stories and found an appreciation for the olden days. Every antique she owned had its own story attached to it; one set of chairs came over on the boat from England more than a hundred years ago, the china traveled the same course, some things were from her side, and others were from her husband, Grandpa Lloyd. They met at the old T-Shop where she played piano for the customers. They used to dance on the nights that she wasn't playing for the silent movies.

She was what I called "fluffy." Hugging her was soft because she had a fair amount of grandmother fat around her bones. It's the kind of fat I loved to squeeze. I always told everyone that I wanted to be "fluffy" like her when I was a grandmother one day. I figured it would be no fun to hug a boney grandmother. She had short, light blond, wavy hair that felt like the hair of an angel. Everything about Grandma Isla was perfect for me. Even her bed. I slept beside her in her soft bed, and it felt like I was sleeping on a cloud. Every Christmas, she would say her traditional phrase, "This must be my last Christmas!" That was her sweet way of saying how good it was. If she died that year, she would have died happy because it couldn't get any better in her mind.

She loved to bake goodies for everyone. She was famous for her chocolate eclairs, cream puffs, caramel pecan rolls, and pistachio pudding. For birthdays, Grandma Isla always made cherry cheesecake. It never failed. Dad always bit the only cherry with the pit in it. He would always look like he just about lost a tooth over it. The unluck of the Mereness family went way, way back. His older sister would tell stories when she was a little girl, and her grandmother died, and they were hauling her casket up the big hill in Kaukauna in the hearse when someone forgot to latch the door properly. She said it was sheer horror when they all watched their grandmother's dead body rolling out of the back of that casket and tumbling down the hill into all the people. To this day we argue whether or not it actually happened.

There was always a story, and the bad luck got passed onto Dad.

The Birth & The Awakening

Between him and his older brother, Tommy, there was always a level of Murphy's Law going on. We later called it the "Mereness Factor." Uncle Tommy loved Bismarck donuts, yet he still got the only donut in the box that was not filled. He would take bite after dry bite in search of the beautiful fluffy cream that was supposed to be there. As he would always look around at all the other people in the room, licking the overflowing cream that would be oozing off one side of their mouth or the other, and wonder why his sweet well went dry. He was tall and thin, a heavy drinker and smoked like a chimney, yet one of the best storytellers I ever met. His stories of unbelievable misfortune and calamity always ended with gut-busting laughter.

One of his famous stories was when he was working as a deliveryman and saw a great big elephant walk past the front of his truck when he was unloading something from the back. He did a double-take and thought it was the alcohol clouding his perception until he turned on the radio to find out that an elephant escaped the traveling circus earlier that day.

Even better than Uncle Tommy's storytelling was his piano playing. Somehow when he would tickle the keys, it would sound as though two concert pianists were playing at once. I would lay my head on the piano when Tommy played. Every song he played was played by ear. He could not read a single note of music, yet he was acclaimed as one of the finest pianists of all time at the university he attended. Years later, when I attended the same music conservatory, they were still talking about his remarkable talent. All I knew was that hearing him play was magical to me.

Dad said he had to work a hundred times harder to master the music and his brother took that God-given talent for granted and never did anything with it. Grandma Isla favored Tommy for his talent and wouldn't let anyone forget it. Dad always said he would have given anything to have that kind of talent, but it never stopped him from doing great things with music. Dad still proved that he could do anything that he set his mind to by hard work and determination. I believe this to be universally true.

Dad traveled the world with his band and was passionate about teaching the love of music to others. To this day, his students still sing his accolades. Some went on to be band directors or musicians of some sort because of the impact he had on their lives. When Dad does anything, he does it with every ounce of passion. His heart was so tied up in his band, and his soul knew that he was making a difference in the world. I remember watching him come home with his head hanging low because the students' parents would not show up to the concerts he would put on. It would break his heart to see the talents of his students overlooked. Dad didn't mix well with people who didn't seem to care.

The high school he taught at did not share in the enthusiasm, and it dimmed the light he carried. Soon he felt he needed to move on with his life and leave the band directing in the past. We picked up and moved from Hortonville to another small town called Little Chute, which was about 30 minutes away, but felt like a world apart. We might as well have moved to another country as far as I was concerned. I was the "new kid" now. I was about nine years old at the time. I left all my friends and all the things I knew behind. Even though I was smaller than the rest of the kids at the old school, my dad was the "cool" band teacher of the high school, making me feel taller somehow. The new school was not nearly as friendly. The kids reminded me every day of how short I was. It was a tough adjustment for me. I went from having a lot of friends to having none and no one to talk to. I had a tape recorder. For a while, during this time, I would speak to a tape recorder for comfort. I did not know about God, so there was only myself or the tape for conversation.

Dad bought a dog kennel and grooming salon. Soon the dogs were my friends. I got my first puppy, and she became my closest confidant. I named her Jolee. I could tell her everything and cry on her shoulder, and she would stay by my side. You get unconditional love from a dog, and that is why I think people call them "Man's best friend." They are always happy to see you when you come home and are the first to greet you. It didn't matter what I looked like, short or tall, if I were mean or nice, dogs would love us, no matter what. Jolee was always there, smiling and wagging her tail because she was so happy to see me. That made me feel loved.

Dad hired me to help work with the dogs in the kennel. I learned a lot about how to work with customers and how to tell them what they wanted to hear. Maybe a dog was nasty and would bite, but Dad told me never to tell the owners this. He knew there was a reason why the dogs would bite and say that it was better to let them know that their dog had a fun time. He said it was NEVER the dog's fault.

The Birth & The Awakening

Dogs only bite when they either have had a bad experience or if they feel threatened; he never blamed the dog. He would say, rather, that the dog had trust issues. He told me that it was mostly the owner's fault. People can damage a dog if they don't train them properly. I saw a lot of similarities in dogs who were traumatized and people who were likewise traumatized. Both react in destructive ways when cornered. Dogs bite with sharp teeth while people use sharp words.

Both cut deep, but a dog's bite heals after a time, whereas words can leave someone wounded for a lifetime.

Most dogs were friendly, and Dad loved his job. He loved dealing with dogs better than dealing with humans. Dad would talk to the dogs like they were his friends. We called him the "Leader of the Pack" because the dogs always respected him, and they seemed to be happy when he took care of them. Together, Dad and I took good care of the dogs and spent quality time in the process, which was special to me.

Dad was always working, but once or twice each year, he made time for a family trip up North to stay at Grandma and Grandpa's cabin. The cabin was painted red and made out of cheap OSB boards and resided in Pembine. There we were, in the middle of nowhere with all our relatives crammed into that small cabin. People lying on the floor, on the couches, or stacked in bunks.

One time Grandpa shot a 100-pound snapping turtle that was found near a pond. The only problem was that the turtle wouldn't die. He had two grown men help lift the turtle over a large stump so he could drive a peg through its head. The poor creature was still trying to move while Dad and my Uncle Henry pulled the back legs, so its neck was stretched out. That's when Grandpa hobbled over and lopped off its head with a sharp hatchet. I was screaming at them from behind a tree, crying for the animal. I could not bear it. He hung the turtle upside down and proceeded to let the animal continue to die. It takes days. How can anyone forget such a traumatic event? They made turtle soup, and I decided that I would never eat it.

Campfires burned long after the setting of the sun. The sparks flew like fireflies from the big logs that would be dropped in. It was a time of loud, drunken laughter, jokes, and many ghost stories. Mom loved to give me a good scare. It made her giddy with excitement to see me shake in fear. After we had our first VCR, Mom would put the

25

horror movies in. I would sit beside her, and when the evil murdering monsters of the films would peek into the windows with their wide-eyed, hungry-for-blood look, I would quickly fall beneath the covers to shield my eyes. Mom would roll with laughter every time. I hated it. Every time it was dark, I was scared. Yes, I was afraid of the dark. I could see these horror movies playing over and over in my mind; I could almost feel the presence of evil. Some say things like this open doors for the evil spirits to come into your mind and haunt you. I would have sworn that I saw someone in the dark corners of my bedroom. And when it was dark enough and I would only hear the pounding of my heart and the blinking of my eyes, I could feel someone breathing into my ear. The feeling of that breath would send me into a state of frozen tremors. I could barely breath as I laid there paralysed and I never wanted to look in the direction of the breath in my ear for fear of actually seeing a real person. Later I recognized the trauma I endured as a child came back to haunt me in flashbacks which felt real to me. Needless-to-say, I had to have a light on or television to fall asleep. To this very day, I will not watch horror movies; however, I am no longer afraid of the dark.

 One time, we stayed in a campground, and after a late night of ghost stories around the fire, when I became scared, I decided to rush to the camper that my parents were sleeping in. They were bunking with the creepy uncle. I knew he was there. Dad was asleep, snoring loudly. I looked over to the opposite side of the camper after I heard the click of a light switch. He looked at me and then made sure I was watching him. I am not even sure why I would stare. I would stare at him as he did awful things. I always thought it was disgusting, but yet I could not look away for some reason. Later, Mom wanted to know why there was such a mess over on that side of the camper and why particular tapestries were ruined. I reported everything I saw for fear that she would think it was me who was destroying the nice camper. She didn't say much. Things like this had happened many more times than I can recount. It was all a part of the course of life for me. Every family function, every party, he would get me alone somehow.

 During a drama class at school, which was led by our school guidance counselor, I started laughing and making fun of what my uncle does because I thought it was funny. After the teacher called Mom and told her, she took me aside and told me to keep quiet about it. I wasn't to ever speak of it because it was a private family matter. I could tell she was quite cross with me. She said that it was just how that creepy uncle was. She also said to me that I always exaggerated things anyhow. The guidance counselor took me into another room and told me that what I was laughing about was not a laughing matter. He told me he would need to inform the police.

After what Mom said, I was scared to upset her even more or get the creepy uncle in trouble with the police, so I cried and got on my knees, begging him not to get the law involved. I told him I made the whole thing up for attention and that I was just kidding around. I assured him that it was a joke. He believed me. I was convincing. Deep down inside, I was scared to death. Because I let it go, it continued for several more years—what a waste. I think deep down inside; Mom didn't want to make waves in the family. She had been used to keeping peace in the family, and keeping me silent was a part of that effort. Stemming back to when she signed off on her baby, she learned to keep everyone else happy but herself. If I was quiet about this, things could keep going on as normal, which was a very dysfunctional form of ordinary.

By this time, I was about eleven or twelve years old. At some family function in his home, I was upstairs, coloring pictures with his grandkids. They loved being with me. I loved being with them. It was one of the slivers of innocence in my life. I guess being with the children made me feel like a child again. I grasped for anything that I could find that would make me feel free. As we were coloring, that creepy uncle came out of his room in his underwear. He started doing very nasty things right in front of those children, and I could see that there was something gravely wrong with that picture. I hated that he was corrupting even these precious little ones.

These sorts of things affect a person for the rest of their life in every area of life. It cripples a person's ability to relate to others. In school, I had a tough time with the other kids. I was withdrawn, and I felt so much inner shame that I never gave myself a chance. The feeling of being worthless was a sting in my mind. I had such deep loneliness. It was a hollow feeling in my heart. I thought the world would be better off without me. The kids at school could see my weakness, and they preyed on it as animals prey on the weak in the wild. The predators attack and beat their prey down until it quivers with the pain of death. It must submit.

I was bullied. I was the subject of ridicule every day I went to school. I was quite a bit smaller than all the other kids, so that did not improve my odds of approval. In gym class, I was always the last kid picked to join someone's team, and the other team leader would laugh at the opposing team's leader who had to 'pick' me. A big, chubby girl named Charlotte was one of my bullies. She loved picking me up off the ground and tossing me down the school steps, locking me in the lockers, and doing naughty things that she would blame me for to the teacher. She was the top of the class, so they never doubted her stories. She would get that evil eye and giggle while I was crying in pain or getting into trouble from the teacher. In some weird way, it seemed to make her happy. Sometimes I would willfully fall into her traps just to make her smile because I loved to see others happy, even if it had to be at my expense.

Often, I felt there was a solid-bold sign across my forehead that said "Pick Me" on it when it came to predators. Somehow the predator knows when there is easy prey. I was repeatedly victimized by the babysitter, the father of the children I eventually baby-sat, a perverted teenage older cousin who thought it was okay to tickle me in places the sun refuses to shine, and of course, let's not forget other boys from school.

Because I was so little and insignificant, I generally could not fit into the popular groups. The only kids that would give me the time of day were the other misfits. In my case, it was the dirtball kids, as we called them back then. They were the kids who came from rough home lives, who would try smoking, used many cuss words, gave themselves homemade tattoos by poking needles in their arms and rubbing ink in the holes, put on dark makeup, and wore the black clothing. They liked me because I was real. I wasn't stuck up like the others. I liked everyone, so it was great to play innocent games like those I generally made up in my backyard. Bog Frog was a game we played, which was a contest to jump on clumps of grass that poked out of the murky, stagnant waters that pooled near the railroad tracks. Our house was situated right beside the tracks. I guess they liked it mainly because it came with a little dirt and danger. When they got full of muck, I would spray them off in Dad's dog grooming tub.

One of the games they liked to play was the Ouija board or performing seances to communicate with spirits. It was always very eerie because one of the girls had a real Ouija board from over a hundred years ago because her dad was an antique dealer and happened to have many old things lying around. One day we took it out to her barn and asked questions that were answered quickly and sharp. I thought that implement moved over the letters faster than our 12-year-old hands could muster. At first, I wanted to believe it was all a joke, but as soon as the spirit was communicating and I got the feeling it was real, I stood up, pulled my hands off the board, and just as I backed up, a whole box full of old records fell inches from my head. It must have weighed a hundred pounds by the looks of it, and it would have killed me had I been an inch closer. The sky filled with clouds, and I felt like I had crossed some sort of realm that day, and I wished I had someone to break off that feeling from my bones. Other things seemed to distract me from all the evil I felt around me, like music and art.

I joined the band and played the trombone. I played the one instrument they told me that I couldn't possibly play because my arms were too short. Just to prove that I could, I picked that one. Dad found an old shoelace and fixed it to the slide of the trombone that I tied to my middle finger. Every time I had to hit a low note, I would release that finger with the string and jerk the slide from the grasp of my hand until it was fashioned to the correct place. Necessity is the mother of invention. I loved that trombone. I would carry it across my back through my backpack straps. It made it awkward, as it would stick out about two feet on either side. I looked, from a distance, like I was carrying a cross, if you can imagine that. Perhaps metaphorically, you could say that I was. I had a lot of things I was carrying in my life.

My life was filled with situations where I was told I could not do something, and I hated it. I wanted to do it just to show them that I was not a complete loser—that I was capable of doing things, great things, if I worked hard enough. I think I inherited this quality from Dad. I was a high achiever, and mastering skills were a part of my new game. It was a way I could have value in a life in which I felt so worthless. People could look at my accomplishments and praise me, and I could feel acceptance. A heart yearns for acceptance.

I had been interested in fine arts since I was a very young child. Dad's eldest sister, Auntie Lois, was a retired art teacher, and she would spend time with me. Of all the people in my life, she was so gentle and kind. She poured into my life so much more than she will ever understand. Auntie Lois lived four hours away, so I only saw her a couple of times a year. It never felt like enough for me. She was a very inspiring person, which made me aspire to be more like her, and I decided that I would be an art teacher. So emerged the artist—one of my many characters in the play. It was a birth of sorts. While I had been trapped in subtle deprivation, the urge to know something beautiful became a wistful passion.

Drawing pictures of beautiful things transformed into worlds of their own. I would sit on the floor and draw for hours at a time. The drawings turned into paintings. Mom and Dad bought paints and canvas. They encouraged the talent as much as they could. Painting forests and seascapes, flowers, and birds brought me to other worlds that I was able to create in my mind's eye. It felt like a safe escape. A paintbrush between the fingers gave me freedom. Smudges of paint mixed together made oceans, and those oceans were vastly glorious. My classmates would praise my work, but socially, I could not keep even one single friend. Somehow, I saw a friend as something I could possess. If I could hold on with all my might, maybe they would stay. Instead, the clutching of my hands forced the things I held the dearest to fall between the cracks. There was nothing to hold on to eventually, for everything I held on to was obscure, except those things I could create. The art was a dependable diversion. The transparent nature of my heart left me so vulnerable.

After completing another painting of flowers and birds, Mom came to tell me something unbelievable. "Erin. You have a sister," I wondered if she was pregnant or how this was possible. It was what I always wished for since I was a little girl. She continued, "Your dad and I had a child when I was in high school." Mom bowed her head, "I was too young to care for her, so I gave her up for adoption eighteen years ago. She just contacted us this week and wants to meet our family. Her name is Amelia." I could tell she was relieved and happy to find her finally, yet I cannot express in words the feeling I had. It was like I won the lottery. I just won a sister, and I could not wait to see what she looked like. I wondered if she had blond hair like me or Dad's dimples.

Soon after, we all packed up and traveled to Minnesota, where a loving family raised her. Amelia looked just like Mom. She was about two inches taller than Mom, but she had the same face and dark brown, lovely hair. I looked more like Dad, so she didn't look anything like me, but I didn't care. I was so happy to meet this beautiful woman finally.

The Birth & The Awakening

You could not wipe the smile off my face as I followed her around everywhere like a little puppy dog who finally found its littermate. She was planning to go to nursing school, just like Mom, and she loved animals like Dad. It was amazing how we lived parallel lives in so many ways.

When we finally got home, I wrote her a long letter with all my feelings about how thankful I was to have a sister. Every day I would run to the end of the driveway to check the mailbox for her letter. When it finally came, I ripped the envelope open so fast, wondering what she would say to my question, "Will you be my sister?" and "Can we be pen-pals?" My eyes filled with tears as I read her words of rejection, "I already have a sister and no time for pen-pals." She didn't seem to want to pursue any sort of relationship with me. My young heart was broken. I had hoped that we could at least be friends, but it was clear that she did not want me. I never wrote to her again. Mom didn't talk of her much after that. I'm sure she had high hopes to be reunited more familiarly, but it was evident that her adoptive family struggled with the anxiety of losing her to us. Even the thought of sharing her life with us was hard for them to accept. Deep down, I think Amelia felt rejected, too. The idea of someone not wanting her and giving her away, I am sure, was a hard place to be even though she could never know the story behind her adoption. Would she ever know how much Mom wanted her? It was a story I hoped I would one day get to share. Either way, unacceptance was something I became all too familiar with.

When a little black girl came to our all-white school, there was no one to accept her. Her name was Trina. She was the most beautiful little black girl. I never cared about what people looked like on the outside. I looked at their heart. All hearts look the same and beat with the same red blood. I didn't even notice the color of her skin because it was lost in her lovely smile. In a world that seemed so void of smiles, a world where I would smile and the smile was not reciprocated, hers was a smile that returned to me a hundred times over. We began a friendship that was not received so favorably among the other students.

"Hey, ni**er lover," they would jeer as they pelted us girls with ice balls gathered up from the dirty melted snow that laid on the ground around the schoolhouse. I would not compromise; Trina was my friend. I would take a thousand blows for her. It was unfair. How could they hate her for the color of her skin? Why would they not get to know her for all of her wonderful qualities? In class, the other kids would stick pencils into her hair, and I would always help pull them out each day as I would tell her how one day I would give them a taste of their own medicine. Ideas of hot gluing pencils in their hair swirled around in my mind. The love I had for that little girl was deep and steadfast. I could love anyone who would smile at me even a little. It was surreal for me to have such a love and kindred heart with her. We would talk for hours and laugh about all the injustice. It could not shake us. I would assure Trina that we were like sisters, and nothing could change that. I had just lost a full-blooded sister, and as far as I was concerned, Trina was my real sister.

I decided right then and there that Trina would be my blood sister. Grandpa Cyril told me how to do it the "Indian" way. Being that he was a Native American, he had to know about these things. He told me about when the natives met up with another tribe, to show peace and brotherly love, they would both cut their arms and then merge their blood so they would be blood brothers. To prove Trina my loyalty and love, I became blood sisters with her, and I have her precious blood coursing through my veins. I was only twelve at the time, but I took all the prejudice with her and for her and would do it again! My parents brought me up to never look down on anyone, no matter what their background or color, their sexual orientation, culture, or how much money they had. I hated injustice of any sort, especially something like this. I mean, there is no excuse to look down on someone for the color of their skin. Racism is taught. You don't naturally notice things like skin color when you are a child. Children just play together. I am glad my parents taught me to love all people.

Sadly, our small white community drove this family away. I am sure people would look at them with that look that says a thousand words for lack of understanding—gawking at them at every stop. It's complete ignorance if you ask me. The abuses became so intense that this precious African American family had to move to another town. I could not even imagine the pain they were going through as I watched them roll out of our closed-minded town. My heart broke for them. It was like a funeral to me. They were gone in a blink of an eye. Now that Trina was gone, the chances of my gaining another friend became as bleak as ever.

I became completely and utterly consumed by the vast sea of

loneliness and despair. The feeling was like a hard spot in my middle. Tossed from one abuser to the next, one user to the other, I had little hope of anything but the grave. The grave seemed to be somewhere where I could finally find peace. Nothing but the art could cause me to transcend life, and the reality was that I was alive. While there was breath, there was pain and sorrow. Nothing could give me a reprieve.

The teen years were not easy. About the time I was nearly twelve years old, the creepy uncle's little Chihuahua got hit by a car and killed. We were all down in Grandpa's smoky basement that was a makeshift bar. Booze bottles and beer signs lined the wall behind the counter that the adults would sit at when they drank. Two refrigerators stood there packed with beer. It was a downstairs tavern if you ask me. Mom was sitting there with her sisters drinking and laughing and carrying on as they often did when she leaned over to comfort him over his dog. She told me to go over and hug him. I felt bad for him, yet I was not too thrilled to get close to the man who had defiled my childhood. I walked over to hug him when, all at once, he leaned into my face and pressed his tongue down into my mouth. I pushed him off of me and ran to the other side of the room, in disgust, trying to figure out how to wash my mouth out. Soap? Bleach? What would take that dirty feeling from me?

He hollered back as I was spitting into the sleeve of my shirt repeatedly, and smearing out any remnant of his presence from my lips, "Hey, Erin, how old are you?" Mom filled in for my silence, which was deafening, "She's twelve."

He concluded, "Just wait a couple of years, and then you'll like it!" They all burst forth in laughter, thinking of it. I am sure every one of them was off in a dream of their first kiss. A forced kiss from an old pervert should not be the first experience, not for anyone.

Human Growth and Development was a course we had to take, which was a fancy name for Sex Ed. I will say that I am not in favor of the class today, where they instruct kids about gender blending, the normalcy of premarital sex in every form, and even in the way of self-gratification. However, this class was a form of salvation for me. It was in that room that I became aware of what sexual abuse was and the realization of what happened to me for so many years. Mom said it was normal for men to do these things, even though, I am sure, deep down, she knew it wasn't right. This was a stark contrast to what I had learned in this class. It empowered me to have a voice—a voice for my little cousins who did not have one. I could stop the cycle. I went to my Grandma Isla and told her everything that had happened to me. Because I was her little angel, she became furious that anyone would do such things to me. She told me that I had a duty to tell on him. When I told Dad, I am sure he was torn. He said, "Why do you always make mountains from molehills?" It was no secret that I was choosing to go against the entire family in telling on the creepy uncle. It was then that I realized that I would have to stand alone, but I did it for the children.

I marched up to the liaison officer the next morning and told everything. By night, he was behind bars, which was the start of a most horrible storm to come. It came with a high price because the entire family turned on me. This creepy uncle was a decorated veteran who saved lives in the war. He also was some kind of officer for a lot of years of his life. No telling what kind of PTSD he must have had that caused him to be so twisted and perverted in the end. Either way, there is no excuse for it. No matter what trauma he may have had in his life, it didn't give him a license to harm others, especially children.

The man was bailed out of jail by other family members, and my restraining order kept me away when the family gathered. I felt like I was the one that everyone was afraid of. I guess they were worried that I would imagine something about them, or perhaps they were in denial. The proof was when I would find out the uncle was invited, and I was not, except for one family gathering. I walked to the basement, where I saw Dad conversing with him as if all was well. When I locked myself in the bathroom to cry tears of disbelief, the uncle came to the door and knocked. It was frightening for me because he threatened my life should I not open the door unto him.

"I will kill you. You can't hide forever," he said in a low desperate tone. I could not answer his call as he pounded upon the door. Each blow sent shivers down my spine, fear paralyzing me. Eventually, he gave up, or another person came past in time. How could my parents, who were supposed to love and protect me, talk with him, and not realize the danger I was in that very hour? It seemed hopeless. No one could see the severity of the situation. How could an entire family of people be bound to one man but not even shaken with grief for the sake of an innocent child?

Later that night, he took out his anger on his wife, Aunt Tess. He ripped nearly all the hair from her head, stripped her naked, and beat her until most of her ribs were broken. When he went to find a way to finish her off, she managed to break through the upstairs window and pull herself out of the house. She ran to the nearest street, naked, bloody, cold, and in fear for her life, to flag down someone to save her. For a long time, I remember my little aunty who was only four feet ten, wearing a wig until her hair grew in. He was off to the jailhouse again for that incident, but I can't even remember how long they kept him there. It seems to me that he was out again not too long after that. Aunt Janice divorced the sick old pervert and tried to get on with her life as best she could, yet the family could not understand how dangerous he was, and some continued to have him babysit their children. I learned that my cousin, who is now a mother herself, was still being babysat by him while all this was going on. She told me one time that she hid under the kitchen table with my mom when he was upset. Mom protected her.

This burden became the deciding factor. I could no longer keep going, and all my thoughts were of only despair. Not even, art was enough to distract me. That evening, I wailed; I crawled on my belly and screamed into my pillow because I felt that no one cared. There was such pain in the rejection of my own family. No one understood my torment, and I thought that the world would be a better place if I would be gone from it. There was no glory in living, no promise of better days, and no paintings that could carry me to faraway lands. I was there, left to myself in total desolation.

Weeping and gnashing my teeth, groaning with the pain of life, with my eyes puffed in tears, I reached up to the heavens. I am not even sure why I reached to heaven. I did not even know if it was real or if there even was a God, yet I somehow yelled out, "OH MY GOD..." and a pause. Then, "PLEASE SAVE ME!!!!!" What a declaration. In total desperation, I called out to a God that I heard about and saw carved from stone and hanging on a cross at Grandma's house. Was I going mad? Or was this reality more real than the pain I was feeling? The room filled up with a light that had the power to chase away the darkness that had held me captive for so many years.

I felt hope at that moment as the life was being restored within me. From that moment on, I just knew there was a God and that He was real. It wasn't only one of those acts of denial like brushing something under the rug of your feelings, a coping by various means, or a painting of a faraway dream; this was altogether different. It was tangible to me somehow. It is hard to explain how real it was. It was more real than the things I could see right in front of my face. It's a reality beyond the seen and known. There was a newness to me and a will to learn more of this. God that met me at my wit's end. How could I feel so loved by something that wasn't there? Love was there. Faith is the substance of things not seen yet hoped for.

Chapter Two
THE BLACKBELT & THE TRAP

Life went on as usual. Everything else had remained constant, but my perception of things broadened. It was as though a blindfold had been lifted, but it was hard to comprehend something I never learned about. I hadn't yet realized the potential of what Christ died to give me, either. The bars and bonds of abuse held me, prisoner, for years to come. I did, however, find ways of coping with imprisonment. One way was through self-defense. If all men were predators, I was determined to fight them with every ounce of my strength. No matter what I did, I fought to do it the best. I invested many hours in learning and mastering the martial arts until I obtained a black belt. If I had been as quick-witted as I was with quick kicking, I might have had a fighting chance. Sadly, I had been so wounded that when faced with direct assault, I would freeze and lose my will to defend myself.

Freshman year in high school was rough. I was still not even through puberty, and the girls loved reminding me of how much of a little girl I was compared to them. I didn't have any friends that year except the ones I met in my Tae Kwon Do classes. That year I trained a lot. Every morning I woke up at four a.m., ran the dogs, and went to lift weights with Dad before school. After school, I would work for several hours, and then my brother, Ian, would bring me with him to train for another four hours in martial arts. He was a few levels ahead of me, but I gave all I had to be the best. I would pick the biggest guys to spar with. Ian would show me no mercy, either. He would kick me right in the head and drop me. I had to work extra hard to learn how to block high kicks since my head was in the target range because of my height compared to most. I came up to most people's chests. Ian and I never did get along. Even when we were younger, I would call my dad at work to let him know that he was "looking at me." I would try to put a cereal box in the way of his face at the table, but he would always tap his hands and peek around the box just to annoy me.

Riding with Ian was never fun because he would give me the rules, and I was supposed to listen to him. I always sat in the backseat because I never wanted to sit beside him. One evening on the way to Tae Kwon Do, he told me to put my seat belt on, and I refused. His fist came right over the front seat and landed square in my left eye. It was a shiner, but he never got in trouble. I always told people that Ian was Mom's "Golden Child." I imagine he was easier to deal with after all they went through with my emotional troubles.

When I would act up and get into an emotional fit, Mom would say, "It is no wonder why people don't like you!" That stuck with me for years. When I was bullied years before, Mom was the one who would call the bullies' mothers and make threats to protect me. She would cry for my sadness but didn't know how to fix me. After I told my uncle, it seemed everything changed, and I was the whistleblower. She stopped coming to my rescue for a time after that. I had to attend a victim support group that year, and those girls were different from me. They all were wearing black like they were at a funeral with dark black makeup around their eyes. They looked like death warmed over them. Most of these girls, because of what happened to them, had given up on life. I think I nearly did before God saved me that night crawling around my floor. We found out after noticing an empty chair one day at our meeting that one of the girls in the support group hung herself. Our counselor told us what had happened to her. The note she left said something like, "I can't handle my life anymore. I am scared. I feel worthless. The guy that raped me is getting out this fall, and I am afraid he will kill me." She beat him to it. They found her hanging from a rope off a deer stand behind their barn. We all cried that day and felt like she was taking one for the team. It was a thought that crossed all of our broken minds at one point or the other.

All of these girls were troubled, but I was the only one who wasn't lighting up a cigarette on our breaks or talking about all the boys they were sleeping with. In fact, I was the only one there who was a virgin. God saved me from that life. I could have been that way. I know I could have. I understand why they did it, too – they felt worthless. Since their bodies were taken through sexual abuse, they figured they were something to be used up, sold, or handed out. What was the use of living when what they were living in was hell? I became quite familiar with those feelings over the years, but I wasn't about to let that be my story.

There was a cute boy that stole my heart that year. His name was Brandon, and he was a black belt at the Tae Kwon Do class I went to each day. I never missed a class, so we ended up spending a lot of time together. After several years, I also attained my black belt, and he worked with me to help me be one of the best fighters there. We would compete at Junior Olympics and would each be the Gold Medal winners in our weight class. I broke boards and cement blocks and won every sparring match. Eventually, he figured out that I liked him, and he managed to get me to kiss him one afternoon. At the time, I thought that meant I was his girl, even though he said we were just friends. Somehow, he always ended up teasing me and making me feel like garbage as he also kissed other, much prettier, girls on the side. We only shared that one kiss, but it was a kiss that I held in my fragile heart because, for a moment, it felt like real love.

No one ever stayed, though. Even when I thought people finally liked me after I got my braces off and could afford more stylish clothes, they found ways to leave me in the dust. I will never forget when I was a sophomore in high school, and the popular girls started inviting me out. I felt like I belonged and that I was important. After a couple of Friday nights riding around with them and going to drinking parties they would find around small neighborhoods, I felt on top of the world. I was high on life and "the life" of the party. I never needed a strong drink to make me act like a fool. I could jump up on tables, showing off my karate kicks, and make everyone laugh without drugs or alcohol influencing me. It was one of my many facades and another act in the play I called life.

It was homecoming week, and I was destined to stick out. One day I was the Statue of Liberty with my hair braided and put into a crown of coat hangers that made my braids stand straight up on end.

Another day I was a disco queen with a flame orange jumpsuit and a pile of makeup on. Every chance I had to be someone or something else, it was apart of my act. I did the Hillbilly and the old lady, and the poop patrol lady. Poop patrol was a part of my life. I picked up thousands of pounds of poop in my lifetime living at a dog kennel.

Homecoming is also a time of pranks. People will toilet paper homes and egg your car if they want to send a message. Since the popular people were so exclusive and had this inherent idea that they were a few notches better than the rest, some of us sought to send them a message that they were not. My message was going to be 75 pounds of poop on their doorstep mixed with gravel. I successfully dumped one sack of poo on one doorstep and proceeded to show off in the high school parking lot that I was going to strike again that evening. I walked about a half-mile to school in the dark of evening with that sack over my back. I walked tall and tough like Santa coming with a pack full of goodies. As I approached the street light, there were gathered half the popular kids and jocks. Everyone laughed at me, and I could feel their acceptance that I was the cool one who goes the extra mile to do the prank right. They had already been talking about the pile left on Rachel's doorstep. Rachel was stuck up enough for everyone to cheer for my job well done. I was trying to find a new target. Who would I pick next? The laughter was like a drug, and I started to swing the sack of poop in a circle, round and round while I could hear them cheering. All at once, a firm hand reached out and stopped my twirling, and I proceeded to try to knock him out with the bag when the deep manly voice said, "Mereness! Mereness!"

I stopped twirling as I looked up to the man. It was the chief of police. I was caught red-handed and had nowhere to run. All the kids were snickering and trying not to laugh that I got caught. He had my arm held tight as he interrogated the top suspect of the poop dumping crime in the town, "What's in the bag?"

I looked like a sad puppy as I lifted my eyes to him, "This.... one?"

His anger started to kindle as he demanded once more, "Mereness, what's in the bag?"

I slunk down further in my shame for being found out and returned with a very sheepish small voice, "Dog poop."

He growled in return, "You and that sh*t get home right now

before I haul you into the station!" I shuffled off into the darkness in my walk of shame with that 75-pound sack over my shoulder and my heart pounding.

Nothing ever lasted. The popular girls in my class would tell me they would pick me up at eight that Friday night, and I looked my best. One time, Mom and Dad were watching T.V. as I watched out the window for their car to roll into the driveway. The car never came. Mom and Dad reminded me several times that they were probably not coming and that I should go to bed. I sat there a few more hours, just waiting. I was sure they would roll into the driveway with a story about a flat tire or something. The next school day, they treated me like a person they never met. I wasn't sure what I did that made them reject me, but I had a backup plan. I never gave up that easily.

That fall, I got my driver's license. It was not only my ticket to drive; it was my ticket back in with the girls. Most of them did not have a license, so they would probably need me, after all. They were your typical fair-weather friends. I also had the loudest stereo around, which made me a tad cooler than the others. I would crank up the rap music. Ian bought that stereo for a lot of money. The bass would make the entire car vibrate, not to mention cause your guts to pulse with every hit. I am sure I damaged some parts of my hearing, cranking it that loud. Those girls fought over who would ride with me because they all wanted to hear and feel that bass. Most times, I would have an overloaded station wagon. That didn't stop me from being reckless.

I would drive down a country road called French Road, known as a place where you could go airborne if you rode fast enough over it. I loved to speed over the bump of the railroad tracks. We would get air and land with a big thud before I would screech to a halt. When Mom and Dad found parts missing off the bottom of the car, I would just act dumb as though I didn't know what they were talking about. My sins found me out, eventually. With a carload of pretty girls, I decided to race over a bump that led right into the Kimberly High School parking lot. I hit that bump at about 60 mph, and after landing, I squealed around in a tight circle, burning all the rubber off the tires in one go. Little did I know, there was a teacher who saw my reckless behavior and took down my license plate number. That night as I rolled in my driveway, Mom was standing in the door waiting for me with a pink traffic slip in her hand. She snarled, "You're grounded for one month, and that is that!" I knew Mom was an immovable force not to reckon with. Her "no" meant no. If you sassed her, you would be slapped in the mouth or dropped to the floor.

When other girls saw Mom smack me, or throw me up against the wall, they would tell me that they wanted to call the Social Services on her. I told her one time what they threatened to do, and she would hand them the phone with a snarky smile on her face, "Call them. Good, I hope they take her. I'd rather go to jail than let her talk to me that way!" No one called on her. I knew she meant every word. She meant business.

Mom did not put up with guff. I begged to use the car on several occasions, but I did so in vain. She never gave in, and I served my time, which was worse to me than anything because, without the car, I didn't have friends, since I was only good enough when I had a car to drive them. Being used was a part of my life, and I became accustomed to it.

Several months later, I had to appear for my citation. Mom brought me in, and as we sat there listening to all the names being called off in alphabetical order, I noticed they did not call my name. They went straight to the "N" names. I raised my hand, and the judge called me up to him. I said, "Excuse me, sir, or I mean, your honor." I was trying to say everything the right way, "It seems as though you skipped over my name. I am Erin Mereness, and I didn't hear you call my name."

He wrinkled his forehead for a moment, grabbed the pink paper from between my fingers, and looked it over after flipping his fingers around in the pile of paperwork that did not include my information saying, "Well, it's your lucky day. We forgot about you, Erin, which means you are free to go with no penalties."

I blinked my eyes in disbelief, wondering if that was true. I questioned, "So, does that mean I need to reschedule this court date?"

He started to laugh as he said, "Nope. It was our mistake, so you get off completely in the clear." Mom was just as shocked, and she told me I was pretty lucky. It would have been a substantial fine, and I would have had most of my points taken off my license. I never did donuts or drove recklessly again after that time. I wanted to keep my record clear.

I was glad to get back into the driver's seat again and get the girls back in my car. In those days, the teens would drive around in cars late at night, preferably down a busy street to hang out. We called it the "Ave," which was short for College Avenue. One night, when I was driving around with these girls who I thought were my friends, I got into a bit of trouble. I always did what they said and went where they told me. Going out in the evening, as young ladies who did not behave with the utmost propriety, was not absent of some risks. The boys we would meet there were not so reputable.

I would wear the best clothes I had, curl my long blond hair, put makeup on, and mist myself with the sweetest perfume, enough to draw any man, good or bad. What was I thinking? Young girls sometimes crave attention so bad that they set themselves up on the auctioning block to the highest bidder. We say, "Pick me" and don't even realize how we cheapen ourselves. I did not have a whole lot of respect for myself, and somehow, I sought out that attention. There was a shady character who asked me for my telephone number and whereabouts. Flattered with the attention it brought, I naively gave it to him, not knowing that he would call upon me amid my slumber. When I was safe and warm within my bed, I heard one ring and jumped to answer the phone before Mom and Dad woke up. It did not dawn on me at the time that it could be that guy.

"Who is this?" I called out in enervation.

"It's Paul. Remember me, the guy you gave your number to?" He chided.

"Oh, yes! I do remember. How are you?" I said, as I suddenly became aware.

"We are planning to come to your home in about fifteen minutes or so and expect you will be ready for us." I would not or could not even surmise what this meant, and I feared my parents would find out.

After I hung up the phone, I hurriedly changed from my bedclothes into the clothing I was wearing hours before. Quietly, I tiptoed out of the house and into the darkness to wait. As the car slowly approached me, I walked into their direction. The two boys came from the car and met me in the cool, dark mist of that summer's night. I thought they would like to jump on my trampoline, and they did. It was far away from the house, so no one could hear the clamor they made.

"See that truck cap over there. Let's go see what's under it," they said, as they pulled me along. I still had no idea what they were thinking because I was lost in the moment of attention. Paul and the other boy lifted the truck cap and invited me under with them. As they laid there for a moment, I realized that I had gotten myself in quite a difficult situation with two boys who I knew nothing about. How could I be so blind? Was it because I was made for this purpose, to be used repeatedly until there was nothing left? Yet, I froze. I could do nothing as they misused me. I could not fight them, for I willingly entered into their lair. I realized at that moment that I must rely on my wits. Suddenly, I had an idea.

"Oh, I think we need some blankets, so we are more comfortable," I said with a confidence I had to conjure up, for I was more than frightened by that point. I knew that this situation could not end well for me, and I had to implore some practical wisdom. I have since realized that this was one of many miracles I lived to experience. God had given me a way to escape.

"Great idea! Let me help you find them," Paul said with earnest expectation. I knew I was not off the hook and that this meant I was still bound to them. "Maybe there is a blanket in this little shed," he said, as he peered into Dad's little tin shed on the end of the driveway.

"I do not think..." I said as he briskly pulled me into the dark hole again. He made another sick attempt at me, but this time, I used the martial art training to subdue him as I fled into the house and locked the door behind me. I ran to the bathroom, where I repeatedly washed my face, ears, and hands, but how could I properly cleanse my mind? I laid awake the rest of that early morn with a feeling of nausea from the evil that was done to me. Weeping until my eyes could no longer bring flow anymore, I pulled my covers up over my head.

When the light of day finally broke into the darkness, it felt so pervasive, and I knew I had to face life again. By this time, Dad marched up the stairs to see why I was taking so long. It was not like me to linger in bed on a Saturday morning. There were dogs to run and kennels to ready for more dogs that would arrive. I steadied myself, wiped the grief off my face, and made my way out of the house, and plodded my damaged body over to the kennel gate. Just glancing at the edge of the property flooded my mind with the gross thoughts of the night before. Soon, Dad noticed the car sitting in the parking lot next door. Both windows were smashed in, and that high-quality stereo purchased by my older brother was stolen. I knew it was stolen by the boys who visited me the night before.

"I think I know who did this," I quivered, knowing that it would disclose that I met them in the night.

"Who?" Dad said with anger in his voice.

"Some boys that came here during the night," I ashamedly answered. I knew they would find out. But would they believe me? Or would they think badly of me? I had a track record already for being irresponsible with the vehicle and too eager to please anyone by acting foolishly. My teachers had a meeting over my unseemly behaviors in school. I would dance in the back of the schoolroom, ask dimwitted questions to evoke laughter, and mimic my teachers, no less. Mom and Dad were well aware of my antics by then. How could they take me seriously if I had said they had caused me harm? They turned a deaf ear to me when I told them about what the uncle had done to me, so why would they think this was any more serious?

After telling them all the things that happened that night, Mom and Dad just stood there in anger. Mom vented, "You liked it, and you know it!" Those words pierced right into my soul! Just a few years before this, my uncle said, "Just wait a couple of years, and you will like it." What a lie! What a terrible thing to surmise. I loathed it entirely! These sick, perverted young men were forcing their way on me. No. I most certainly did not ask for this, but I was naive. Going out in the night was a very senseless affair altogether, one that I will always regret. Mom and Dad made me call the police about the thieving. Not about the other situation. That just got brushed under the rug. Nothing could be proven anyhow. The stereo was long since sold and the money most assuredly spent. There was no way to trace it. I didn't even know their full names. Besides, my parents were growing weary of my foolishness and the consequences that would follow me because of it.

I wanted so badly to understand God since He seemed the only one who reached down to help me in my time of great need. I did not own a Bible, but I could talk to God. He still seemed real and like a friend. Even when I was quiet, I learned to speak to Him in my thoughts. I begged God to help me to cleanse my mind from those horrid thoughts. The thoughts stretched across my life like a banner of depravity. So many thoughts I could not erase, and they would replay in my mind like videotapes of nasty things. Some of the things I replayed were those vial things that I experienced. Other things that would replay were the pornographic videos and the graphic images that were etched in my mind from my youth that I had to watch with the neighborhood boys. How could I erase them? Only the power of God could blot out such things from my brittle mind. This was a power that I did not know how to access because I had just started the journey to know my Savior, Jesus. The only thing I could do was find more things to fill my mind with.

At this time in my life, I babysat a lot. Now that I had my driver's license, I could pick up my little cousins and bring them to the zoo or on nature hikes. Being with them got me the feeling of childlike wonder and purity. Children are like that, and that is why I think Jesus said we all need to become like little children again. Most of my weekends were spent with these precious children.

I also joined the softball team. It was a big mistake. I did not have what it took to stand in the field because my mind tended to wander quite a bit. The other girls on the team would scream at me to pick up the ball and throw it to them because I was in a daydream. I had my little moped, and I would drive it to practice. Mr. Church was the coach, and he had very little patience with my personality. He was my Biology teacher. When I stared blankly ahead, he would shout to the entire class, "Ding, ding, ding, elevator going to the top floor, Mereness?" If I raised my hand with a question, which he suspected would be a dumb one, he would rebuke me with, "Mereness, I am convinced that you have what I call, diarrhea of the mouth and constipation of the brain." The rest of the class would laugh at me. I laughed with them because I probably enjoyed the attention. In softball, he was not too impressed and kept me seated on the bench for the most part.

I wondered if I should even keep going to practice after a while. I didn't want just to sit there all the time. I nearly fell off the bench one day when Mr. Church told me that I could be a "pinch runner" or whatever that was. I had no idea. I just got excited that I would get to play in a real game for the first time. I sheepishly asked, "What do I do?" The other girls told me that I would take the first base for the pitcher. I thought that seemed relatively easy.

There I stood behind the chain-linked fence in front of the bench with my helmet on while I watched every move that the pitcher made. My heart was racing as she had her bat lying across her shoulder, waiting for the pitch. The ball slammed into the catcher's mitt, and I jolted forward, ready to run. I took a deep breath and watched intently as the next ball was thrown. Crack! The ball was hit, and I took off out

The Blackbelt & The Trap

of the dugout, raced the batter to first base, and slid in before her. I thought I did my job all the while everyone was screaming at me from the stands, "You idiot!"

The coach had the ugliest look on his face as he motioned for me to get back on the bench. We got an out. It was all my fault. I was only supposed to trade spots with the batter "if" she made it to first base. I was just a substitute, not even a batter. I never lived that one down. They forever reminded me of being a lousy pinch-runner. I quit after that episode because I had to cut my losses. I knew the longer I would be in softball, the more things I would get wrong, and the more the girls would hate me. That incident cost us the game, so they were upset.

Mom's best friend had a daughter named Nikki, who was a champ at softball and who I knew my entire life. She was going to get a full scholarship, not only for her academics but also for softball playing. She was more like a sister to me, but we were nothing alike. She liked boy stuff and sports while I played barbies and dolls. She cut off all the hair on her dolls and drew nasty markings all over their faces because she hated them so much. I always thought it was such a waste to destroy so many pretty dollies. When I would stay at her home, she "had" to watch WWF wrestling, which I hated just as much as she hated dolls. Ian and Nancy always loved it and would jump on the beds like wrestlers. On her walls, she had posters up of Cubs players and professional wrestlers.

When she would stay at my home, I would always forget to eat, so she would have to call her mom to pick her up. Our moms always got together, and because she was the only child, Ian and I played with her. I think she enjoyed playing with Ian the most, but I looked up to her. She was twice my size yet only about nine months older than I was. We camped a lot in the summer together in her Grandpa's old RV. As she got older, she and I started collecting Precious Moments dolls, which seemed odd to me at that time. I guess she liked them because they were the kind of dolls you just put in a glass case to look at now and again. We always got another pretty doll for our special collection each Christmas.

Not only was she twice my size in the body, but she also had to have been twice my size in intellect. In later years, Nancy became a legend in her town. She excelled at everything, her education, her sports, and her friendships. She was everything I was not: popular, smart, and athletic. Her future was filled with promise.

Memoirs of a Keeper: Angels & Demons

At this time, when we were both in high school, we started to hang out at the parties that were in her community. I met a guy there named Sam. He was a star basketball player, tall, dark-haired and handsome. I could not believe he even noticed me while standing among the most popular girls in my school. I was the one he gravitated towards. Nikki and I would talk more because she liked a boy that was his close friend. Strangely enough, she and I were always the only ones at the parties who did not want to drink or smoke. Sam smoked, but that didn't stop me from kissing him. I found out he did a lot more than kissing with his last girlfriend because she thought she might be pregnant.

However, he took his time with me, never pushing me or pulling me in any direction that would bring me harm. We would go for long walks in the woods near streams, and he would lovingly hold my little hand. Soon after hearing my whole life story, he slowly pushed me away. It was how it always worked out. Most people don't want to know EVERYTHING. It makes others feel awkward. I like to think he was a gentleman and possibly because he did not want to add to my grief. He was a lot more experienced in the ways of women, and his needs were beyond what I could rightly satisfy. My wounded past thwarted young love at its sweetest, but again it was a miracle from God who would keep me from giving this guy my body willingly. I was broken when he told me that it was over between us. It was only a couple of months. There was nothing I could do to take back my words and stories, no persuading words to keep what was lost.

That July, we drove out to Minnesota to attend my long-lost sister's wedding. We were so thankful to be invited. We were seated at the furthest table like we were the most distant people they knew, which was probably right, but she and I were full-blooded sisters. That had to mean something. From where we sat, we could not even see the head table as our table was around a corner in the ballroom near the back door. I just wanted to see her with my eyes.

She was so beautiful in her white dress. It was perfect. She had met a nice guy who looked smart. We managed to sneak a photo of us with her as she came to say hello to us. I still have that photo in a box somewhere. I secretly wished that I could find a way into her heart, but I knew that she wanted us there but not in her life.

As I tried to move forward with a broken heart, I had no idea how much more heartbreaking the next few months would be. That summer, we found out that Uncle Tommy had stage four cancer. Between Mom, Dad, his grown children, and I, we went to his house to care for him. There he was, lying on a hospital bed in his living room, next to his old piano that would never feel the weight of his fingers again and no more rides on his big boat that he loved so much. It was evident that he was dying fast. It was like I could see his final trip into the sunset that rippled over the water he would sail. I made a painting of his boat on the water. His body was withering away to nothing. There were no more jokes and stories or laughter. His hair was gone except for a few wisps, and we were taking him back and forth to the toilet. The nights I stayed with him, I would use all my strength to hoist him in and out of bed. He mostly wanted to die watching boxing on TV. He was only 57 when he passed, so it was a hard funeral to attend, knowing that all of his married children were just at the point to start families, and we all swallowed hard when we realized he would never get to see all of his grandchildren. At his funeral, Dad played old recordings of Tommy playing piano and singing. The pureness of his Tenor voice sent goosebumps over everyone that day as we heard him one last time singing Ave Maria. Not everyone gets to be heard singing at their funeral. Dad always made weddings and funarals special.

No sooner did we clean Uncle Tommy's place after his death than Grandpa Reichel became very sick. He had his recliner parked in front of the television that he would sit in to watch the news, read his paper, or watch the Packer football games. He wasn't always in that chair. He would go to the basement or the screen porch outside for all the family gatherings. The more he drank, the funnier he would get, and the more old songs he would sing. One of his songs went something like this, "There was an old gal like Mary." All his songs sounded like that old song we sang on long car rides, "45 bottles of beer on the wall, 45 bottles of beer, take one down, pass it around, 44 bottles of beer on the wall!" You would count down until you had nothing.

That fall, he was sitting in the chair all the time and using an oxygen machine. One day, while all the family was out in the screen porch for another Kanadle Feast with Sour Bratan, I sat there at his side and held his hand. I didn't want him to sit there all alone. Kanadles was everyone's favorite, and Grandma spent the week before souring down the meat and making those big Kanadles. It was an ancient family recipe that had been passed down for generations. Grandpa sat there eating his meal in between trying to catch his breath. He had mesothelioma, which he got from all those years working in the paper mill that smelled so strong of sulfur.

Soon he was in the hospital, and I would go and visit him. Mom and Grandma were usually there every day. I came to relieve them on occasion, give him a back pounding and a hair washing. Mom showed me how to do everything. She taught me how to cup my hand over his back and start pounding up and down to loosen his fluids that were clogging up his lungs by that time. He would cough up fluids after that, and the nurse would suction his lungs. I loved washing his gray hair and making him feel like a king. He was part Mohican Indian and would tell me so many stories of his heritage while he still had breath in him. He said to me if you are near a campfire and the smoke starts coming your way, the old Indian trick was to say, "I hate rabbits!" He told us that this repeated over and over was sure to make the wind shift directions and the smoke out of your way. The one thing he said that stuck with me for my entire life was, "You're only as old as you feel. Always stay young." He said that with tears in his eyes. He was like a big kid, always having fun, and being childlike.

About a week later, he died with all his family around him. Mom was there. She was so dear to him. She told me later that he said he saw his parents and other people he knew who had died. He refused to take pain medication because he said, "Jesus suffered for me. I will suffer for him. Forever and ever, Amen!" She said he would repeat that phrase, "Forever and ever, Amen," over and over, and as he was gasping for his last puffs of air, he said, "I can see Jesus. He is coming for me. I will be with Him." He was a church-going man, a staunch Catholic man, who paid his dues and never missed Mass. God isn't in a box like we humans like to put Him in. Those last days when I looked into his eyes when he could barely speak, I could see that he understood what I understood about God at that time. Neither one of us had it all figured out, I didn't even own a Bible at the time, but I can say that as our eyes met, we knew God was real and that he was with us.

Grandpa's funeral was a happy one. I think we all were glad he had a long life. I don't think any of us remember him not being satisfied. He loved hunting, fishing, and being with his family. I was asked to sing "On Eagles Wings," and I also said the eulogy for him. It was something

The Blackbelt & The Trap

I spent the day before writing. I shared many funny stories, and besides everyone laughing, they were crying because he was a good man who would be missed.

No sooner did we scatter his ashes on Lake Winnebago than my world became even darker with grief. Two funerals in one season seemed like a lot for our family. We had many family friends visiting during this time to help us cope with our losses. Fall pressed on, and we hoped that life would settle back into our version of normal. Everything seemed like it was going smooth, until one horrid night. A night I will never forget.

The phone rang. It was four in the morning. No call at that hour is a good call. Mom tiptoed down the steps to find the phone. She bellowed and wailed, screaming, "Nooooooooooo!" I dashed down the stairs to see who had died, for there was no other cry that can compare. "It's Nikki! She is dead!" My heart pounded in my throat. It would've been understandable if it were someone else, someone older, but not Nikki, an only child, one with so much promise. It was incomprehensible.

It was on that cold October evening the night before that Nikki had gone out with some friends to see a haunted house. As they drove her home around one in the morning, they stopped at a stop sign. Everything was completely dark, and there was no traffic coming that they could see. A couple of drunken men were driving a car about 70 mph with their lights off. As the girls passed over the county intersection, that fast-moving car with the drunk driver smashed into the side of their van. The fires could be seen from Nikki's home. Her body was thrown from the vehicle, and she died instantly.

How could God take her so young? I went down into the kennel and fell to my knees. "Why? Why? Why?" was all I could utter. This was the very first time I had ever questioned God, and the last time. For some reason, the situation was so evil, and I could not understand. If God was good, how could he take such a young and innocent soul? Why I blamed God, I can't say. I was so angry at the time, and it did not seem fair. I know better now. It was not God's fault. It was just a very tragic thing.

Mom was soon to be absent most of the time. She was a nurse for a reason. She could feel the pain others felt, and she could stand in the gap for them. Most people would call upon my mother in a crisis because they knew she would drop everything to come to their aid. If there was nothing she could do to alleviate their pain, at best, she could be there to listen. Sometimes that was all they needed. For Nikki's mom, there was nothing that could take her pain away. It was most grievous, indeed. In this situation, nothing could make this mournful mother see better days.

I was also lost in grief; I could think of nothing else. I pondered the idea that it would have been better if I died instead of Nikki, who had the whole world by its tail. After all, I was so self-destructive, it would have made more sense if I'd have been killed in that accident rather than her. Someone so loved and accepted, Nikki would be sorely missed by so many. I could not say the same for myself, and it seemed to me that no one would even notice if I were gone. I figured that if God saved me from ending my life, He must have had a purpose for my future. I just did not know my value at that time. It's weird how in life, those that have a will to live and so much purpose die, while others who don't even appreciate life go on.

The funeral was the most dreadful experience. As I paced toward the open casket that held Nikki's lifeless body, I buckled. Holding the sides of the wooden coffin, my tears poured down the side, and I touched her frozen hands folded across her chest as if she were praying. Though nothing could be as final as the grave, it seemed like something could still loosen her from the grips of death. Maybe her body was just sleeping, awaiting my call. I prayed she would open her eyes, that she would wake. I had faith that God could raise her from the dead somehow. It was possible.

Nothing happened while I was begging God for a miracle, so it dimmed my faith for a time. Nothing obscures my faith now, but it has been exercised so often that I have learned to stand fast in an immovable hope. I did not even have a Bible, so I had no proper instruction on keeping my faith strong. As I walked away from Nikki's lifeless body, I felt like I was walking away from all possibility of hope. A whole future was gone in a second.

Mom kept vigil with Nikki's mother in her sorrow. When someone is grieving without the hope of better days to come, life becomes a bitterness to endure, and they grasp for anything that could take away the pain. Alcohol can never take the pain away, and it is not a consolation, but it was a way to cope for some. I was no stranger to being around alcohol. Interestingly enough, it had not been long since

Dad had given up his drinking.

One evening, five years before, Dad sat across me at the table. I will never forget this. It made a significant impression on me that would last a lifetime. He sobbed as he recalled the kind of father he was, how his drinking caused such a poor example. Most times, his drinking went unnoticed by me because he would drink the most when I was already in bed sleeping. I loved him for every word, for every tear, for I could see promise in it, the promise of a life not bound to vices such as alcohol.

"It is your future, your body. You can pollute it if you want. From this day forward, I will never drink another drop of alcohol. There are consequences to drinking," he steadily declared. "I was a bad example, and I am truly sorry." I could see it in his eyes. It was never going to happen again. All those years of rowdy drinking parties with all the relatives were over for him. I remembered seeing him swaying with intoxication loading the family in the van, and proclaiming that he was okay to drive us home. They would forge ahead in blind stupidity, weaving back and forth all over the road, but yet the Lord protected all of us every time.

My relationship with my father grew stronger after this. I inherently agreed that drinking was not the path I would ever choose. Alcohol can be a dangerous thing, indeed. For some it is a prison and others have the freedom in their conscience to enjoy it on special occasions. Later in life I learned that alcohol can be used responsibly but at my young age, all I could see it was as another form of bondage that I didn't want to be chained to. In my mind, it looked like bars that hold a person prisoner. I think that's where you get the name "Bars." Bars are like prison bars. Traps. From what I learned from Dad, an alcoholic cannot see that they are held captive. They reckon they are free to do as they please, with no thought of how it affects others. That is not true freedom. Until Dad saw the chains, he couldn't see his need either. When he saw how he was bound, he was able to spring free.

Memoirs of a Keeper: Angels & Demons

Chapter Three
THE VISION & THE ESCAPE

It was mid-winter in the year of 1994, shortly after the death of Nikki, when I found myself on a skiing trip for school. Nikki always loved to ski, so I thought it was worth a try. Up the ski-lifts to the tops of the snowy hills, the students would pick the path that would give them the most incredible thrill. It was my first time skiing, and the others knew it; they preyed on that fun fact. Their first trick was to tell me that you don't get off the lift at the top of the hill; you have to ride around to the other peak. There was no other drop zone, so I went back to the bottom of the ski hill. Everyone was laughing like a pack of hyenas at me.

    I went around back to the top of the hill and made it to the drop zone, but this time I got off the lift. Of course, they figured they could convince me to go down the steepest hill. It would be funny for them, and they thought I would figure out how to stop. As I flew down the slope, feelings of terror overtook me, zipping down at a very high speed while hitting various bumps and ramps along the way, soaring in midair at times and violently hitting the icy ground below, I still managed to stay upright to the bottom of the hill. At last, I saw the lodge and rows of unsuspecting people. The only salvation was a pine tree bustled out with soft needles. I wrapped my body around the boughs to stop finally. Soon after, many of the girls came down after me in laughter. They thought it was the funniest thing they ever saw, me flying full speed down the incline, not knowing how to stop. Determined to learn the skills of stopping correctly, I made sure to ask a professional and stayed away from the advice of the other kids.

I learned to ski just fine, and by the end of that evening, I could ski as well as any of the others, but because of their tricks, I tried to stay out of their way. Around ten p.m., the bus was loaded again for the journey back to school. I sat in the very back of the bus by myself. A boy named Jeff sat beside me. For some reason, I unloaded my whole life story on him. He sat and listened very intently. When I got to the part of the story where I cried out to Jesus, his eyes widened. It was a different response than what I had received from the other kids in a Catholic Catechism class. It was unorthodox. Somehow, he understood my divine encounter with God.

"You should come to my church sometime!" He said with enthusiasm. "We are Pentecostal-Charismatic, and we understand the salvation of Jesus Christ."

Not too long after, Jeff picked me up and brought me to his little church. His parents wanted to make sure that I said a specific little prayer to ask Jesus into my heart. "Erin, did you ask Jesus into your heart?" his mother, Marge, asked.

"Not specifically, no. But I know He is real, and I want to know Him more," I returned.

"It is simple...just say to Jesus right now after me...Jesus, I know I am a sinner."

"Jesus...I know I am a sinner," I paused with my head bowed down low. I was good at mimicking and saying what I was told to say, so I just followed what Marge was demonstrating even though I did not even understand what "sin" was at the time.

"Please forgive my sins and come into my heart," Marge went on.

"Please forgive my sins and come into my heart," I repeated.

"In Jesus Name...Amen!" Marge said as she clapped her hands and smiled with delight. "You are saved now!" I thought I was saved before, but I guess for safekeeping, I said the canned prayer anyhow. Marge gave me a New International Version Bible with study comments. This was the first Bible that I ever owned, and I devoured it. Each day I would take my new Bible out into the grooming shop while waiting for customers to pick up their dogs. Marge told me to start reading the Gospel of John. Every word on the page was filled with meaning to me. I drew pictures in the margins and highlighted verses that stood out to me significantly. Soon the pages were solid blue, green, and yellow with underlines and tears that stained through the printing. It was the word of God.

The church was a Four Square Gospel Church. I soon became a devout member. I came for all the Sunday mornings and the mid-week youth group meetings. Red carpets that were worn and off white walls. The church was very out of date. The front of the church was a small, raised platform with just an empty cross. I was used to the Catholic churches with Jesus on the cross. Jesus being displayed on a cross never made sense to me growing up. Here you have a man dying on a cross in a world that is dying. Where was the resurrection of life? Where was the hope? It all was very bleak when you look at death and pray to a dying savior, not a risen one. The empty cross was supposedly showing that He was no longer on the cross. He defeated death. I am sure most of the Catholics understood they were praying to a resurrected Christ, but I was perplexed at the time and did not have enough teaching to answer the questions that flooded my mind. Oh, I had so much to learn. Cross or no cross, I was happy to be among people who seemed to understand the saving power of God.

They spoke in tongues. That was strange to me. Sometimes I saw people flopping on the floor who were suddenly "slain in the spirit," they said. During the music, which they called worship, the people would cry tears and lift their hands above their hearts like they were reaching out to God. It was no wonder when I brought my parents to visit that they thought I joined a cult.

I thought it was strange in a way, but the people loved Jesus. They were genuine, and they took me under their wing. I was ready to learn everything and be open to whatever God had for my life. I am so glad now that I wound up at that little church because it was there that I saw Jesus.

One Sunday morning, as I was sitting in the back playing trombone on the worship music group, I had a vision. It was a time when all the people started swaying and crying out different things. Some were speaking in tongues, which sounded like babbling. Nothing made sense. I set my trombone down as I felt this presence surround me. I went out of my body, and I saw myself standing there naked. Jesus, robed in white, came toward me. I saw him walking. I was crying. He took off his robe, and he wrapped it around me, thus clothing my shame and nakedness. He took his finger and collected my tear into his hand, and said, "Don't cry."

I felt safe. It was surreal. We walked together, I in his robe and holding his hand in mine. There was a great big gate that we walked through. Beyond the entrance was a garden filled with every flower and tall plants. There was a waterfall. The path was golden, and we walked toward the waterfall. I could hear the tinkling of a thousand strings for every drop. Each drop was like a diamond. The flower was something I could experience with my hand pressing through the layers of glistening jeweled beauty. It was not like an ordinary flower. I even could see the air. It was of every sort of color, and I could touch it somehow.

I blinked my eyes, and it was all gone. I was still there behind the man playing his guitar and singing a melody to Jesus. The room was bland. The smell was of old carpets. I did not forget my vision, not by a long shot. It gave me hope. I saw the reality of Christ at that moment. Later I painted Jesus wrapping me in his robe. I still have it hanging in my office as a reminder.

Mike was the worship leader. He was a big man with an even bigger heart. He found out that I loved to sing, so he asked me to sing along on the songs he wrote. God so anointed his songs. His songs freed my voice. I found the harmony to his melody, and it became another way for me to draw closer to God. This was the church that Jeff and his family attended for many years.

Jeff would not leave me alone. He kept bothering me to go out with him. I liked him as a friend but not in the way he wanted me to. I wanted time to heal. Marge gave me a book that was written to help girls that were sexually abused. After writing me a lovely poem with a card, I got suckered into giving him a chance. It was a mistake. I could not handle relationships at this stage of my healing.

We were in band together, the high school musical, the church worship team, and other various classes at our local high school. We started a rock band, and I was the electric bass player. I spent a lot of time with him but soon found out he was a typical guy driven to use me. I allowed myself to be manipulated by him. He would use his image of God to control me. He would say we were married in God's eyes. I owed him my body. If I did not yield to him, he would tell me that he would do as my uncle would and find pleasure in another way. I couldn't bear it. It was all so confusing to me.

The Vision & The Escape

He became aggressive and expected me to do things with him that I wasn't ready for. If we were watching a movie late in the evening, I had a tendency to fall asleep, and he would push me off the sofa and say, "If you're just going to sleep, I am leaving!" When I ate, which I admit I did not have proper etiquette, he'd get so upset. I remember his cold stares as he would drop his fork waiting for me to correct my behavior. When he would drive, if I would fall asleep, he would slam his brakes so my body would fly forward and hit the dashboard. It was like I had launched myself into a constant state of control. He could be kind, and he was talented, but he had power over me, and I felt very much like a piece of meat rather than a treasure.

On one occasion, he became so violent that I disagreed with him; he started to shove me around and push me. It was in front of a restaurant where people could see. Someone called the cops, and in a moment, we were surrounded by squad cars. I was shoved into the back of the police car, and he was pushed into another police car. When I was in the car, the cops attempted to get me to incriminate Jeff. I wouldn't. They said, "You stupid girl!" I heard that before and now landed myself in the courts for obstructing justice.

When you are a victim, you keep yourself in that realm. That's the way of life. I thought all men were just like this. My mom told me they were. Maybe she was right. I certainly was losing hope that there were any guys out there that would not use me.

He would string me along. He would say I was his girlfriend when he wanted to use me. I had to pay for meals if we were out. When we graduated from high school and started our first year of college, he wanted us to be "just friends." That way, while he was in college, he could explore his options. How convenient! On his weekends home, he would want to get with me, and then I was his girl again. When I disagreed with this scenario, he forced himself on me. I lived in fear.

I graduated high school with a whole bunch of what seemed to me, drunks. Everyone was into parties and drinking. I think I was the only one that wasn't. I was the life of the party without the substances to control my mind. I could have a high on life and an adrenaline rush if I could make people laugh. That was my drug. I acted like a drunk with no alcohol because the rush I would get would leave me feeling so good. I never could understand how people even needed to drink or smoke, for that matter. How boring to be like everyone else and get hammered, pass out, puke, and not remember anything. It's all so dumb. Yet people do it. I didn't keep many friends from high school. I'm not sure if they are still mean or even if they remember me. If they remember me, they more than likely laugh. I did a lot of dumb things to get attention.

One time I dressed up like a fat man. I had my legs stuffed up to my arms; my belly hung over the waistline of my thrift store plaid suit. My hair was slicked under a short curly black wig, and my face was decorated with a three o'clock shadow. I talked in a low, gruff voice and went around to each class and told them I was the scheduled motivational speaker. The teachers would let me in, not knowing it was me, and I would give the kids a speech. I was putting on a play about a man in a van down by the river living on a steady diet of government cheese. They all would just laugh. When I arrived home, even Mom didn't recognize me and thought I was one of Dad's dog grooming customers.

I was very much into acting because it was an escape from the world I lived in. I found that playing another part was freeing. Making people laugh was my currency. The more I could make them laugh, the more I felt better about myself. I acted in the musicals as the Wicked Witch of the West or Princess Winnifred in Once Upon a Mattress. I had no fear of making a fool of myself. I could get up in front of hundreds of people and let loose.

My first year of college started, and I was ill-prepared for the party scene. I had a roommate, and she was a party girl. She would be out all night, and it was loud in the halls. I could barely sleep. Most weekends, I would go home to try to get a good night's sleep only to come home early on a Monday morning to find some random naked couple occupying my bed in my absence. Yuk. I soon plotted to get myself in the private dormitory where I could be out of the way of loudness and depravity. The only way was to live in the special needs section. Special needs? I made an appointment with a psychologist and got myself labeled with an emotional disability and a label for ADHD while I was at it. I had PTSD from coping with my past and found out my flashbacks; my anxiety was a part of this. They even labeled me with bipolar disorder. I had it all. The conclusion was that I was a disturbed person, just trying to make something of my life. It worked because I got the labels I needed to move into a safer environment.

I started on all the pharmaceutical drugs, which messed with my mind. I would walk out into the street and did not care if I got hit. I was numb, but by this stage, I was very much dependent on these drugs. Even though they were supposed to make me feel happier, I found myself feeling like an unfeeling zombie. I hated that. Out went my creative energies, and in came the demons.

You would think that I was getting a bit smarter by this time, but I still was pretty naive. One guy asked to do homework in my room with me, and I thought that meant doing homework. When he came to my door, I let him in. He sat on my bed, and I looked on the desk to find the books when he grabbed me and pulled me on top of him. I quickly jumped up and told him that I was under the impression that we were doing homework, and he was upset that I did not want to have sex with him. What is the deal with guys? I opened my door and demanded he left that instant.

That was not the last time a guy would try to get into my dorm room to mess with me. I had another guy who was in Tae Kwon Do with me and somehow ended up convincing me to strip down naked and run out into the hall with a blanket on while he was in my room laughing. It was a stupid dare. He had a friend with him, and because he was a black belt, I was no match for him, and on went the abuse. Thankfully, I did not go too far with him. The way I felt was utter disgust with myself for being this stupid and falling for his tricks. After he left, I tried to wash the poison of his lips off me. How can you clean your inner heart from all the shame? I felt responsible because I kept letting perverted men rule my world. I opened doors I never should have.

Jazz was one of my escapes of that time. During college, I was in a jazz combo playing the big double bass, an instrument twice my size. It wasn't the first time I picked an instrument that looked to big for me. There is a lot of emotion in jazz music. It rises and falls, and each instrument converses with each other in a language no one knows, but the message is beyond words. In the imagination of music, the trumpet and piano might argue when I come in there with a bass line to fix it. I might sass the saxophone when the guitar comes in for his two cents' worth. If you ever listen to the old jazz standards, you will hear the instruments arguing, meddling, sassing, caressing, gently speaking to one another in song. When we all have had enough, there is a time we all come into agreement, we prove our point, and the music hits the climax. It sort of builds. You hear the frustration and a passion, yet you want to breakthrough. After the top moment, the instruments wind down, and all is well.

I can't clearly explain how I knew how to do this. It came as natural to me as breathing. Talking to the instruments with my fingers was sometimes the only way I could be a voice in my life that seemed so gray with confusion. The old jazz standards of Miles Davis, Duke Ellington, and Thelonious Monk are among the greats of that time. Their music takes you on a trip.

The music people at the university were different folk. They were chill yet intense. We called them "the Connies" because they were from another planet resided in the Music Conservatory. The Con was another world, indeed. The people were so caught up in their music that they were not conversing with others on other topics besides music. I surely did not fit in that world either since I would hate to talk about music all the time. I did not fit in with the Art folk either.

Todd was an art professor who changed my life. He saw beyond the facades I masterfully created. He knew I was a true artist. He taught me that art is not just what you make on paper or with your hands; it is a state of being. "Patience and urgency" was his motto. Let me explain... It is not to be in love with what you are creating but in love with the process. It is diving into the realm of feeling, of emotion, and of the journey that creating is. The music is a journey, a conversation between the instruments' voices, and art is a conversation between paper, hand, and the voice is with the eyes. I learned to draw what I saw instead of what I know. The challenge was not for perfection but to lose myself in saying something with my eyes. My eyes communicate with my hands, and you see what I see, so my message is clear to the audience. Art is a form of communication. Todd told me that I was a true artist because anyone can draw correctly. Anyone can pick up a brush and paint a picture. Every human can learn or master a skill. But the real art is with your mind's eye. He said it was a rarity, and I possessed this quality somehow.

If I were drawing a self-portrait, he would come and smear the entire thing because I was getting too precious about it. He challenged me to get out of my brain and be watchful to express what my heart was saying. Slash it up, tear it down, build it again, erase this, add color here, and pull the elements together to make something from humble beginnings. I see this creative force as something we have from God.

The Vision & The Escape

He is the ultimate creator. His words He creates the universe and sets it in motion. All life, all that we see, was made as an expression of what was in His heart. If for just a shadow of what God is, I understand, in part, being a creator. As we are made in His image, so we are created to create. We are designed to be an expression and to express.

If I wasn't plucking my bass or creating artwork, I was reading my Bible. I had a whole list of books I was required to read for my first year of college, and I did not even read one of these books. I listened to lectures, and I could tell you what the book was about. It is common sense, mostly. I had perfect scores on my papers that I would write even though I never read a word in the books. My prayer was that I could dedicate that year to the Lord and be immersed in His Word. I wanted to grasp every aspect of who my creator was. I believe it was a miracle that I could study His word, and the knowledge for all the rest was given to me. With tests, papers, lectures, my mind quickly understood it all without much effort. I would compare historical figures like Plato and the Apostle Paul when writing essays. I was reading the New Testament at the same time as hearing lectures about Plato's Republic. My university was a Liberal Arts school. That means it is pretty liberal. The professors loved the arguments that I would form of the vast sea between God and the wisdom of man. All I wanted was more of God each day.

That summer, I found out about an opportunity to escape to the North Woods of Wisconsin. Fort Wilderness. It was a family and camp for kids of all ages. There was a volunteer position there for camp counselors. That was a dream job for me. I applied for the position, and because it was a Christian camp, I had to tell them what I believed. Putting into words the depths of how much I loved Jesus was easy for me, and for them, it meant that I was qualified.

When I told my parents, they were not happy. Why would I go to a place where I didn't know anyone to volunteer when I have an education to pay for? It did not make sense to them, but I had to go. I wanted to work with the children, and I wanted to be away from town when Jeff was home so that he could not weasel his way back into my life. He did come home and tried to convince me to save my heart for him. I was a people pleaser, so I told him that I would save room for him upon my return, but I needed to have this time to draw closer to Jesus.

As my parents drove down the lane that led to the camp, it was like a tunnel of pines. "I hope this is not a cult, Erin." I ignored it and brushed it off as I did all the other times; my parents ridiculed me for my faith. My dad said many times, and the memory still rings with me today, "Who do you think you are to talk about religion with me? Let people believe what they want! No one cares about what you believe!" I had gotten used to the fact that my parents thought I was in a cult and that I was nuts.

The smell of pine lingered in the air with each breath. I said goodbye to them and went forward to my destiny. As I watched their car roll beyond the trees, I felt a sense of freedom from all that had happened to me in the past. No one could tell me I was stupid anymore or worthless. Mom could not tell me, "No wonder why no one likes you," when people did not understand me or lost a friend. I did not have to worry about getting slapped in the face or getting my hair pulled with my head being slammed against the wall for the times I tried to defend myself or when I didn't agree or if I didn't listen fast enough. Nor did I have to cower in a corner in fear of my life. I could wake up each morning to the birds, the rays of sunlight bursting through the pines like golden stripes on my window.

It was like I was beginning a new chapter of my life—a glorious chapter of just me with my God in the woods.

Chapter Four
THE CAMP & THE CANOE

The camp was everything I had dreamed of. Tall pines, birds singing, the sun shimmering across the beautiful lake beside the pines. Cool breezes and the peace of God is what I remember most of all. I didn't know anyone, so I enjoyed my solitude. The walks I had in the woods with Jesus were the most incredible. I would talk to Him, walk with Him, and feel His presence in the gentle breath of the breeze.

In the evenings, all the staff at camp would gather in a big room. This big room was all there was between the men and the women. We all had rooms with bunk beds. I picked an empty bunk room. One evening as all the young adult staff was laughing and carrying on; I decided to announce that I was a first-degree black belt. I couldn't stay long in my solitude as I am quite a social butterfly. Some things can't stay at bay. They have to be revealed.

There was this tall guy, Mark. He was a typical guy, the kind I am all too familiar with. He started to tease me for my karate. He lifted his hands in a Kung Fu motion and made a high- pitched sound as you hear on those old Kung Fu movies. It irritated me. He was a jerk in my mind from that moment on. I wanted to beat him up. He never attacked me, so I had no reason to, so I devised a plan to level him.

I had a meeting with the head of staff at the camp to discuss my other duties while watching over a flock of ten little girls around ten years old. When the kids are off doing their classes during the day, we had to have something else to keep us busy. I was already signed up to help at the Nature Center. When I asked them if I could also teach a self-defense course, they were delighted. This was my ticket in. I wondered if that guy named Mark could be my dummy. They chuckled because of our size difference. He is six feet five and very athletic, and I am a mere five feet one. "Okay," they laughingly said. "This ought to be good!"

There was one purpose in my mind, and that was to teach this cocky, jerk a lesson: " You don't mess with me. I may be little, but I am feisty." I had been through enough jock-type guys like him teasing me, but they always get worse, until they eventually use me.

In high school, there were packs of guys trying to take me down once they knew I was in Tae Kwon Do just to prove that I could not break free. I was locked in lockers, stuffed in gym bags, thrown down the stairs, tossed around in the air, and bullied not only by the big girls but also by the guys. When you're so small, they find it fun to toss you around a bit.

One time I had had enough of the teasing, and when this guy named Lance came to punch me in the arm, I twisted his arm behind him, and round-house kicked him in the solar plexus. It knocked the wind out of him, and he fell to the floor. The others stood in amazement. When they all ganged up on me one day, I could not fight them off. "We could all have our way with you, and there is nothing you can do about it." They were right. I could not fight off that many. Their sheer number would have consumed me. After all, I was no Kung Fu Master. Those were my fears. I did not want this new guy, Mark, who was the same size as the guy I kicked to the ground, to think he could corner me.

The first day he was standing across me in the presence of all the staff and the campers, I said, "Come on, hit me!" He looked down at me with the most genteel look. He actually couldn't do it at first. I felt like David staring up at Goliath. How do I get him to attack; do I throw a rock at his head? Finally, I convinced him to grab me by my wrist, and I twirled so fast under his arm and tucked my little body behind his long muscular leg, which was practically the size of me, wrapped my arm in front of him, and threw him over my legs in a flash. There he was lying on the floor while everyone laughed. I guess you could say I swept him off his feet.

There was something different about him. He was timid and quiet. You could hardly get him to say, "boo!" There was this expression of innocence in his eyes. They were gentle eyes. He honestly looked like he would never harm me. Not even for his pride. Nevertheless, I kept flipping him over my body day in and day out to show the kids how to defend themselves. It was good to show that on such a massive person because if you know what you're doing, size is of no consequence.

In the evening that week, I had a cabin full of these little girls. They were on bunks all around me, and I got to talk with many of them and become like a mother to them. Some had also been abused, and I was someone who could understand and help them in a small way. After we woke, we would gather for a big camp breakfast in the main hall, which always tasted delicious, even though it was not the healthiest. It was all you could eat of the finest, fluffiest pancakes, toast, bacon, or sausage.

After our hearty breakfast, we would all convene at the big top tent. Under the tent, I would play my bass with the worship team, and we would have these fun revival meetings. The kids would be jumping up and down, crying, and even kneeling in prayer. It was quite a sight to see so many kids getting on fire for God. When the meetings were over, and we heard a life-changing message from the speaker, we would all head to our classes. My first class in the morning was teaching at the nature center with a very nice young woman named Angela. She was tall and slender wearing the typical outdoor-type attire in all neutral colors. Her soft brown hair was cut to her shoulders, and she would always greet me with a wholehearted smile. Often Angela and I were left in the nature shack for hours with no class to keep us occupied. When we weren't off in the woods teaching the kids about insects, frogs, and the type of fauna on the forest bed, we had Bible studies together.

She was a person who I thought I could completely trust. I started unloading all my stories on her like I did so many times in my life to find out that it was a mistake. Somehow it felt safe. She was older, more mature, and seemed so eager to mentor me. When I told her about all the times I had been violated; it broke her heart. She took me under her wing and started to show me great Bible verses that would comfort me in my sorrow and help me heal.

"I never want to marry. Men are pigs!" I told her with all the conviction of my being, "I want to be a missionary in a foreign land and be a mother to the motherless children of the world." She looked at me with the most confused expression I have ever seen. It was as if I said something wrong.

"No, Erin. You can't do that," She said as she began to prove her point, "You are called to be a helpmate to a man. You need to be a helper to a man and become a wife and a mother. That is God's will for your life." I was so confused at that point, but I wanted to believe her. She was so convincing.

"Me? Marry a man?" I said in total disappointment, my head hung low. "Who?"

Angela began to instruct me step by step, "Pray for your mate," she continued, "Ask specific things when you pray. Tell God what your goals are and pray that He will give you a man who would share these same goals."

As soon as I could break free, I bolted for the woods to talk to God in prayer. "Okay, God," I said with a bit of sarcasm. "If I have to get married, he has to want to settle down in the country, want to have a big family, have a bunch of animals, and have a farm." I figured this was a long shot. There are not many guys who want to settle down, much less have a large family and the family farm to go along with it.

I had no idea God was listening. The very next day, Mark and I had to take the campers on a long canoe ride. I watched as the canoes started to fill up one by one until we were the only ones left. I sighed as I gazed at him. In my mind, I was thinking, oh, no, I was stuck with Mr. Dull, the guy I had been flopping over my shoulder, the big guy, who was good looking but not my type. My type was the Jesus-looking guys with long hair who can play guitar, not the basketball-player kind. Besides, what would we talk about? We had nothing in common. How can you converse with a guy who doesn't speak? How awkward will this long journey across the lake be?

We walked over to that lone canoe and started paddling on the lake. I wasn't interested in him and was kind of irritated that I was stuck in that canoe with him. After a long silence and the sound of water being pushed over the paddles, I thought I would try to talk with this guy.

I asked him a typical Erin question, "What do you want to do with your life?"

He responded, "Well, I would love to settle down, get married, start a family, have a bunch of kids, and live out in the country. Maybe I would get some farm animals..."

The Camp & The Canoe

I jumped to my feet that instant before he could even finish his sentence, nearly dumping the canoe over, "We're getting married!!!!"

He steadied the canoe and said in a gentle voice, "Okay."

I ran back to the old Nature shack to tell Angela that God had answered my prayers. She was horrified and said, "No, that's my brother!!!" I had no idea that they were even related. They looked nothing alike. They did not even talk the same. She spoke and he didn't. His hair was thick and black, and hers was thinner and light brown. Yeah, they were both tall, but their faces were nothing the same. I was shocked at her reaction. She was the one who recommended that I pray for my mate. How was she to insist on such a prayer, yet not accept the answer? That was the end of our friendship for a time, as I became opposition to her ideals for her brother. If it were any other guy at the camp, she would have been happy for me.

I felt the beginning pains of rejection that day, but it did not dim my will to follow the call I know I heard from God toward being a wife and mother one day. To me, I took his words of confirmation as the writing on the wall with the very finger of God. Going my own way, against God's call, meant I would be going against God. That never ends well. I had read stories in the Bible where people did not obey God, and one such individual ended up in the belly of a whale. This was serious business as far as I was concerned. Just because she disagreed didn't mean that it was not from God. At the time, I did not feel I needed any other form of confirmation.

Thankfully, a trip was scheduled later that week, where all the staff gathered to have a little downtime, enough time for Mark and I to talk. The waves crashed into the shore, the moon was shining, and we had sand in our toes as we held hands and stared out into the horizon that seemed to stretch far beyond the water's edge. I think it was time for me to get to know this guy who I just proposed to and would give the rest of my life to. I didn't know him. He didn't know anything about me. We sat all night just talking on the beach of Black River Harbor on Lake Superior. He made a fire from driftwood. The logs crackled and popped as we sat there. I can still see the glow of oranges and reds over his lovely face. The light was dancing in his eyes. Our hands held fast to our new love.

For starters, I found out he was from Milwaukee. He was half English, part German, and part Irish. His parents were divorced, and I remember him telling me about his growing-up years. I told him my life story until that day, stories of pain, rejection, and loneliness. His story was one of such discouragement. One thing that sticks out was that he said he felt like a failure in all that he did. It sounded like he was the black sheep of the family. My oh my, two broken souls. Sounds like a match made in heaven, right?

Some of his close family members felt wholehearted that I was too full of baggage to be the one for their beloved son/brother. I don't blame them. I understand that when you love someone, you want the best for them, not a girl that was half-used up with mental problems. That's not the sort anyone would naturally want to pick.

I was sorry that I disappointed these lovely people so much in the beginning, but I would like to argue the point that God can use someone who has a broken past. He can use someone who has been through the wringer a few times and learned some lessons from the hard knocks of life. After all, God doesn't call the equipped; he equips the called. He called me, so I knew He would also be faithful to prepare me. All I knew was that I was a perfect fit for this soul, and he was likewise my ideal match.

It was not easy trying to win their respect, but I had to come to grips with the idea that it may never happen, and if God wanted to join us together, we just had to go ahead without their blessing. I know how deeply it must have grieved his family. I can't even ask forgiveness for that decision now because I knew it was the right thing to do. It was God's perfect will for our lives.

Months later, as we had gotten more used to the idea of "us," I noticed one remarkable thing. I was eating with him, and I dripped a bit of food out of my mouth. He quickly grabbed a napkin and blotted the smear off my cheek with a smile on his face. I could not believe his kindness toward me. I was used to being made fun of or abused by guys when I crunched my food too loudly. I did not know a man could be so kind.

He said, "I won't bring you flowers, nor candy, and I am not romantic like other guys are, but all that fades anyhow. My love will never fade." Was I dreaming? I sure did not need any of the fluff. Just kindness. I asked him, "What can I ever do to thank you for being so good to me?" He returned, "I will tell you later!"

He took me to the bluffs of Lake Michigan in the dim moonlight.

The Camp & The Canoe

We stood there looking over the vast sea of ripples, the waves crashing into the shore. He did not say anything at all for some time. I was in awe of God's creation. It was marvelously beautiful, how the moon lit up the waves below as the water shimmered. Then he grabbed my little hands in his much larger hands, "Erin. Do you remember when you asked me what you could do to thank me?"

I said, "Yes!" The man of few words stared down at my hands safely tucked away in his. He slowly looked up from his gaze upon our clasped hands until our eyes met. "You can thank me by spending the rest of your life with me." Then he pulled out a ring; it was my favorite kind, an antique one, nothing fancy. He slowly went down to his knee, and he was the same height as me at this point. "Will you marry me?"

I guess my proposal was not official. This was official. It sealed the deal. He said he was not romantic. I don't care what anyone says; that was about the most romantic story ever! And it was mine! Of course, I said, "YES!" I would have been a fool to say no!

The top of the mountain moment was short-lived, sadly. I was not prepared for the battle ahead—the cold stares that cut through my soul. One evening at his place, his mother noticed the ring on my finger. She grabbed my hand and asked me, "What is this?!" I replied in fear, "This is my engagement ring from Mark."

Still holding my hand, she pulled me out of the kitchen and into the living room where my love was sitting. She said, "What is this?! Erin said, this is an engagement ring! Is that correct?" She put my hand in front of his face. My heart was pounding, and I waited for his approval when he looked at her completely confused and said, "I have no idea what that is or what she is talking about."

I burst into a flood of tears as I tore my hand from hers, and I ran for the door. I just kept running. I could not believe that he did not acknowledge our engagement. Was he ashamed of me? Was I out of my mind? Did all the good happen to be all taken away like everything else in my life? That worthless feeling so quickly came back, and I felt hopeless. I imagined that she must have thought I made the whole thing up. I must have. It could not be true that someone good loved me. Indeed it must have been a dream.

As I walked into the darkness, I did not care if I knew where I was. After all, why would it matter if I got lost? My only true love had forsaken me. I sat beside a pond just watching the streetlights flicker their dim reflection on the still water, perhaps miles from the place I ran from. Then I heard footsteps. I didn't dare look back. Mark found me and sat beside me. I ignored him, stared straight ahead with wells of tears blocking my vision. As the words of contrition poured from his lips, it fell on me like a healing balm.

What now? How do I face her? Where would I go? I told him I could never return to that place. When I was around her, she would stare at me with such disdain. Sometimes I felt the stares pierce my very soul like a knife freshly sharpened. Never have I ever felt the darts of the enemy so strong against me. I prayed every day that she would see that I was trying to live for God, that I was a broken vessel who just needed a mentor. I begged God that she would soon pull me under her wing and teach me the truths of God's word. I imagined that I could have been so much better a person by her teaching, her divine example of a Godly woman, or by her love for me. I craved her approval.

He drove me to his dad's house on the other side of town that evening. His dad was so gentle and kind to me. He was everything Mark was, just a bit older and with a cool English accent. I found out he was born and raised in England and moved here to marry Mark's mother. They had three children together, Mark being the one in the middle. He and his wife were very welcoming, and I will never forget their act of kindness. It meant so much to me in the light of my severe rejection of his mother's side of the family. They were the ones who I was told were the bad ones from his family because they had an affair when Mark was only eleven years old. I guess we undoubtedly were the outcasts together—the bad ones. The ones you ought to stay away from, but I felt loved by them. I could see past their past.

Things became very confusing for me as I attempted to process this rejection. Laying aside my conflicts with his family, I had to work hard to not lay this offence to their account personally. As I put my thoughts into a broader scope, Christianity in general, It was not what I believed Christianity to be. I wasn't raised in a Christian home, so my perspective was limited at best. After being abused by others, I can still say that I was presented with more love in my family than what I had found in Mark's home. I just figured Christians would be like Christ. After all, the name! Christians were big into reading God's word, so if they read it, why not apply his all-encompassing love toward them so that it overflows to all those lives they are blessed to touch. I figured the

Christians would love more unconditionally, forgive quickly, minister to the broken, and would accept others because I read that in the Bible. Was I misled? I found myself measuring people's faults with the same ruler stick of judgement I felt measured by. When trying to figure out the intensions of another humans' heart, no matter what the offense, it lends to some serious introspection. My own heart began its' decent into bitterness and hate, a path that only leads to spiritual death. By calling out the hypocrisy I witnessed, I essentially became one myself.

That was my first disappointment with Christianity. I could not, at the time, figure out how to get past the idea when a Christian, a follower of Jesus Christ, acts in such a hateful, bitter way towards someone who was already so broken. It didn't make sense me and I had a strong tendency at the time to dwell on the negatives. I can't rewrite the past. I can't take this page out. It was something that shaped me. I found out that just because someone calls himself a Christian does not mean that they have joy, peace, patience, forgiveness, or love. It is always a choice.

Thankfully, I didn't allow this to turn me from Christ. Many people hate God because of the bad things that happen to them or sometimes because of hypocritical Christians. Well, I can't blame the free will choices of humans to act in such hateful ways on God. I do know this…God would not have approved. I never once blamed God for the bad things that happened in my life. I never shook my fist in his direction. I always felt like anything right in my life was God's mercy. I didn't have an entitlement attitude that God owed me anything. If only others could accept all the injustices of life and not hold it to the account of God. It would be one of my sincerest prayers. God is good. Bottom line.

From those hurtful experiences with others' disdain, I wrestled with the feelings of being unworthy of His love and God's mercy upon my soul. I questioned whether or not they were right about me, whether or not all I deserved was to be left in the trash can where I belonged. A piece of me wanted to please others and let them have their way. Break it all off and be done with hurting others by being loved by Mark.

I pushed Mark away. I said hateful things to him. I threw things at him and treated him like a piece of dirt. I could not break him. His love for me was pure, and he knew that I was simply acting out. He still says, "All women are crazy. It is just a matter of what level." He waited out my crazy phase. He did not move. He would not go. He just stayed. He took my abusive words. It was then that I knew he would never forsake me. But I had to test him. I had to know for sure that he would stay, no matter what. I could not reinvest my heart to be broken. And from that day until this, he has never broken my heart again. He has never wavered in his devotion to me. For that, I am thankful. For that, I am in awe that he would love such a one as me. It is my miracle. Mark is – and has been – my gift.

Here is the thing I learned about disappointment. It is also a gift. It is like the rain. It pours down, and the sky is dark. Clouds are looming over. The sun ceases to shine for a time. It can seem hopeless. But rain is essential for life. Without rain, all that is alive would become thirsty and dry. It would be a deserted wasteland. Life would cease. We need rain just like our souls need disappointments once in a while. We learn more during times that make us question than those times that the sunshine of life will ever teach.

So that you know...I forgave her eventually. I certainly do not share this part of my story to justify myself or make myself look better. Nor do I share this story because I want Christians to look bad. I know she only meant well. She did not know any better at the time. I forgave her based on Christ's example. After all, His own people spit upon Him, reviled Him, rejected Him, and cursed Him. And He still died for them. He even forgave them.

I also chose to forgive my parents, as well. All the pain of feeling like they did not understand me or the times I thought they hurt me, I decided that I was wrong if I did not learn to let go and forgive them. They did the best they could. My mom ran to my rescue more times than she ever meant me harm. I knew that she did everything she could to help me, and as she stood with me in my engagement, it bonded us so close together from that day forward. We planned a life together. My parents were now my closest friends, and I would endeavor to become Mark's mother's friend as well. Life will be more fun when you live it alongside those you call your friend. Enemies make the journey more difficult. If Christ did it, I knew I could too.

As our bloody wounded savior hung on that cross, the only thing He would say about these murderous, hateful people was, "Father, forgive them for they do not know what they do." If Christ can forgive in such circumstances, my situation was so easy in comparison, then why could I not forgive? I held fast to this verse, "With men this is impossible; but with God all things are possible." Matthew 19:26

The rain was coming down like crazy. I was brushing a dog and adding the finishing touches, thinking Mark was tending the kenneled dogs. The evidence of no barking silently told me that he was still there beside me. I was just too busy to keep track of where he was.

"Take the dogs out!" I said in his direction, "It's raining!" And there Mark stood, blank-faced and oblivious. He moved to my hometown to be near me, and he worked with me at our family business, the dog kennel. Was he tired or just being stubborn? I couldn't tell you. It wasn't like him. I grabbed his shirt and tugged him toward the door that led to the kennel. We walked half hunched over into the rain as we guarded our faces. One by one, we let the dogs out—each one to its outdoor cage. As Mark stood in the kennel, he stared across the room at nothing. It was bizarre, but I needed him to help. These dogs had to go to the bathroom and get back inside out of the rain. We needed to clean the cages, fill the water bowls, and feed those that needed their dinner.

"Feed the dogs, Mark!!!" I yelled, "They are soaking out there!" So he went for the food. He grabbed the scoop, and he loaded the dish up, and everything seemed normal until he started overfilling. The food was pouring out the sides of the dish, and I was getting frustrated at this point with his odd behavior.

He still did not move around much. I just decided I needed to work around him. Why was I so clueless? I think back to this, and I am bothered by my lack of sense. I think it was because the dogs were getting wet, and you know what a wet dog smells like, right?! Well, try the scent of about twenty dogs! The smell is thick in the nostrils. I rushed around, feeding and watering when I saw Mark leave the kennel. Where was he going?

He came in with two dogs: a big one and a little one. The big one was a wet, hairy Airedale, and the other was an itty, bitty Yorkshire Terrier. That little darling must have been about three or four pounds. It just quivered under his arm. He corralled the big dog into a cage and then tossed the little one in there with it. WHAT?! You don't just throw the dogs around like that! Then – there was the strange thing – he reached over and grabbed this big dehumidifier and proceeded to add that to the dogpile up in the cage! I grabbed a water dish filled with water, and I threw that water right in his face to wake him up! What was his deal?! He did not get mad at me. He just stood there and took the water in his face without any aggravation.

I had to shove him aside, "Are you out of your mind?!?" I took the dehumidifier out of the cage and gently scooped the frightened little dog out of that cage and put it into its pen. After every last dog was adequately put away, I led my big, odd-acting fellow up to the back door of the house. He stood there like a robot. I went in, and he was still outside the back door, just standing there until I opened the door for him. After he was all the way in, he lifted his foot and kept it there hanging above the floor. He said, "Hello!" in a very sarcastic, rude manner, "Aren't you going to help me?" I stared at him, thinking, what in the world is going on?

I walked over to humor him, and I pulled his shoe off, "There, are you happy?" What was his deal? Then he did the same for the other foot. I started to laugh and think; this guy is such a goofball. How fun! How on earth I did not suspect this as something that was ailing his mind; I do not know to this day. I am ashamed of how I made fun of him and let this behavior keep going as it was entertaining me. I know. I was a fool.

After I was able to lead him over to the table, I sat him down, and my dad, by this time, was a bit concerned that he was on drugs. I guess we did not know him that long to judge. We looked over at the table where my mother had brought home some hospital food for us to eat. Yummy hospital food, right? Not. My mother typically made the most nutritious and delicious meals. She had to be somewhere, so she brought us hospital takeout. Mark just sat there, poking a fork into the Styrofoam container. I started to laugh because it looked so funny to me. I opened the box so he would be able to get to his food, and he just kept motioning the fork over the food but never could touch the food and bring it to his mouth. I grabbed the fork and put a jiggling piece of fat on the end of it just to see if he would eat it. He hated the fat, and every time I ate with him, I noticed that he would precisely cut the fat from the meat. So this was a real test. He gobbled it up, and that is when it dawned on me that something might be wrong with him!

Soon he acted more normal and finished eating by himself. What was that? I had not seen him ever behave like that. It was strange, but I never thought much of it after that day until it happened again.

That summer we had many relatives over for a wedding

celebration for my brother Ian and his new wife, Michelle. He brought her home the Christmas before with a suprise. My brother who was never a risk taker, met Michelle in Florida while in music engineering school, two weeks later, he drove out to Las Vagas where she was visiting her family and married her. Surprise! I was so happy to finally have a real sister. The rest of the family wished they could have been at the actual wedding but I was glad they were happily married with a new baby! I was an auntie for the first time to Lila.

  The celebration was in our backyard and we tried to get Mark to play basketball, and he just sat there saying, "What's it to you?" It was rude, and I think my family thought he was a jerk. He sat on the edge of the chair with his legs straight out. People had to walk around his legs, and his toes pointed straight up as he slumped in that chair. It was very odd, yet I still did not put two and two together. Finally, I was able to pull him out to the court. He didn't participate. He just stood there staring blankly ahead. This was very strange because Mark was an excellent basketball player and he loved the sport. He never missed an opportunity to play. I wanted to show him off to my family. I wanted them to see how amazing he was. Instead, he repeated the same rude phrase, "What's it to you?" The ball was thrown right at him, and then he fell back into the fence. It was a very tall wooden fence, and the way it shook with the weight of his body got everyone's attention.

  He fell to the ground and started to flop around violently. People were huddled around the scene. My mother called 911, and the ambulance came rushing into the driveway. I was so scared for his life. I wondered if he would make it. Most of all, I wondered what caused this. Just an hour before, he was acting completely normal. The paramedics asked for his family, and there were none to be found. I piped up, "I am his fiancéé!" They loaded my love onto a stretcher and stuffed him into the back of the ambulance. They invited me to ride along with him. As we raced down the freeway, I saw IV bags dangling and hitting the long pole that stretched high above Mark's head.

  I watched as they reached for testing supplies and tried to help him. Finally, they discovered that he had such a low blood sugar level that caused him to go into a seizure. They had to give him some glucose to bring him back. The doctors had never seen a person have an episode like that without being a diabetic. They questioned whether he took a dose of insulin from a diabetic, but we could not remember being around anyone with diabetes. It took over a week to diagnose him after they sent lab work to a much larger hospital.

He had a sporadic tumor in his pancreas. If he did not have it removed, he would die. The tumor was called an Insulinoma because it produces insulin. One in 10 million around the world have this kind of tumor. The specialists came into the hospital room where he had been sitting for a week and explained his condition and how they planned to cure it. The only cure is to remove the portion of the pancreas that contained the two-millimeter-sized tumor. It was July, and the surgery was scheduled for that September when I would be in Peru studying abroad for my Junior year at the university.

After the doctors left us, he looked at me with helpless eyes. I knew what he was thinking. "I won't go!" I proclaimed. How could I leave him now? I would be halfway across the world, and he would remain here in need. He quickly grabbed my hand and said, "I will wait to have my surgery until you return." Was that even possible? "Your trip is planned, and even though I wish you would not go, I know it means a lot to you. I don't want to hold you back!"

His life was more valuable to me than anything. My response was, "No, I won't leave you!" Now, I didn't want to go at that point, but Mark always had this generous heart that begged me to follow my dreams wherever they led me. He gazed into my eyes, "You NEED to go!" To this day, I find it hard to share certain things with him because he will lay down his own will to prosper mine. All the pain of our broken way flooded into my mind, and the more he loved me, the more I responded to that love. The more he proved his devotion to me by his endless acts of selflessness, the more I wanted to return that devotion. I'd never been loved so deeply.

He would put his life on the line so that I could travel far from his side. It did not make sense, and I hated the thought of it, but the part of my heart that wanted to please was willing to honor his request. Mark begged the surgeons to reschedule this necessary surgery until December when I returned home from Peru. They agreed but had to put him on medication to keep him alive until surgery. I didn't want to go, but I had to put my trust in God, who would be in both places at the same time, watching over my love. Anyway, God does a better job of caring for the sick.

Chapter Five
THE INCA TRAIL & THE ABDUCTION

*S*aying goodbye to Mark at that time, knowing he was sick, was one of the hardest things I've ever done. Our last embrace before I boarded the plane was filled with emotion. I think we knew that we were both headed in an unknown direction.

The flight was long, and I slept most of the way. We arrived in Lima, Peru and the place where we stayed in the inner city was dirty. There was no chance of sleeping through the horn honking and dog barking—it was deafening. It indeed reminds me now of why I live out in the country. I like the peace the country offers.

I went there with a group of college students because we were required to study abroad for one semester to get our degree. This trip changed my world. I'd never seen poverty like poverty in a third-world country. When you are poor, you are truly lacking. They do not have welfare programs or disability checks. The first time I laid eyes on a needy person in Lima, I was so moved.

This poor man had no arms, yet he found a way to provide for his family. He carved beautiful things by placing a carving instrument between his teeth and holding the board with the arms that were halfway gone. It inspired me because it showed me that no matter what your situation looks like, there is always something in which to thank God. It must've been a hassle to carve this way. How much easier it would be if he had hands. And most of us have hands, and we don't even try to carve things. We have so much ability, yet this man with a disability did more for his family than most of us will ever understand. We have it so good. I bought things from him. I wanted to help him support his family, and in return, I was able to keep some of his beautiful creations that I will always cherish. Many things were handmade, like the tapestries by the hands of nearly blind, impoverished grandmothers and like the jewelry and knickknacks made by the small hands of homeless children from the rocks they find.

There were even people who dressed up in traditional Peruvian attire and would ask for money to take a photo of them. There were children on the streets begging for pocket change, undoubtedly starving or without hope. After touring the catacombs where thousands of people were buried, and their bones were displayed in perfect artistic designs. After visiting the countryside, we got on a plane that carried us to Cuzco. Cuzco's elevation is over 11,000 feet, so we were told to drink Coca Leaf Tea for the altitude sickness we might get. The city was congested but a lot prettier than Lima. When we went to the top of the mountains, there were little villages where they sold all kinds of items in the open markets. Meat hung in the heat of the day with flies on it. Things were very different from what we Americans were accustomed to.

The village people who live upon the mountainside seemed like good farmers. I noticed the women took their children to work with them in the fields as they gathered things needed to make provisions for their families. They grew their corn and other vegetables on terraces. It is the only way that they can make the mountains yield a harvest. They had to build the terraces to hold the earth to plant on a flat surface. I thought about how much work that would be, and it boggled my mind. They have done this technique for thousands of years. I felt like I was on top of the world. The Andean mountains were so beautiful. God was with me there. That's when I realized that God was everywhere.

Each day we would have to walk to our class. I thought it very strange that they didn't feed us in the mornings. In this country, the main meal was around noontime. Every place in the town shut down so that families could come together and have a meal around a table. This was a stark contrast to what I was used to in America, where families ate at different times because they are too busy or they ate in front of a television. I had to adjust to that schedule. In the morning, I would pour a cup of hot water that the servant would prepare ahead of time, and

I would add a tea bag to it. You couldn't drink the water unless it were boiled because it could make you sick. After tea, I would walk to class and find a vendor who baked fresh bread and buy some to sustain me until the noontime family meal around the table.

The first family I stayed with was a lovely, upstanding family with a comfortable home. There were a mother and a father, two brothers, and a sister. One of the boys was around my age, and the other about fifteen years old. I remember seeing the news that Princess Diana had died on a little black and white television on their kitchen table. It was all in Spanish, so I had a hard time figuring out what had happened to her and had to look at the photos and try to piece it together somehow. They were all crying. I couldn't understand why at the time because they were not even subjects to her rule. I grabbed a lock of my hair between my fingers as I remembered when I used to have her hairstyle and how I hated it, yet I felt sorrow for her family, especially the little boys who would never get to grow old with a mother to nurture them.

The bathroom had a toilet with no seat, and the water only went on one time during the day. There was a trickle during the time it was turned on. There was no toilet paper, so I'm not sure what they did about that. All I know is that my first phone call home, I asked Mom to send me a box of toilet paper and baby wipes. Baby wipes were invaluable in such conditions as this. I used them to clean my hands when the water was not working. I hated the thought of using the restroom and not being able to wash my hands.

Each home in the city seemed to have a young lady who did the cooking, cleaning, and laundry. She was usually a very meek and quiet lady who had her living quarters. The homes were made of clay, and their walls surrounded them. If you had a window, it was just a hole in the wall that revealed the wall around the house. On the top of the walls, there were sharp shards of glass protruding to stop a burglar from coming in to steal. Laundry was done by hand. I mean, by hand. You were given a bucket of rainwater and a bar of soap. I learned to conserve my clothing and rarely bathed. The shower was another issue. If I could get my head to line up just right, I could get a trickle of ice-cold water to stream on my hair, but the part when I applied the soap proved difficult. I couldn't get the soap out. I grabbed for the rain bucket and poured that over my head to rinse it more appropriately. It was a rude awakening to us spoiled Americans.

Memoirs of a Keeper: Angels & Demons

The younger brother started showing up in my bed in the middle of the night, and it became very frustrating to me. He must have had a crush on me, but I didn't feel comfortable with him climbing into my bed. The three years of Spanish I took could not prepare me to tell someone I didn't want them in my bed. I called my professor and asked to be removed, explaining that I was scared and had a past of being abused by men and didn't want something to happen again. She put me into a second family who happened to be close friends of hers. In that family, there was a mother and father who were also professors. They had two adult daughters and a servant girl. The bed that I slept upon was made of hay and covered with a sheet. Most of the time, I was home alone at this home. The oldest sister, Gabby, could speak English. That was handy.

The stench on the streets was nauseating to me. It smelled like dead animals and urine. I think they had issues with waste management there. The food didn't taste like anything I tried before. The meat was boiled in water and then put on your plate with no salt or seasonings. It was flavorless. Papaya was a common fruit served with the noontime meal and unsweetened papaya juice. I could never get used to it for some reason. My house mother would point her crooked finger at me and nag me to eat. She would say in her language, "Eat! Eat! Eat!" It made me nervous about facing her each day, the food, and that dreadful, crooked finger pointing at me. And yet I felt like I was such an ungrateful person not to be more thankful for what I had.

One time I was served a guinea pig! It was staring at me with its teeth glaring. I could not eat it. That's where I drew the line.

I made phone calls home to my parents and also to Mark while I was away. I missed all of them so much. It was a very happy day when I found out that Mom and Dad would meet me in Machu Picchu, the ancient ruins of Peru. They were planning to celebrate their 20th wedding anniversary by visiting Peru and their long-lost daughter. We took a train to this particular checkpoint where we would begin the trek of the Inca Trail. It was three days' journey on a trail, sometimes no more significant than the width of the pack you were carrying. There were sheer cliffs down thousands of feet, so you had to be mindful of every step you took.

All the way down was the Mighty Urubamba River. You could hear it roaring from up on the trail far above it. The first night after hiking all day, we stayed in a hostel on the side of the mountain. There were waterfalls that we got to bathe in because it was a hot and dusty climb in the mountains. Each morning we would wake at the crack of dawn and get back on that Inca Trail. It was treacherous at times, and I thought I would fall. I even got sick on the hike with diarrhea, which was inconvenient to have on the trail. It was hard to figure out how to go without falling off the side of a cliff. The views were spectacular. Nothing surpasses the majestic Andean Mountains.

  The third day as we woke, far before the sun came up, we walked the trail by moonlight. They wanted us to see Machu Picchu when the sun came up over the horizon. And there it was. This ancient world hidden in the clouds was revealed to us as the sun appeared. I strolled through the ruins, and there found my parents waiting for me. I cried when I saw them. It seemed so long since I was around familiar faces. I was homesick. Every ruin was so tightly constructed with huge rocks that were somehow cut precisely to fit so close that you could not even get a piece of paper between them. All the buildings were created to face a certain way for the sun, and certain times were dedicated to sacrifices to their gods. The people were one day found by the Spanish Conquistadores and murdered, raped, and plundered. It is a lost city now that we can see only a sliver of what they had. Religion, of course. Not God.

  Later that day, we took a bus down the side of the mountain, and it led to a little tourist village. We stayed there that night. When our group went out to dinner that evening, we all did our usual complaining about the terrible food. I noticed the little starving children outside the window. I had never seen that before. When I glanced at all the food that the others had wasted, I cried out and begged to give the food to these children. I placed the plate of food, by that time with all the scrapings, had created a large mound in front of the starving children. They grabbed handfuls of the food and smashed it into their small mouths as if they had never eaten. I wept for them, and it changed my outlook on life forever. I learned more about Thanksgiving that day than our once-a-year turkey dinners, and pumpkin pies shared in the presence of family.

  One little girl stole my heart. Her name was Carmela. She was selling these pins that she made from painted stones. Later I brought her to the hot springs with me and cared for her like my very own daughter.

Memoirs of a Keeper: Angels & Demons

I gave her everything that I had with me in my pack. I hated that she had nothing, so I gave her things like a toothbrush, toothpaste, hairbrush, clothing, sleeping bag, and much more. I taught her how to wash her hands and how to brush her hair and teeth. That evening when I walked her home, she told me her mother had died, and her father was dying. I found her house was just a few pieces of tin propped up against each other to shield her from the wind and rain. The floor was dirt, and it was tiny. The father was curled in the corner, barely breathing, and my heart broke. I prayed with my entire being that I could take her home with me, but it was not allowed. When I hear children complain about the little things, I often think about this little girl and how little she had yet how happy she seemed.

The next day we traveled by train to another village. The train ride seemed endless, and the wooden seats shook as the train shoved through narrow passes. Ten hours of sitting on a wooden bench was difficult. The bathroom was a closet with a hole that revealed the great wide open tracks below flickering like a strobe. As fast as we were going, you could barely see the wooden beams laid across the tracks and the rocky surface. But when you go, everything just has to be aimed in the hole, and then it just goes on the tracks. Very primitive.

We were in a market train. There were stops every so many miles. People would Jeffer with those who came on from that stop. The lady who sat beside me had quite an odor. I was feeling very sick, smelling it. I was not sure what was in the bag that she was clenching in her fists. When all at once, at a particular market checkpoint, she stood up and unveiled her creature. It was a skinned animal that had been dead a while, yet she proceeded to hang it for its weight and sold it to another passenger before exiting the train. I hoped the buyer would find somewhere else to sit than right beside me. That stench was awful!

On one of the stops, there was a woman selling oranges. She was yelling out, "Naranja! Naranja! Naranja!" which meant orange in Spanish. She had these oranges all gathered up in a big blanket that she had tied around her shoulders. Like a flash, police officers appeared, coming from all directions, toward this lady, who happened to be right in front of me. There were guns and lots of yelling. She was guarding her oranges with her life. Not sure why, but I thought I would help. I stood up and grabbed her belt loop and pulled her away from her oranges so they could take them. After she left go of her sack of oranges

The Inca Trail & The Abduction

for a moment, they seized the blanket, dumped the oranges, and out came the cocaine. It was a drug bust, and I was there to save the day! Not really, but I like to think I helped.

They left with the lady and her oranges, and off we went again. This time we stopped somewhere for the night. It was another hostel. It had plenty of rooms and an entire animal sanctuary! Wow! I was in my element. There were monkeys and all kinds of exotic animals in the jungle caged there. Some roamed free like the black spider monkey I enjoyed looking at. He became my new friend. I would feed him little bits of rolls, and he followed me all around the complex. There was another small animal that I think was a baby wombat. My dad was holding it very carefully. I wanted to hold the little creature. I had no idea that it would be aggressive, but I thought it was cute. All of a sudden, the small animal went crazy, chomping my arms, or belly, anywhere it could until I released it.

That evening I went out to find fruit to feed to the animals. I found plantains and bought a bunch of them. We were in a tropical zone, so there were lots of fruits growing. We passed a church on the way and decided to go in. In there, I saw Jesus in a casket. He looked real. It was like a wax sculpture of him lying in a coffin with his arms folded as if at a funeral. It was extraordinary. I have never seen him depicted that way. What was even more bizarre was that it was a little, ratty, old church. It was convincing artwork on the depiction of Him, yet unfortunate because I served – and still serve – a living God, not a dead God that is buried.

When we got back to the place, I went out to feed the animals. I started handing plantains to the raccoons and the monkey when I felt a crushing thud on the top of my head. I looked up, thinking a coconut had dropped. And then BAM, BAM, BAM! Another few knocks to the head. It hurt! I turned around to find an angry white-tailed deer, wild on its hind legs with its ears back to show its fierce temperament toward me. He wanted my plantains. I threw the rest of the plantains at the deer and ran for my life. I didn't know deer could attack at that time, and I must say, they are brutal. Those hoofs are healthy and to prove it, I had little knots all over my head from each blow. From that point forward, I had a more profound respect for wildlife!

The next morning we all had planned a trip that was about ten hours away. It was a small ancient ruin up in the mountains called

Memoirs of a Keeper: Angels & Demons

Vilcabamba, the hidden city—a place that the Inca people escaped to when the Spanish Conquistadors were there to kill, steal, and destroy them. We loaded up into the back of this dump truck to get to this place ten hours away. I think Mom and Dad were a bit shocked that we all paid money to have such a struggle. With twenty people crammed into a small dump box, we had to sit on each other's feet or legs. Dad said his legs had gone numb from it. It was a long ten hours, flying around in the back of that truck, bumping into others, not to mention the one-lane roads that led there, sheer cliffs on either side—one straight up and the other instant death straight down for thousands of feet. It was a little freaky! We were given five bread rolls for the trip to share among all of us. That was all, and we didn't see a miracle of the five loaves feeding a multitude. We broke off a small piece and passed the bread to the next person in the dump box. I figured it was the last I would ever complain about a long car ride in a comfortable car.

When we arrived at the village beneath the hidden city, we were already not in good spirits. I know I was not happy about my parents having to endure that ride. They didn't know what they were signing up for that morning! We needed a lot of adrenaline to survive that level of anxiety and fear of plummeting down the side of the mountain every time a vehicle passed. We felt like we were dangling over the side just barely, so we all looked a bit shaky at that point.

Everyone was grumpy, especially after holding our urine for ten hours in that truck only to find out there was only one outhouse that had a dirt floor and a hole. Ready. Aim. Fire! It was hard to manage to hit the target, and there was no toilet paper. Then we found out where we were going to sleep that night—on the dirt floor crawling with guinea pigs! Did I mention that those little creatures were there for our food? Why yes, I looked across the room where the maid was knocking the little creatures over the head and putting them into the oven, fur and all! That was our dinner! I became a vegetarian that day and proclaimed it loudly for all to hear! Those who had enough energy went on the hike up the mountain to see the hidden ruins. I was not in the mood! I found allies to work with me to overturn the decision to sleep on that floor. We banded together to make the ten-hour dump truck ride that night. We got our way but had not thought about how scary it would be to ride in the back of that dump truck in the pure darkness with a dim headlight to guide the way through the winding mountains on the one-lane dirt road. None of these students were Christians, but prayers were going up, and when the choir major started to sing a hymn, we all heard it as if it were an angel in heaven singing. I will never forget the way we were all huddled together that night, holding hands and praying to return alive.

Thud! We all began to wonder, what was that? The truck stopped, and the rear end started to float. Yes, we were floating and drifting to the right! We were stuck in a river that was a huge waterfall! And you could hear the water rushing down the mountain into the darkness. We couldn't see where it was or how close we were, but it sounded like we were inches from flowing down the waterfall, truck and all. We all screamed and jumped out of the back of the truck. Mom and Dad, on their memorable anniversary trip, were also jumping out the back into the river. Mom was not happy! We could see nothing except the dim rays that came from the headlights shining on some rocks. We all had to push the truck out of the river and back on the road ahead. There we were, half in the water, half in the cold night air, scared, pushing a two-and-a-half-ton dump truck up the bank.

Safety was the last thing we were feeling at this point! We still had another five hours to go and no idea if we had more unexpected adventures to come! On this trek back home, we only had a full belly IF we ate guinea pig. I was not only scared; I was cold and hungry.

We arrived home safe, thank the Lord! The next morning we were stuffed back into the market train for another ten hours back to Cuzco. Mom and Dad were a bit stressed and were glad to be flying home where things could be normal again. My only regret was that they left me there. I told Mark about the crazy adventures, and if he could have, he would have jumped through the phone and rescued me. I was there to stay for another couple of months. That crooked finger and force-feedings were in full force again.

I started to get sick. I needed to go to the doctor. I was not sure if it was the food or the pills that the lady was giving me. I called up my professor and told her how sick I was. She promised, "Be ready tomorrow. I will come in a taxi and pick you up to bring you to the clinic." My body was weak. I felt like I had lost some weight, and I think I had a fever. The next day, I gathered myself together and made my way to the gate on the wall surrounding my house and waited for that taxi.

A taxi pulled up and in that taxi was a lady I had never met. She told me that my professor wasn't able to make it, so she came instead. That seemed fine. What could happen? I should have never gotten into that car! We did drive to the clinic. It looked like an average clinic with a waiting room, tile floors, and pretty pictures on the walls. I sat there until the lady brought me back to the doctor's room. We looked at the doctor for just a moment and kept walking. She pointed and said we had to go this way. Okay. I just kept walking down this long hall until we got to a door. She opened the door up, and it appeared to lead into a dark alley. Still, I thought it must be okay, a tad bit weird, but chalked it up for third-world-country backward methods.

As we walked down the alley, it never crossed my mind that I was in danger. On the left, there was another door. She opened the door and led me in. It was a very fancy home, marble floors with a grand staircase. We walked past the stairs and entered a small library. Books lined every wall, and there was a pretty fancy desk sitting there in the middle of that room, which looked like a rich person's office. I was standing there, admiring the beauty of this home when they wheeled a dentist chair into the room and instructed me to sit on that chair. I sat there when I heard another cart rolling in from behind. It was an ultrasound machine. I wondered what on earth was going on? I was sick, but why on earth would they need an ultrasound machine? Again, I just figured at this point it had to be normal in that country. They put the cold jelly on my tummy and started to roll that instrument all over my stomach, chest, sides, everywhere!

"Vamos a operar," they said in their language, which meant, "We are going to operate!" Oh! What?! I was learning to speak pretty fluently, but medical terms, not a chance. I had no idea what they were saying, only bits and pieces I could understand. I started to become very anxious. "Can I call my family?" I asked in Spanish, of course. They said, "No." No is the same in most languages, so no meant no. That is when a red flag started to go up. Why would they not want me to call home? They told me to undress and put the hospital gown on to prepare for surgery. I did. I can't believe I did. And then, in the dining room, the grand dining room, with fifteen-foot ceilings and a huge chandelier hanging down over a ten-foot table, I was wondering why we were in a dining room. The table was fancy, with carved wooden chairs, and they proceeded to move it to one side of the room. After the servants moved the table, they left the dining room for a moment. They walked with a small stainless steel table that looked like one of those tables they have in a morgue. They told me to lay on that table, and I tell you what, at this point, I am thinking, I must need surgery that they are going to all this trouble.

I got on the table, and as I laid there, tears rolled down over my temples and started to soak my hair. I looked over at the giant painting of Jesus on the wall across from me. The wall was this bright aqua blue around that painting like the sky. It made me think of my life. I had a good life, and I knew as well as anyone else that we were only here for a short time, and you never know when you will draw your last breath. People die during surgery, and I could die. So I thanked my God for all that He did in my life, for Mark, my family, and the many other gifts I was so graciously given. It was weird. I kind of felt like I was on my death bed that night. Was I? Do you know when you are going to die? I thought that was it for me. I did.

They grabbed my arm and plugged in an IV. I took a deep breath, prayed, and had to have faith enough to go home to Jesus. I was ready. Something was fishy about the whole ordeal, and I just knew I was not in a good spot. I just knew I was going to heaven when I closed my eyes. It was not because I was good, nor did I do anything that warranted a heavenly prize, but only that I had great faith. I knew that Jesus shed His blood to make me pure. He took that punishment for my sins so that I could be called a child of God. It was a sweet moment of peace, as my number was drawn for the last time. Yet my last prayer was that God would save me again, just one more time, and give me a way of escape if it was His will.

Suddenly, the people were scrambling, and the surgeon called because he could not make it until morning. They never did put the medicine into my IV port to sedate me. Oh, heavenly days! I was not allowed to leave! I was put into a tall structure that could have been a baby crib in a horror movie, but kind of looked more like an animal cage. It did not look like I was going in there to enter and exit as I needed freely. It was at the height of a standard bed, and the metal bars went nearly to the ceiling. They locked me in that cage structure and gave me a bedpan since I was not free to get out at any time. The IV was still fastened to the inside of my elbow with a steady drip of what appeared to be a clear saline solution in a bag dangling somewhere above my head attached to the bars. That seemed normal. I felt like the

IV was helping me feel better, and it was giving me more strength. The room was more like a large walk-in closet with a tiny window, not much bigger than a standard-sized piece of computer paper. I knew I could not fit through there, but I knew that I needed to develop a plan to get myself out of there.

The lady who brought me there sat on a chair, staring at me for a while until she decided to go home. There I waited in the utter darkness, cold, alone, and frightened about the morning. I had to get out of there. I laid awake all night long, waiting for the first light of dawn. It is that subtle light that barely shines the way, yet enough to see your surroundings. And there it was, the dim, purple light of dawn. My salvation! I couldn't see the metal bars, and I needed to get busy devising a plan of escape.

First, I needed to get the IV out of my arm. I ripped out the line and clenched my hand over the spot until the blood clotted. I didn't need to leave a trail of blood. I had to think about everything. I climbed up the side of the metal bars and hoisted myself up and over, squeezing myself through the pass between the top of the cage/crib structure and the ceiling. Good thing I was little. Being little comes in handy when you are trying to escape. I let the weight of my body pull me to the floor, and I was free! Free from the cage, but I still had to get out of that place somehow. There was a pile of my clothing right where I had left it the night before they told me to put on that hospital gown. I reached into my pockets and found that all my money was gone! Someone must have taken it. I quickly put my clothes on, and ever so quietly opened the door that led to the dining room. No one was there. I peeked my head out and looked both ways.

Down by the grand staircase, I could see a big door. I waited. Some footsteps echoed with the marble floors. I heard them from that direction and held my place. I pulled my head ever so slowly back behind my door. The room was beginning to light up by now with the morning rays of the sun coming breaching the horizon. I could only see buildings out the window, but it was much brighter, and I could see everything by that time.

I heard the big door open in the hall. I peeked my head out again until I could see the servant grab a newspaper or some wad of papers from outside the door. They kept walking down the hall away from the door and further away from my room. All seemed still and quiet, except my heart beating louder than a drum. The door was still closing as I watched that stripe of light on the floor, getting thinner and thinner. I made a mad dash for the door. I never ran that fast in all my life. I grabbed the handle of the door, shoved it open, and made my way out into the street. My heart was racing, and I kept running. I heard in the distance behind someone coming for me. I would not look back. I could not. I knew what became of Lot's wife for looking back and a pillar of salt was not what I wanted to become. I just kept running down this alley and then that alley. I wanted to be hard to find. Not knowing where I was or how far I ran, nor whether anyone was close behind, I flagged down a taxi. With no money, I had to pretend that nothing was amiss. I had the taxi take me back to the house that I was staying at.

When I got there, I jumped out of the car and pushed through the gate as the taxi driver was out there yelling at me to pay him. I just ignored him. I couldn't pay him anyhow, and I heard him peel away in a fury. I didn't have money, but because I was a Gringo, I am sure he assumed I would have had money. I came to the door of the inner house, and the door was locked. That was unusual, and the other strange thing was that no one was home. The day before, no one told me they were leaving on vacation. Strange. I knew that in the house parents' bedroom there was a phone. Normally, I could walk into that room to use the phone through the doorway, but it had been locked. I could only enter through the window on the side, but the window was boarded up and locked as well. I had to get in, so I looked around the patio area for a chair or something. There was a chair, and I quickly picked it up and began to smash it over the boarded window until it popped open! I crawled up and over the hard window opening. I was running solely on adrenaline at this point. No food. I was still sick and weak otherwise. Adrenaline is a powerful chemical, not to mention the strength of the Lord.

I got in and found the phone. "Mom, you are never going to believe this!" I went on to tell her everything. She was worried that maybe I needed surgery. What if I had a ruptured appendix? Being a nurse, she had a concern that this could have been a legitimate surgical need. My sister-in-law was Dominican, so she told me to get to a real doctor's office and get the doctor on the phone with Michelle so she could hear the Spanish and know what was going on. I went into my room; I had enough money to get to the doctor's office. They looked at me and talked to Michelle. They told her I had Campylobacter but no need for emergency surgery.

My parents wired me the money to change my plane ticket, and I got on the first flight back to the states. Still concerned, I scheduled a doctor's appointment with someone who did an ultrasound on my guts. I just wanted to be sure that there was not something wrong with me. The doctor said, "You're lucky they didn't harvest all of your organs! There's nothing wrong with you, and your organs are perfect. You would have been a perfect host for them." I was sitting on the edge of my seat as I took a long hard swallow and listened. "AND…what they do is, take all your organs out, sell them for millions of dollars on the black market, and then they just get rid of your body. Erin, it's a miracle you are alive!"

I knew that God saved me. When I prayed for a way of escape, He had provided it. It is a miracle. I'm sure I would not be here to write this if God had not intervened. I stood firm on this verse,"There hath no temptation taken you but such as is common to man: but God is faithful, who will not suffer you to be temptedabove that ye are able; but will with the temptation also make a way to escape, that ye may be able to bear it." 1 Corinthians 10:13

Why was the housemother so urgent about feeding me and giving me pills? Why was my professor sending someone else there when she took a plane to Texas? And why was my Peruvian House family mysteriously gone when I escaped without giving me notice? I still don't have answers to these questions, but I'm just thankful to be alive today!

Chapter Six
THE WEDDING & THE WITCH

Surviving nearly getting my organs harvested was something I had no time to reflect on. Mark had scheduled the surgery for when I returned. We had to move forward with his procedure. I remember the day he had to be prepped for the surgery. I had given him a golden ring as a promise to marry him while I was gone to Peru, and he was not wearing it.

He took my little hand, and in his fist, he revealed the gold ring. He proceeded to hide it in my hand with a silent promise of coming back to me alive. A tear rolled down my cheek, and it dripped off my chin. Mark caught it in his hand. I pressed my forehead upon his, "Oh, I want to call in a minister to marry us this day!" I was scared that his mother, who disapproved of me, would bar me from my love if something went wrong. The whole scene plagued my mind as I thought the worst. It was a ridiculous request. I just needed to trust the Lord. After all, the Lord, who saved me from the hands of those who meant to kill me, was the same God who could keep him safe.

I watched them wheel him out of the room, and I sat there waiting for hours to find out if he was okay. It was no simple operation. They had to make a cut over a foot in length up the middle of his abdomen. I rested on the fact that God was with him. Out came the doctor, and I could overhear him telling the others that Mark made it through okay.

I did not approach them. I held my peace. I wanted to see Mark, but I was not family, so I waited until later. I sat in the waiting room until just after the last visitors left, and I begged the nurse if I could only see him for a moment. They granted my plea, and there he was, a dim light above his head, tubes coming out from his mouth, nose, and around his sides. He was sleeping, and I just prayed for him. I had hoped he didn't think I abandoned him. When I saw his eyelids flicker, I rushed beside him and held his hand. "I am here, my love!" I felt a weak squeeze over my hand. He was okay!

The time he was at the hospital, I knew I had to wait until after hours to see him, for the nurses had to keep me away otherwise based on the request of his mother. It was hard to feel like I had to lurk in the shadows like a criminal just to make sure he was okay. Eventually, when Mark could speak, he could permit me to come as often as I wanted. After that point, I never left his side. When he was able to sit up, I fed him. I washed his hair in a basin behind the bed and cared for him anyway I could. The day he was discharged, I took him back to my home in Wisconsin because that's where he wanted to stay so I could care for him. It was a long road of recovery for him, but I knew he would be okay.

Mark and I had not kept ourselves pure in every way. I found out from his dad what the word fornication meant. I thought if you become intimate with another person physically, you were married in God's eyes. It was taught that way in the church I attended, so I felt that Mark and I were married, but we were planning to make it official. We had found an apartment on the water and moved in together. After praying about what his dad said, I started to feel a solemn conviction about this immorality and decided to move out. I moved in with our pastor's family for several months before the wedding, and I begged God to forgive me. I know Mark was not happy about this decision, but I had to live my life to please God, no matter what the cost. If it was wrong to fornicate, then I wasn't going to do that. I don't believe it's a sin until God convicts us, and I know God forgave me and washed that sin away so that I could be pure on my wedding day.

We started to plan our wedding for the coming spring. I was still studying at the university, so in between my classes, I planned for it. Mark didn't want a big wedding. He didn't want bells and whistles, nor pomp and circumstance or tuxedos and frills. To his surprise, I didn't either. I ended up finding the dress that Mom wore on her wedding day. Grandma made the dress some 25 years before. I tried it on, and it was a perfect fit. Mom and I just happen to be the same height. Wearing this vintage dress was very special to me. The white polyester had barely aged. For the veil, I went to Grandma's home, and she pulled out something antique. It was about forty years old—my mother's First Communion veil that she wore when she was only five or six years old. Grandma made that as well. She was an amazing seamstress and keeper of the home.

One afternoon as I was visiting my mom, she pulled something out of her jewelry box. It sparkled and shined with bright blue light. The ornate design around the pendant was incredible. It was a big blue translucent, precious stone about the size of a quarter. So old, so beautiful, I gently allowed her to place it into my hands. "What is this?" I asked. She answered, "You can borrow this for your wedding." My eyes lit up as she continued. "This is my great-grandmother's necklace. It was given to her by her husband. Since I am her namesake, it was passed down to me." This was a very special piece to wear at my wedding. It made the old saying, "Something old, something new, something borrowed, something blue" work for my wedding.

I found the perfect place to have an intimate wedding. It was a little chapel in Door County right on the shores of Lake Michigan. The chapel was all handcrafted from the hand-hewn beams and timber frame construction, the paintings on the walls, the hand-carved pews each with a part of the bible story pictured, to the needlepoint work on ever seat. Everything had meaning. A married couple, fifty years before that day, built the chapel. They put their whole heart into every square inch of that little place. It was the perfect place for us to start our journey—a handcrafted place. At that time, I had no idea that we would also continue down a similar path as the old couple, leading us to become more self-sufficient one day.

I called to tell him about it. "Mark, it is the perfect place! You will love it. It is simple, just like you wanted for our wedding," I said with such excitement.

He returned, "How big is it? You invited 75 guests!"

"Oh, it's plenty big enough," I said with complete confidence. I always had a way to see things more significant than what they were. I did not read the fine print where it said the maximum capacity for the chapel was thirty adults.

At the university where I was studying art, I engraved a picture of us in an embrace to use that as the cover for our invitations. I found some fellow music students that I hired as the string quartet. Mark was able to find a nice suit, coat, and tie for this joyous occasion, and we were ready to start our journey together as a married couple. His dad bought it for him, and his step-mom bought all the table favors and helped as much as they could in the planning. It was indeed a gift to have both my parents and his dad helping us plan our day. We would have loved to have his mother's approval, but that approval never came. She fought against that day with every ounce of her heart, yet it was the one time of my life I could not make everyone happy. Mom called her a couple of weeks before the wedding and told her not to come if she was so against us. I wasn't sure if she would even go because I hadn't talked with her since Mark's surgery when she wasn't happy with me. I sent her an invite because we wanted her there with all our hearts and wished she could find a way to be happy for us.

May 23, 1998, was a misty morning in Door County. I put my mother's dress on and stared in the mirror. I wasn't the perfect bride. I knew I was spotted, but I had faith that God had washed me white as snow when He forgave my sins. Amidst all the old things I was wearing, I was something new. I felt brand new. I felt perfectly clean and white. If the only one who saw me in that light was Christ, I was okay with that. Only Christ knew my heart. It was a heart that yearned to serve and to yield to His perfect will for my life. That day I learned that His perfect will was that I would be Mark's wife.

I gazed out to the waves on the shore and felt the breeze brush my hair, and the sun caressed my face. The sun was peeking out from behind the clouds with the promise of clear blue skies; how I loved the mornings. I loved how the sun cascaded its glorious light through the trees until it flickered on the ground. Having a morning wedding was perfect. It was nearly ten o'clock, and all the guests were arriving one by one. I was told that Mark was very nervous because he saw the actual size of the chapel. While my head was swimming in the clouds dreaming about sunshine and roses, my love was back on earth, trying to figure out logistics.

As I approached the chapel for my journey down the aisle, I noticed half of our guests standing outside. My heart raced when I saw his mother standing there on the other side of the trees blocking me from all the other guests. My maids were in a row. The first was carrying the word of God, the lamp to our path, and she represented FAITH. God's word was something we wanted to stand on. After the first was another maid who held within her hands the candle which symbolized HOPE, this candle that we would both light as one. The next maid carried with her LOVE in the form of our rings. I walked down behind the last maid, who sprinkled the floor with flower petals for me to walk on. My father's arm joined with mine as we walked to the beautiful concerto of the string quartet.

Every step brought me closer to my precious husband. As my father put my arm into the hands of my love, I knew I was home. He was my new home—my new life. Everywhere he would go, I would surely follow. We listened to the scriptures being read; candles lit the small dark chapel. I could see the candlelight waving across the beautiful paintings on every wall. When we faced each other for the first time, I could see tears welling up in his big intense eyes. I couldn't stop my tears from flowing. They were happy tears, and my emotions were high. I could see people crying for joy with us and others who were weeping because they were sad. For some, it was a symbol of rebellion to see us go forward in our forbidden love, and yet to others, it was a moment of rejoicing. But to God, it was sacred. It was the day he brought a man and a woman together to become co-heirs to his glorious plan. We were, from that day forward, one flesh.

We gave our vows one to another. We did not say, "I do." We said, "I WILL." "I will" is making a declaration. It is declaring that no matter what, I will promise to be faithful and endure whatever may befall us in the life that was laid before us. Come sickness or health, good times or bad; we stood firm in a promise that would not be broken. When my pastor began to play a song, my dad accompanied with his flute, and I sang harmony as we lit the candle that represented HOPE, hope for growing old together, starting a family, and following Christ. As he pronounced us husband and wife, my sweet husband reached out to hold my face within his large hands as he wiped my tears away and pulled me up for a kiss.

Words cannot explain the feelings I had that day. We walked down together, and together we could face anything. We had already survived some unusual close calls in the year before, so we knew the strength and miraculous work of God would carry us onward.

Watching the sun setting on Door County's shore was more than a dream to me. We spent a day relaxing after the wedding going on hikes and visiting art galleries down in the old fishing villages. Waking next to my love was like a dream, a dream that I never wanted to wake from. I was Mrs. Harrison. He was my husband and I, his wife. I remember that morning filled with our calls back to each other "husband!" or "my darling wife!"

We were married on Saturday morning, and Mark had to be back to work Monday morning, so we drove back to our apartment that Sunday evening. When we opened the door, we saw the stack of gifts in the living room. I asked my grade school bully, Charlotte, to drop them off. She was always pranking, tricking me, and getting me to do all sorts of mischief through school to make her laugh. We eventually became friends along the way. When she offered to drop them off, I thought nothing of it. To our surprise, the entire apartment had been booby-trapped and pranked. There were cracker crumbs in between our sheets. Everywhere we looked, there was something wrong. Cream of broccoli soup splatter was dried on and smeared all over the shower. Ketchup was drizzled all over the bathroom mirror and toilet seat. All of our underwear was frozen in a block of ice in the freezer. Every shoe had sticky candies in them.

It took us hours to clean up the nasty mess of tricks. I sat there, not sure if I should laugh or cry. We were exhausted from the long drive home and just wanted to enjoy our first night home, and all we were doing was scraping stinky messes out of the bathroom, thawing our underwear, and changing bedsheets. I think we found more hidden treasures over the next few weeks as we lived there.

I was glad when it was all finally cleaned up, and we could start our life together. I had an Educational studies class that Monday morning. We studied how to be teachers in that course since I was planning to be a K-12 art teacher.

The walk to school each morning was nice from our historic apartment building. We were right on the Fox River. Views of rushing water through the dams and under bridges were powerful. Seagulls were flying everywhere, searching for the carp they would eat off the top of the water. The building we lived in was over 100 years old. It was an old Cotton Mill. In our apartment, there were massive arches made with clay brick of pink, peach, and yellow colors. As I walked past the buildings, I felt like I was walking past an old castle with a moat around it. Now that I was married, I truly felt like a princess.

I sat there around the big table as the announcements were made. One student chuckled and said, "I was in Door County at Bjorklunden and saw Erin getting married at the old Boynton Chapel." They all looked at one another in disgust as the professor took his snobby jab, "Oh, well...speaking of rushing into things...don't we have something important to discuss?" I knew I was in the minority. I was the odd one out. Marriage was not an accepted thing at my school. I was subsequently not one of them. I was an outcast because I chose to marry a man instead of just sleep with him. They were intolerant of my lifestyle even though they were professing to be tolerant of difference, tolerant of people of a different culture, gender, race, or sexual orientation, but against the Christian, the pro-life, the straight, and the morally upright. I didn't even speak against others and showed all the love in my heart to every person, no matter what their lifestyle was, yet I was persecuted just because I was married. It was altogether confusing and hypocritical.

Marriage was one thing but having children another—wanting children, I should say. I wanted children. Desperately each day, I would pine away in prayer for my children. I was told the devastating news when I was examined after I came home from Peru that I could never conceive. The condition I was diagnosed with was called Anovulatory Bleeding. When I was only sixteen years old, after I started my first period, I was put on the birth control pill to keep me regular, resulting in breakthrough bleeding. Before the pill, I had painful periods that only came every few months. I remember being doubled over with pain, passing huge brown clots. When you are sixteen, you don't understand the severity of a condition such as this since you're not trying to have children. I just took my pill every day.

When I came home from Peru, they explained it more precisely as they studied my records. It was then that the news sunk in. Newly married, I was sorry that I might never be able to give my husband children. I begged God, and when I felt I could not shed another tear, I came up with my plan. "God, if I can't have my children, I will just become a mother to orphans and adopt them one day," I said with a knot in my stomach knowing we were as poor as church mice with no way to afford adoption. I went on to say, "I will go on to get my Masters and then become an Art Professor so I can make enough money to afford adoption." I knew it would be a long time before I could hold a baby, but was in it for the long haul.

I stopped taking the pill, and I started weaning off the anti-anxiety medications I had been on for years. I figured if there were a chance for a miracle, I would not want to be on any drugs that would harm the possibility. The Paxil was a beast to get off. I had this aura and delayed, dizzy, movement in the room. It was nauseating. Standing up was difficult for several days, and I began having severe panic attacks to the point my throat felt like it was crushing my breath. I would lay on the floor, gasping for air and pawing at my throat until the world stopped spinning around me.

I started throwing up several times each day. The dizziness was so intense, and all I wanted to do was lay still under my covers. Mark was at a loss at what he could do to help his poor wife, who was neither willing nor interested in him. "Don't talk!" I hated to hear anything or feel anything, "Don't touch me. Don't look at me!" He would try to get me a drink of water, and I could not drink. If I took one little sip, I would run to the toilet and vomit. Thankfully, I was on summer break, and it had only been three months since our wedding. My final year of college was soon approaching, and I was not eager to start. "I can't. I can't go to school like this!" I said in utter desperation. "I quit. I am done!" I hadn't eaten in days. I was wasting away. I regretted coming off the drugs at this point, thinking I was enduring some crazy continuance of withdrawal symptoms. By this time, I was throwing up nine or ten times a day. Mark had become increasingly concerned about my well-being. He brought me into the ER when I started to weaken even more.

They had hooked me up to an IV for fluids since I was severely dehydrated. "You're pregnant, Mrs. Harrison," the doctor said. I sat there for a moment with my jaw wide open and eyes as big a saucers. The moment I had waited for my entire life was there—a child in my womb. We had not been trying to conceive since I thought there was no point, and here I was throwing up because I was pregnant! I could not have been more proud of hugging the toilet, for enduring the pains of hunger, and the suffering of morning sickness. It was a miracle and one of the happiest moments of my life.

"You have to drink to live. You and your baby will not survive if you continue to like this with no food or water. There is a drug that I can give you that will stop nausea and allow you to eat and drink again. It comes with some risk. The side effects are that the unborn child could have ADHD from it." I had already been diagnosed with that condition, so I thought it was not that bad—it wasn't life-threatening. Before I could sign up for the drug, he went on to say, "You do not have a choice about this. It is either the medication or possible death. I had already lost ten pounds, and I was only 105 to start with, so I agreed to take this drug.

Mark took me home, and we rejoiced for the life that was growing within me. The drug took the edge off, but my nausea had been so unusually severe that I still felt nauseated all the time. I could keep food down, but an aversion to food still lingered. The only food I could eat was Spaghetti-O's out of a can. I ate cans of it each day. It was better than starving. Feeling that sick all the time was hard to bear day in and day out, and I still didn't want to finish college. "No. You are going!" Mark said with authority. "You have come this far and paid all this money. It would be a waste not to get a degree." I wondered why I would finish now that I will be pregnant my entire year, sick, miserable, and what was the point? I was going to be a mother, not a career woman. As determined as he was, I decided to listen to his reason and started school that fall.

One of the classes I had on my schedule was printmaking. We had to handle many very toxic inks and things like paint thinner to wash the ink off of the tools. I was already feeling very ill from my pregnancy, and these smells not only made it worse, but I was also quite worried that they might harm my unborn baby, breathing them in for so many hours each day.

There was an upside-down purple triangle on my professor's door with the word, SAFE ZONE, written in bold letters. This sign meant that if you were a homosexual, you would be safe to enter her office. She would not judge you for your lifestyle. You could go in there if you were gay and be safe from harm. You were safe if you had any other alternative lifestyle or religion. It meant you could be yourself.

I entered into the SAFE ZONE, thinking I would be safe, but boy was I wrong. After I told her I was pregnant and asked her if there was any way I could work from home with non-toxic substances for the health of my baby, she violently rebuked me, "You have a choice! Get rid of it!" Excuse me? Did she just tell me to kill my baby? "This is your last year, Erin. You can't be bothered with a baby right now. You can always terminate this pregnancy, and then when you are more settled, you can start a family later if you want. If you miss class, because of this, I will not pass you, and you will not graduate." Well, she was my academic advisor. She was in a position to advise me on my academics. How could she think it was her place to suggest me to have an abortion?

"I will not get 'Rid of' my baby!" I yelled as I stormed out of her office in a flood of tears right under the SAFE ZONE sign. My baby wasn't safe in that office, and neither was I! That sign wasn't meant for us. I went to the Dean of Students and told him about my experience with my advisor, and it was clear he must have already talked to her. I think this man was a believer. He treated me with such kindness and respect for my choice of life. Later my professor did end up sending me home with non-toxic inks to finish out my course. She did not act very warm towards me after that day, but she tolerated my presence.

As my belly grew, the stares of disgust grew from all the onlookers. Every class I attended, every lunchroom, every hall I walked down was met with people staring me down and then whispering into the ear of another person. For being so against bigots and racists, I sure felt the pain of their prejudice. Some places on campus would not serve me without rolling their eyes. It was either snickering, rolling eyes, or cold shoulders. It was a shame because I was happily married.

The only person I could find on campus who was kind to me was a witch. Yes, a witch. She was a red-headed medium-built woman with a sincere smile. Each lunch hour, she and I would sit across from each other and discuss what we believed. I found it interesting that in her Wiccan doctrine, they also believe in Jesus. She said they see him as good energy and light. Their religion recognized many deities as it is a form of polytheism. I found out this pagan belief has two main deities, a Horned God and Goddess. Of course, I sought to win her to trust in Jesus as I did. I told her how God had miraculously saved me from suicide, from being killed, and for life in my womb. In short, I told her my whole life story. To my surprise, she was not put-off by my crazy accounts. Instead, she wanted to know more.

"Did you know there are up to five generations in your ovaries right now? When you were in your mother's womb, all your future generations were present?" She asked as she placed her hand over my belly. I was astonished by her words and captivated by my newfound friend. I could not wait to meet with her each day.

It was late fall, and I made a bargain with her. I told her that if she came to visit my church one Sunday, I would visit one of her Wiccan meetings. She was delighted at the prospect and promised if I came on Halloween night to her Witch meeting called Samhain, she would come to my church service. It sounds more like "Sow-in," rhyming with cow.

My faith was so steadfast and fearless that I thought I could go to a witch meeting, and it wouldn't affect me in the least. I knew God, and she would never convince me to follow her religion. I hoped that she would trust Jesus eventually. The tricky part was to convince my new husband to come along with me.

"You've got to be kidding me! A witch meeting on Halloween?" He said with contempt. "No."

"But if we go to her meeting, she promised to come to ours." I pleaded with all my heart, "Please, it is for Jesus!" How could he argue with anything that was for Jesus? We packed ourselves into his little Honda Civic and raced off to the river's edge, where the meeting would take place in the cool dark of the night. Mom came along with her friend that lost her daughter. Mom always loved a good scare, and the mystery of a witch meeting on Halloween was something they both were giddy with excitement for.

As we approached, I looked as far as my eye could see, squinting to pull the shadows of witches dancing in the flicker of the flames. There they all gathered around a fire in a circle, all wearing long, black-hooded capes that draped over the damp field beside the river's bank. Mark was staring at me with that, 'what have you gotten us into,' look. I shuffled forward toward the fire and the witches that surrounded it, like the blind leading the blind. I had no idea what I was getting myself into at that point.

"So mote it be" was chanted around the circle. One large man with a very evil, gruff-sounding voice said it, and when he said it, all would tremble. You couldn't make out their faces because black, ominous-looking hoods shaded them. I could see the red glow up the front, revealing the noses only. "To the spirit of the North..." and then silence which ushered another, "So mote it be." They recited as they looked to the north and continued the same ritual to the South and the East and finally, the West. All spirits they turned to greet with the same rumble and horrific end phrase of "So mote it be." It means "so may it be," said at the end of a prayer, similar to "amen."

The incense came out, and the witches said incantations as we stood in a line. My witch friend came to me and held her hand over my womb, and she said something I couldn't understand while waving the smoking stick of incense around her hand as if she were casting a spell on me or my unborn child who was only three or four months' gestation.

As soon as we could break free, we bolted over the field in a mad dash. The darkness had penetrated our hearts that night, and we seldom talked about it. She never did come to our church.

The winter was just around the corner, and we had an opportunity to buy a home that belonged to one of my relatives. He was married to my first cousin. They had two kids before they separated. It was a small home situated on a busy neighborhood street corner near an ice-cream stand called Dick's Drive-In. I used to babysit at this house many weekends taking care of his two kids after the divorce. He was a chiropractor, and he had helped so many people with pain and even illnesses. He was the only member of the family who stood up for me when I told on my creepy uncle who happened to be his ex-father-in-law, and he also had an interest in protecting his children from him.

He had died near the house, actually in the parking lot of Dick's Drive-In a few months before, after trying to hide cocaine in his throat. He seemed such an upstanding man; after all, he was my only ally. It was shocking to find out that he had a long-standing addiction to drugs and even dealt them. When we moved into his home, I could see little strange pipes and other odd items hidden around in the nooks and crannies that could have been used for drugs.

Having a home of our own was such a rush. We ended up getting a whole trailer full of antiques from Grandma. It was like a dream for me to have my place with my loving husband, and to be able to finally make this house a home, furnishing it with all these old relics of the past. Grandma Isla was in the process of moving out of her apartment to live in Chicago with her daughter. I was so thankful for the old pieces of antique furniture that she gave to me in the family for over a hundred years. All the stories attached to each piece would be stories I could retell for a lifetime as they graced our home.

Every piece of furniture smelled of old smoke and had a haze of orange tar to be polished off. It brought back a lot of memories as

The Wedding & The Witch

I carefully polished through the stains. I remembered her sitting beside me with her alcohol and puffing on cigarettes as she would tell the tails of years passed. She drank hot toddies in the evening with her cigarettes. Smoking was like breathing for Grandma Isla. She was born in the early part of the last century, so she lived through the Great Depression. Living through those times made her very frugal. She would suck the smoke into the deepest part of her lungs and hold it there to get her money's worth. I would watch as she would slowly allow the smoke to escape her lips in such a way that she would snort the remnant clouds of smoke into her nose. It looked like a tornado cloud running into the nostrils.

Having her furniture held a lot of memories for me. Every chair, every table, and every dish had attached a story to them. I now owned the chair she would sit in when she was just a little girl, no more than four years old, the same chair she was sitting in after her mother died and had that supernatural experience. Then there was the old violin I stared down at, which was from a German man who gambled it away in her father's saloon. She remembered hearing the man play it one last time before he forfeited it. It was probably his only possession if that was all he had to give. She said the violin sang so beautifully.

The dishes were from England and were gently carried over the ocean by boat and by train to the Midwest of Wisconsin. She gave me her very first doll with the porcelain face and long locks of pipe curls. So much history. So many stories. I still love old things.

I placed each piece in my new home, painted the walls, and decorated it to look like you took a step back in time. We celebrated our first Christmas that year with a tree and family gathering around. Mark's family came that winter, and they were all so happy about the new baby coming. His mother, especially. She would put her hand over my tummy and talk to her future grandchild. This would be her first. My heart met hers halfway. I was still holding on to the past at this point. I was confused with how all the rejection could just be brushed under the rug, and now we are all acting like we are happy and excited.

A part of me wanted to give her a taste of her own medicine and tell her since she didn't think I was good enough for her son, then she didn't need to be a part of our life. I wrestled with it a lot, yet I knew it was wrong. It was an ugly thought. She never said she was sorry, so I never knew if she had changed her mind. I knew that I was not responsible for her actions in the past and that I was only responsible for handling it. I chose to embrace her love for this child and take it as a way to win her affection.

She started to talk to me and became quite friendly over the next months as she wanted to share in our happy new life together. Some things don't have to be spoken; some truces in life are just felt. I could feel her love. Little by little, my heart let go of my hurt. Love comes gently at times. My heart was happy to have her a part of our lives and the future life of our child.

I had an ultrasound soon after and found out we were having a boy. I was still in college and performing with my jazz combo at coffee houses, so I named him Miles after the great Miles Davis, jazz composer. I played one of his songs when I found out we were having a boy, so it made perfect sense. Mark added Patrick for his Irish heritage and because he thought it would be neat to have the initials, M.P.H. My husband was a sports car enthusiast, and he liked the idea of having a son with a Miles Per Hour abbreviation.

As I got bigger and bigger, I cut my hair shorter and shorter. I started to wear my husband's large shirts to cover my enormous belly. My Karate pants were very comfortable, so I would often wear them under his sweatshirts. I no longer walked to my classes, for by this time, I was waddling. There was generally always a gay pride parade going on at my school with rainbows and purple triangles decorating the campus. I knew a lot of homosexuals, and I was friendly with most of the ones I met. I never tried to tell them what to be or not be. I loved them. I hated when Christians paraded around with hellfire banners damning them. I knew it was not the right way to win someone. I was a bit of a liberal-minded democrat at the time because I was raised to see people, not religion, race, or sexual orientation. My parents taught me to let people do what they want and treat people with respect.

One of my classes was Sociology. It was a required class for my teaching degree. I sat in between two lesbians. They had hair like mine, and we often talked. As we were speaking about some insignificant matter, in walked a very scandalous-looking woman as our guest speaker that day. She had long wavy hair with long legs covered in fishnet tights. A little leather mini-skirt was around her waist, and the clicking of her high heels announced her presence. We all stared straight at her with our eyes bugging out of our heads, wondering why we had a woman who looked like a hooker speaking to us. Or anyway, that was what I was wondering.

"Hey!" He said in a gruff voice. It was a man. We all sat there, every one of us, gay or straight, with our eyes wide in disbelief. He introduced himself as a married man who was straight and married to a woman with two sons at home. For some reason, I was so appalled, so confused, and felt the gumption to stand to my feet and say, "How can you dress like a lady in front of your boys? Don't you think that's confusing?"

He stopped and took a long, sharp look at me, running his eyeballs up and down my figure checking me out. As his expression became cynical, he said, "Well, you look like a guy. How come it's okay for you to dress like a man, yet it is not okay for me to dress like a woman?" I was stopped dead in my tracks. My face changed five shades of red as I pondered his reaction. I had to examine myself for a moment, think about what I was wearing, and figure this out. Yes, he was right! I was silent. There was nothing I could say as I sat my humbled self back down. I was dressed in men's clothing; my hair was cut short. I did not have any makeup on. I was looking more like a guy than a girl. I'd never thought about this before. It was a wake-up moment in my life.

I started to see a very valid point. More girls look like guys, and it's entirely socially acceptable. I also know that a guy donning dresses and makeup is considered "drag." It's not everyday attire. You don't see guys dressing like that, and if they did, it would not be as acceptable as a girl dressed as a tomboy. I felt this overwhelming sense of the gender blending of our society. When I returned home, I looked at myself in the mirror, unlike I've ever looked at myself before. For the first time, I saw what he saw that day, a boy. My entire wardrobe was jeans, karate pants, unisex t-shirts, and big boots that looked militant.

It took a bit for me to allow this to sink into my heart, but even to this day, I have tried to remain consistent. If I feel it's confusing for a guy to dress like a woman, I should not dress like a guy—bottom line. It was not a religious reason, nor did I put that on anyone else, even though it would prove to be another reason people would persecute me.

I remember the first time I started wearing dresses. People would say, "Why are you dressed up? How come you feel you need to wear dresses? You are getting legalistic, and that is a dangerous spot to be in." I couldn't believe the reactions I was getting for dressing like a lady. It made me want to do it all the more just because it was such a controversial way to dress, interestingly enough, even in the church. I had Christians saying this to me, which was strange since it was only several decades ago that all women wore dresses or skirts to church.

It shouldn't matter how a person dresses so long as they feel right in their heart about it. I found that I had a conviction from that day forward. My wardrobe changed, but that did not change who I was. It's a sensitive subject I have found because others think you're judging them by your choice in what you wear. It's just clothing, nothing to argue over. It didn't matter what I wore at that time, I was big, and most things just didn't fit anyway. I set aside the urge to buy a new wardrobe and focused instead on getting ready for the birth of our son.

Chapter Seven
THE GIFT & THE LESSONS

*E*verything was ready: the changing table, stacks of diapers, the crib, and baby boy clothes folded. My belly was stretched out far beyond the view of my toes by this time. I could feel my little boy kicking and moving around within my womb. My due date was just around the corner, so I pleaded with all my professors to take my finals early to focus on the birth. It would've been challenging to go into labor during the stress of finals and not be able to finish because I was set to graduate in June of that summer.

As I sat there taking my finals, I found it extremely hard to concentrate hunching over my paper, taking the exams with a big belly in between and a baby who decided to have hiccups. I was rocking him to try to settle him so I could get these tests over with. I'm not even sure if I did well, but my grades were always so high that even if I did not pass, it would not prevent me from graduating with a high grade-point average.

The birth pains started coming faintly at first, and since I'd never been in labor, I asked Mark to take me in to be checked. We were sent home several times. It wasn't until the third day that they realized I was in actual labor but that something was wrong. The doctor I chose was a general practitioner, and he did not have the experience to recognize a complicated situation such as I had. After 72 hours of no sleep, crunching under the pressure of each contraction, I had become exhausted.

My cervix was not opening, and they did not know why. Until this day, I was bound and determined to have a natural delivery with no drugs or medical intervention. The choice was taken from me as I began to slip in and out of consciousness. On went the oxygen. In went the epidural and the Pitocin. They put a dilating cream over my cervix. I went from nothing to full-on dependency on whatever they could do to help this baby come into the world. By this time, his little heart rate was falling, and he needed to get out of my womb. Mom was filming. Being a nurse, she knew that something was wrong but didn't say a word. In her heart, she feared the worst.

Mark was holding my hand as I laid there, half-conscious and half asleep, trying to conjure up the energy necessary to push when the time came. The doctor came in, gloved up to the elbows, and a clear-looking shield over a helmet, making it look all the more serious. "Let's get the baby out of there," he said with a farmer's fortitude. He was under pressure like a farmer whose crop needed harvesting before a storm, or he would lose everything. He looked like he was wearing a bug shield, but I wasn't sure why. "His hand is there!" It was a complex presentation with the baby's hand below the head in labor, called Nucal Hand. That explained the long delivery because the head was not pushing on the cervix to open it properly. "Push!" I gave it all I had. When I am determined to do something, I go beyond the call of duty. I pushed like I was birthing the world.

Mom was getting more nervous by the minute, shaking as she pointed the video camera at the little hand that was dangling as if to wave hello. The doctor grabbed the hand and put a suction cup over his crowning head. "Keep pushing; you're doing great!" He was in a hurry to pull the distressed baby out of my body. At this point, we were all getting a bit concerned.

Heaving with all the might I could muster, moaning, I was bearing down against the numbness of the epidural. I couldn't feel anything but pressure. With all his weight, the doctor pulled, like a farmer with the chain on the calf's legs, removing it from the mother cow. I saw the video, and it was intense. You could see veins popping on his head, sweat beaded down his brow. As he pulled the hand and the head at the same time, the baby's elbow tore me open wide. It was a third-degree tear. As Mark and I held our wet and chalky child for the first time, we felt like we'd been through another close call, another battle for life, with another cry of victory. The victory cry was an infant announcing his beginning. It was a cry that calmed our fears, our baby Miles, our gift.

For an hour, I laid there being sewn up from one end to the other. I could not sit for weeks. My bottom was so swollen and painful. I don't think the doctor sewed it right. It was mangled, and nerve tissue was on the outside. I was so excited about being a mother that I simply looked beyond the pain. Seeing Mark holding his son was so beautiful. Father and son. Miles was the most handsome, contented baby boy. He would just stare into our eyes, and it seemed like he was aware of everything. I could not stop staring back at him.

Nursing was another difficulty because when my milk came in, I was literally like a cow. I made enough milk for an army of babies. Milk was everywhere, squirting, and rushing out whenever he cried. He would choke when he nursed because the pressure of it spraying out was more than he could handle. I could set a large glass under the other breast while nursing the other side, and the glass would be overflowing at the end.

Two days after the birth of Miles, I had to walk on the stage to receive my Bachelor's Degree at the University. Mark was holding the baby out in the crowd somewhere. I did not know where they were; I just nestled a little inner tube under my graduation gown. I had to have it for any time I sat. As I walked up to the principal of Lawrence University, who handed me my diploma, I could hear my baby crying in the crowd. My milk let down right there, and the gown was now wet in two spots, and everyone stared. The disgust they had was confirmed in that brief display. I paid no mind because I knew my baby was hungry, and I would not listen to another speech nor sit another minute, and I would find him by following my ear.

There is a powerful force between a mother and her child. Science has yet to figure it out. Nothing can match it. It is like gravity. When one tries to defy gravity, they meet certain death. Every woman who is separated from her flesh experiences a death of sorts. I can see how my mother must have died a thousand deaths for every passing year parted from her child she gave up for adoption. They say when a mother has an abortion, she never fully recovers for the life that is ripped from her. It is sacred. Life is sacred.

I was adjusting to motherhood, the sleepless night feedings, the long hours of trying to figure out what each cry means. You eventually get in tune with the patterns: what they like and what they do not like when they are hungry, tired, and when they just want to look at you because you're their mother.

No sooner did I align myself with my new infant when I got the call for my first teaching job starting that fall. I thought I would have jumped at the idea. It was what I had worked so hard for. Mom worked. All women I knew worked, and it seemed fair to say that working was the way of life of the modern mother. Leaving your child was all a part of the program. When they are five years old, we send them on the school bus. Was that going to be my path? Why did I feel so sad to leave?

The morning I woke for school came too soon. I bundled up my baby and rushed him off to the babysitter for the day. She had a few other little ones and was happy to have a new baby on board. It was a home daycare. She seemed so trustworthy. I touched the soft, delicate skin of my baby boy's cheeks one last time before I fled out of her back door in a state of grief. I felt a sense of loss. My breasts cried out to feed him, and the artificial pumps were no consolation.

All-day working with little children of all ages, I started to wonder if I was doing the right thing. Why would I be spending the day with others' little ones while someone else is spending the day with my precious son? She would be the one who would get to observe all the firsts. The first step, the first rollover, and she would have what was rightfully mine as his mother. I could not change it; I had the job; I could not let the school down. After work that day, I drove to the babysitter's home to pick up Miles. As I picked his carrier up, I wondered if he had been in there most of the day. I wondered if she was too busy tending to the other children to notice him.

I unhooked him after coming to our home down the street. I smelled him. I took the deepest smell of his skin to remind me of the scent that I missed all day, and I started to cough. He smelled like an ashtray. She had told me that she didn't smoke. Obviously, someone there did. Who was the one blowing smoke around my baby? Would I bring him back there? That was the real question that begged an answer.

I bathed my baby, washing all the smoke that penetrated every inch of his little body. The night was quiet, sober, as I held him so much closer. Tossing and turning with fear of what the morning might bring. I couldn't leave him ever again. It was decided. But who quits their dream job the second day? Only a person who finds a more fulfilling dream to replace it.

Motherhood that day became my calling, and I vowed never to step outside the home for anything or anyone. This calling became something etched into my heart that morning. My life's work was staring at me through those little eyes, and I knew that my purpose was far beyond credentials, paychecks, and classrooms filled with generations of families marching their children off to school year after year. I traded a career that morning, a job that could have spanned a lifetime, for a humble title: the keeper of the home.

Motherhood was the gift. It came with a little package wrapped in flesh, a tiny heart beating in sync with the creation and the plan of God. He created a woman to bring forth life and to nurture its very essence from the beginning. I realized in that short time that there was a battle in society that rages against nature – against the natural pureness of marriage, motherhood, and family. There was a lot to learn, for I was not educated in the ways of the home.

At this point, I only knew how to make food that I could dump out of a box or can and warm in the microwave. Macaroni and Cheese or Chef Boyardee were about the only things I could make. Anything beyond an instant or packaged meal was a burned and charred mess. I needed a teacher, someone who could take me under their wing. The perfect person was my mom's mother. Grandma Reichel was a true keeper of the home, as were most women of her era. She would know how to teach me.

The first time I invited Grandma over for dinner was a disaster. I was living in an apartment at that time. It was shortly after we were married, and I was pregnant. I wanted to make the most beautiful table setting graced with the most elegant set of dishes. She had given me this set of dishes for a wedding gift a few months before the wedding. I had gone to help her haul things off to Goodwill when I saw a box filled with the most beautiful china.

There were pink and red roses painted on each cup with a gilded edge that shined, plates with the same pattern, having the same whimsical edge that caught my eye.

"Grandma, are these dishes going to the Goodwill?" I asked in utter dismay. Who would give such treasures away?

"Oh, yes. I have held onto them my whole married life and

never really used them. They just sat, tucked away in my cupboard," she replied without a trace of sentiment.

"Where did you get them?" I begged for the story. I knew there had to be a romantic story to grace these beautiful teacups and saucers that I delicately handled between my hands. "I got them during the Depression. The grocery store was trying to encourage us to spend money. It was a reward for buying so many things. You got to pick out a piece each time, and I ended up collecting this set over the years." She went on to say, "You can have them if you want."

"That's the best wedding gift I could ever have wished for," I gleamed as I wanted her to know that she didn't have to give us any other gift. That was the best gift, and I would use them. She plopped the box into my arms with a smile as I walked carefully to my car to give them a new home.

Mom had given me a salad shooter, and I hadn't the faintest idea of how to use the thing. I figured it was for vegetables, so I ran hot boiled potatoes through it to make them mashed. Grandma was on her way. I had the table set with candles and the rose china. The apartment smelled of baking chicken. The only way I knew how to make chicken was from when Mom would put the breast in the bag of Shake n Bake. As a little girl, I would shake the pork chops or chicken breasts in there before mom would plunge them into the oven on a flat baking sheet. I knew I could handle that. The chicken was cooking in the oven with a coating of breading on it. I had whole potatoes boiling. After pricking a fork into the potato, and it seemed soft, I proceeded to load them into the salad shooter.

The machine made a gruff noise, and all at once, there were boiling potatoes being shot all around my little apartment kitchen, burning my hands and up my arms. Some remained in the bowl below, but in the frenzy of scraping hot potatoes off every surface, I smelled the dreaded smell of smoke. Yes, the chicken consequently burned, and my meal was a disaster.

Knock, knock, knock. It was Grandma. She most certainly couldn't know I was lying on the floor, pregnant and defeated. I brushed myself off, wiped the tears from my face along with the other fragments of dried-on potatoes, and welcomed her into my humble home. She never winced at the smell as she passed the cloud looming over the candle-lit table. My burnt offering was motionless on our plates alongside the chunky, bland potatoes. She acted as though it was a masterpiece. Gnawing on the chicken, she smiled. "Maybe someday you could visit me, and I could teach you." She did not have to say anything as both Mark and I already knew I needed her training. I couldn't go on cooking like that, and the only other alternative was unhealthy packaged food.

After I quit the job and decided to be a keeper of the home, I started making regular visits to Grandma on the hilltop of Kaukauna. The same house she raised her five children and lived most of her life was now my new classroom. She loved seeing the baby. His smiles and soft kissable fat cheeks were payment for her long hours of teaching me. Her hands and mine would knead bread in the big metal bowl. "Punch. Punch. Punch. Fold in like this. Punch. Punch. Punch," she would say with little patience. It had to be this particular way, or it wouldn't work. The result was the most glorious baked bread, golden and fluffy, with a delicate crunch to the crust.

"Will your hair grow longer, Grandma," I asked with perplexity as I examined both the ingredients and the resulting crusted bread, knowing there was not a special coating to the outside. It couldn't possibly have a specific vitamin on the crust, yet as far as I could remember, I was told that if I ate the crust, my hair would grow longer. I always wanted long hair.

She chuckled, "No. I always told you that so you would not waste the crust!" Grandma was brilliant. She knew all the things to say to make everything more meaningful. I laughed out loud, thinking how gullible I had always been and how my trust was still so steadfast, even when I believed outlandish lies to my detriment. Child-like faith is not a bad thing. Even Jesus told us to become like little children. I think it is because when we are like a child, we are quick to forgive, trust without guile, and have unfaltering faith.

If I wasn't learning the art of baking, I was learning how to make pot roasts with potatoes. Grandma taught me how to be a clean cook. She demonstrated, "When you are cooking, you have to set the spices down after you use them. So, instead of setting them down on the countertop, just set them back where you found them...in the cupboard." The knife she used to cut the meat went in the hot soapy water while searing on the stovetop. It was rinsed and then put away while the food was cooking. The kitchen remained clean; it was streamlined and simple to understand. She taught me everything she knew, and everything she knew was such a value to a young mother as myself, who was so eager to learn. Miles would sit there in the pram, watching us work in the kitchen until we could not help ourselves but break down and cuddle him, eating up all his cuteness. He was such a delight.

From then on, when my parents or Mark's parents came for a visit, I could whip out a beautiful meal, all thanks to Grandma. Learning the art of keeping my home and of hospitality to those who entered through the doors of my house was something I would continue to press into for a lifetime. She gave me a treasure that is so beautiful, a gift that you can't touch with hands, but it makes you rich in the things that matter most in the heart. It is a gift that keeps on giving. From mother to daughter or older woman to the younger, it was a cycle that's worth repeating.

Chapter Eight
The Slob & the Demon

Miles grew so fast. Little blond curls covered his round head, and everyone was enamored with the dimple in his chin right beneath his small sweet smile. He was always smiling. Everywhere I went, people would gravitate towards him and his giggling little character.

His joy was something that brought people together. You could forget the past, the pain, the bitterness when there is a giggling baby between you and any person you might be at odds with. Laughter is good for the soul. Mom and Dad would come to see our little one quite often. I wanted to have a family over as often as possible. Now that I was learning to be a keeper of the home, I loved preparing meals for others to enjoy and having a tidy home.

Mom may not have had the time to teach me how to cook when I was young, mainly because I did not act interested. I followed other dreams. Every delicious meal Mom prepared was placed on the table for us like clockwork. We would come home from school, and there was a hot meal waiting for us. She learned from the best, so from mother to daughter, the art of cooking a tasty meal had passed down. I was the missing link! I broke a long chain of mother to daughter cooking lessons which have now since been redeemed.

Mom did teach me how to clean when I was younger. She cooked, and my job was to clean up. Not only that, I had to do the weekly cleaning. Mom never liked dirt. Every surface had to be scoured and scrubbed till it shined. I knew how to clean. I had to. If I did not clean it right the first time, I had to do it again. You learn to be mindful of the dirt when you are made to go back. My problem was not cleaning. It was stuffing things away. When people would visit us in our new home, I would quickly stash everything under the bed, in the closet, or cupboard so no one could see it. My house looked shining clean at first glance.

Truth be told, I used to be a classic hoarder! Mom knew it. When I was young, Mom would threaten to throw all my junk onto the driveway, which she did once. I had to run outside around the back of the house and gather up my junk, hauling it back to my room, making fifty or so trips. Mom was taught to clean well by her mother, who kept a fine home. I should have been better in my own home since I learned from the best. When I talk to Mom now, she tells me how frustrated she was with my stubborn slobbish tendencies. In fact, she made me shut my door to keep from seeing it and allowing it to drive her to want to run me and my junk out of her home for good. When I first got married, she invited Mark and me to their home for a meal. When we pulled into the driveway, there sat what looked to be a caravan of plastic bins streaming from the back door fifty feet.

She looked up at my tall, handsome husband and said, "She's your problem now!" Thankfully, my husband is not a pushover. He looked at me, dumped two of the tubs out, and said with steadfast authority, "Okay, you have two bins. Whatever you can fit in these bins, you may keep. The rest is going to the dump!" All I could think was how merciful my dear husband was to allow me to keep a few of my special things.

I searched through bin after bin of school papers, my dog's baby teeth (weird!), dolls I saved, rocks (really?), stuffed animals, and old, worn-out clothes. I saved everything. There were over forty bins, so it was a long, laborious afternoon–the afternoon this hoarder was caught red-handed. I love that my husband is strong for me when I am weak. This was a purging that needed to happen for me to grow into a better homemaker. Today, I do not miss that trash. I cannot even remember what I threw away that day. For the few years after that, there would be more bonfires filled with debris purged from our closets. My transformation did not happen overnight. The habit of saving everything was a hard one to break.

It frustrated my husband. He hated all the clutter and especially

The Slob & The Demon

how I would stuff his things frantically in places that only God would know to look. Going on a mystery treasure hunt right before he would leave for work was not a game my husband wanted to play. It embarrassed me when his mother would come for a weekend visit. She was not fond of me from the beginning, so it was a hard battle to convince her that I was worthy of her son. I wanted her to like me so badly. I wanted her to think I was a good wife and mother. She loved seeing the baby and took every opportunity to come around. Because she lived two hours away, she generally stayed on long weekends overnight. It's hard to prevent someone from discovering the mess behind the doors when they live there with you for days on end.

Finally, I did what most women would not dare to do...I asked my mother-in-law to help me organize my home! She could be my next teacher.

One closet at a time, I let her pick through all my stowed-away messes, while she would ask me the dreaded questions, "Why would you keep this?" "Do you use this?" "Is this garbage?" Usually, it was something that I should have thrown away! She taught me to put each thing in a specific place, "its HOME." When I was done using it, I had to return it to its "home." Wow, this went against my nature. It took years of training to get me out of some pretty bad habits of laziness. Now I am known as the "Clean Freak!"

In some ways, it bonded her and I together because we were working as a team. I was thrilled for her help. I must have been the most blessed young mother in the world, getting to sit under such amazing women who taught me. Mom had already taught me how to clean things during my growing-up years, Grandma taught me how to prepare meals, and Mark's mom taught me how to be organized.

I wanted to be organized in all areas of my life, for that matter, even with mothering. Mark's mother had a beautiful baby shower after the baby was born, and I met Janet, the wife of one of Mark's cousins. Janet gave me a book that taught me how to have a schedule for my baby. I read the book and found it to make so much sense, so I applied it like everything else in my life. The book taught that a baby is more contented and stable with an ordered life. It is a life that is family-centered, not child-centered. The child learns to eat at scheduled feedings, sleep through the night, and wake cheerfully. It worked. I had Miles waking to be nursed. He would then be changed and played with.

I would sing, read books to him, and have a beautiful time with him. At the end of our time, when he would get sleepy, I would lay him down for a nap. He would fall asleep quickly and take nice long naps. When he woke, no matter the exact time, he would be fed, and the sequence would continue. It made my life so much easier. I felt free to enjoy mothering instead of feeling constant fussing or crying and never knowing what to do. It was terrific because he was so content and happy as a result.

Storms were brewing in our young marriage. It wasn't the first time. Even at the apartment, after I first became pregnant, I remember demanding to have critters just like my dad did. Mark didn't see sense in caring for little creatures. I had a ferret, a kitten, two parakeets, and a hedgehog. He hated the loud bantering of the birds and having to watch where he walked in the night for fear of stepping on Saul, the prickly hedgehog which I insisted needed time to forage during the night. One such night Saul got lost, and I was frantic. We looked under the bed and dressers and in the closet when finally Mark spotted a spine protruding out from the wall. Saul was on the wall. Mark said as he heaved a sigh of disgust, "Oh brother. I guess I will have to get him out of there." He tried to poke his long finger in the slit near the register, and the hedgehog hissed while jarring his spines right into that finger. Next, he grabbed a wooden spoon and tried to pop him out, which didn't work at all. Finally, he started cutting a hole a little bigger than the width of that prickly ball so that he could grab the poor little creature with a pair of tongs. He wasn't too happy about having to patch that hole. I could tell he was running out of patience, so I made arrangements to find the hedgehog, the ferret, and the cat a new home since I was so sick at the time, and all these nasty smells were getting to me.

I talked Mark into letting me keep the two little birds. After class one day, I remember trying to clean out the birdcage. I hauled it over to our sink in the apartment, and all at once, the birds started freaking out, and the wind from their wings broke out a massive cloud filled with empty seed husks that littered my entire kitchen. I was so mad that I threw the cage with the birds in it clear across the room. One of the birds flew around the room, and the other just laid there limp, and I ran to the poor creature and started crying. I was so ashamed of myself and had to blame it on my pregnancy hormones of all things. It was such a stupid temper, and I couldn't seem to get my emotions under control at that time. The bird lived, and I vowed to keep it alive.

Later that same year one cold winter morning, I woke up and saw the two birds lying dead at the bottom of the cage. I screamed in horror as the tears streamed down my face, "Mark! The birds are dead!"

He was in the closet, fixing something as he emerged with a very calm resolute, "Good." That infuriated me. My blood was boiling, and I could not believe he could be that heartless. I asked him kindly to remove the birds from my presence, so I did not have to continue to look at their dead carcasses. It just made me cry all the more. He said he would get to it when he was done, but that was not good enough for me. I was not having it. I rose angrily off the chair and stomped toward the kitchen to grab a garbage bag, and I steamed, "I will do it myself!" I marched myself, passed him, and toward the dead birds, and I could hear much louder stomps coming after me. He grabbed me with the most fearsome look in his eyes, and he bit a piece of the black plastic bag off and spit it at me. He later said he was doing this to prevent himself from doing worse to me.

I would chase him down with wooden spoons and scream at him, threaten to divorce him, cuss him out, and he would just stand like a statue and hold himself back from killing me. I admire him for being that self-controlled. I knew how to push some serious buttons. Ask my folks. They will concur.

Since we were now parents and caring for a little one, we were that much more frustrated and easier to find something to fight about. I remember, at that time, he would blare the terrible devil sounding heavy metal music in the basement whenever he had to get away from me and my whining. I would be harassing him, and he would just wave his hand and say, "Whatever!" as he would storm outside or to the basement below. I could sometimes hear a crack or thud when he would chuck something or punch a wall to get his anger out. I think he would even sneak cigarettes because I could smell it on his breath. More than likely he woud do it to calm his nerves. I told him before I married him, it was me or the cigarettes. I didn't want to marry a smoker.

Soon everything came to a head when I asked him a simple but probing question, "Do you know where you are going to go if you die?" He looked sad. He looked almost defeated and I knew something was amiss. His silence took me by surprise, and I knew he was not who

I thought he was. I thought I had married a Christian man. Anytime I tried to coax him to church or plead with him to trust Jesus, he would tell me I was treating him like a child and storm out. It truly felt hopeless that he would ever come over to the other side. I sure wasn't a good example of a Christian, so I am sure it didn't appeal to him in the least.

I knew I needed to work on my own heart. I needed Jesus to rule my heart and help me be the wife he created me to be. I started watching TV evangelists on the T.V. and jotting down the things I was learning. For starters, I realized that if I wanted him to lead, I needed to help him to be a leader. I was the one who was in control, who wore the pants. I started asking before I did anything to give him an opportunity to lead. It was hard when he would say "no," but I knew it was for my growth. Little by little, I let go of my controlling nature as a woman and learning to trust God to lead my husband to Him.

One weekend he told me he wanted to go to a men's revival meeting and just about fell off my chair, knowing God was listening to my prayers. He came back a different man. The very first thing he did was go to the basement and came up with an armful of satanic music. He began to throw them into a burning pile, and I could not believe my eyes as I saw the shining plastic melt. I asked,
"Why not sell them?"

He quickly replied, "What? Sell them and lead others to hell? No, they need to burn!" That was rather radical for him. He wasn't a true radical man, but a steady sure one who did what always needed doing. That was a turning point for our marriage, and I was delighted that my husband was lost and now had found Jesus too.

"Grandma had a stroke!" Mom told me over the phone, her voice distressed. Grandma had been put into a hospital for recovery, and the entire family was trying to figure out where she would go. They all knew that the time had come that she would no longer be able to care for herself. It was quite sad because she was such a productive woman. She woke before the crack of dawn to work with her hands, mending, sewing, baking, cleaning, doing laundry, gardening, and canning up the extra. You couldn't stop her. All things run out of steam eventually. Every machine that ticks like a clock with perfect precision must wind down. She was in her late 80s, and she put her time it, burning her candle at both ends. She never asked for credit, nor did she expect anything from anyone; she just kept her nose to the grindstone. In my book, she was incredible. I only wished for more time to learn from her. She was what I wanted to become.

"Can I take her in my home?" I offered. The thought of this great woman, this hardworking woman who never complained, put into a nursing home felt wrong. She needed to be wrapped in the care of her family in her last years for all the care she gave in her lifetime of putting others before herself.

"We will have to ask her, Erin. She wants to be in her home," Mom replied. After telling her that she had no other alternative, she agreed to live at my home, and I think the thought of being able to see the baby every day made her happy.

We moved her in over the course of a few days and tried to make her as comfortable as possible. She was a spitfire with a whole lot of sass. As independent as she was, it was hard for her to adjust to someone taking care of her. "Grandma, do you need to go to the bathroom?" She would say, "No, I can get there when I need to." The only trouble was that she couldn't get up unassisted. Because I was respectful of her wishes, she would mess herself every time. I would let her boss me around and tell me that I didn't need to help her, which always ended up a miserable situation. I had to help her up and then clean up a huge mess.

"The renters just got evicted!" That's what Grandma would say every time she pooped herself. Even though it started out with a bit of sass and a bit of humor, she always ended, saying she was sorry. She felt terrible that I had to clean up after these so-called renters, but I ever calmly and gently returned, "Oh, that's okay, Grandma. Everyone poops. It's no big deal." I had to help her shower and dress her. Everywhere I went, she had to go with me. I could never leave her home alone. I would cook, take care of her and my six-month-old baby boy at the same time. I would be off changing his diaper when she would fill hers. It was a constant whirlwind of work, and I was wearing down quickly.

She called me Flossy. It was short, she said, "for Florence Nightingale." Her other children would holler at her and demand her to do things when I would ask her nicely and be patient with her. I guess that made her feel like I was her Florence Nightingale.

I enjoyed the calm when Miles was down for a nap, and I could sit in a chair beside Grandma and talk with her about her life. There were so many stories. She enjoyed reminiscing about the past eight decades. It was a good thing she taught me how to cook when she did, or she would've had to eat some pretty lousy food while staying at my home. It was like God gave me that little window at just the right time, although I wished I would've started learning much earlier. How is it that you can go through life and miss the most precious teaching moments? I guess I just didn't know the wealth of information that I had my whole life from my mother and grandmother. It's no use regretting what I didn't see in times past, for now, I laid hold of the precious gift.

Back in college, when I was preparing for graduation, I did ponder my role in society. I sincerely wondered if I was blindly walking in a circular motion of being what a woman was meant to be. My pregnancy felt like a prison, and I was held captive. It's all in your perspective and what you're around as the tides of popular culture dictate. Here I was in a university of liberals who detested the natural role of the woman and cried out for her right in society. I bought into the lies for a time. In my art, you can see the struggle I was having. There were paintings of a pregnant woman behind bars with her hands tied tight. She had no choice. I made a teakettle of a pregnant woman that I placed on a table in front of a window.

I called my feature painting, "The Cult of Domesticity" (I was the child in the painting. The portrait of a little girl with no eyes running from one window to another to sit behind like a shadow, kept, and put there). The table was set with china, and I had this displayed in my Senior Art exhibit. My teapot was placed there in the middle to pour out as a mother does. We pour out, and the breasts were the spouts that could fill two cups at one time. The wrestling I did in my heart ended the moment I saw my sweet child. I knew this was right where I was supposed to be. I can understand how women raised in this present culture strive to find their destiny in every other place than as mothers in a home. Grandma was the norm for the culture she grew up in and for thousands of years before. Hearing her stories even confirmed more solidly in my mind that a woman and her home are the same.

Soon I began to grow weary of the night changing of the two at the very bookends of life—one at the start and the other at her end. The smells started to make me very sick, and I was back to the bathroom wondering how on earth if it was possible that I could be pregnant again. My baby boy was barely six months old. I started to feel very depressed and overwhelmed. There had only been one occasion that I came together with my husband since the delivery because of the pain I had in that area. The mangled mess from the stitches prevented anything with the exposed nerve tissues. I had been to the doctor, who said it was something that had to be surgically reconstructed.

The mystery was solved after taking an over-the-counter pregnancy test. I was expecting my second child, and it seemed bittersweet. I was excited, but I had to make a hard decision to stop taking care of Grandma. Extreme fatigue and nausea made me ill-equipped for the job. All I wanted was to do was lie down. Mom made arrangements for Grandma to be put into assisted living, and I could go and see her anytime I wanted. It worked out for the best.

I found a new doctor, this time, an obstetrician. For what I endured with the last delivery, I wanted to have someone who knew what they were doing. She was a good doctor. After so many months, we decided to find out what we were having. It was a girl.

I loved knowing I was having a little girl. Pink clothes, ribbons, bonnets, and little dresses were things stacked on the changing table. I found a nice lady from church that taught me how to sew a pretty quilt for my new baby. In the excitement, I refinished an antique dresser, crib, and nightstand for her new room. The theme was little white lambs, and I painted little stuffed lambs to hang on the wall.

Most of my days were filled with nature walks to the park or potty training, Miles. Yes, I did potty train him when he was just an infant. Growing up at a dog kennel, I had to potty train many puppies over the years. I figured people were so much smarter than animals, so it must be easier to train a baby, right? After changing Grandma's diaper and his at the same time, it made me want never to have two in diapers again. Whenever I could see he was trying to go, I would slip his diaper off and set his little body on a potty chair. He would get used to the feeling, and we would have so much fun spending time together.

When he was crawling about the floor, I would keep the diaper off, and when he started to wet, I would clap my hands and get his attention. He would stop going, and I would pick him up and set him on the pot until he would finish. It became a very natural fun activity. I even read him stories while he sat there. We made it fun, and he found it easy and natural to begin taking himself to the potty once he could walk. By the time he was one year old, he had worn big boy underwear and rarely had an accident.

I did not realize how unusual that was until meeting so many other women who had children three and four years old still using diapers and how hard it was for them to train them. I guess the children were so used to peeing and pooping in their pants that they found it scary to sit over a bowl of water. In essence, the child will do what they are taught. They are either taught it is natural to pee and poop in a diaper or a toilet. I thought it made more sense to train them how I do it—on the toilet.

Later in the pregnancy, I found out that I had placenta previa (which means the placenta covers part or all of the cervix) and would need to take special care. My due date had been scheduled in case of the emergency for the placenta being birthed first. It's very dangerous and life-threatening. I had the whole church praying for it to move, and when we went in for the final ultrasound, it had safely moved out of the way, but we stuck with our scheduled delivery to be safe. Because of the last traumatic delivery, I had varicose veins in that area, which had become painful alongside the nerve tissues, so I was glad to have all hands on deck.

Mom did not want to be at another birth, so my brother's wife, Michelle, came to film. She was always kind to me. As I laid there in the hospital bed, she brushed my hair and fixed it nicely for the photos. The doctor had induced me, broke the water, and did an epidural so that we could make sure there were no complications. As I recall, the Olympics were going on, and I was bound and determined to win. There were many other women giving birth simultaneously, and I wanted to beat them so I could see my baby first. I grabbed the metal bed rails every contraction, and I pretended to row the boat with all I had in me, thinking I was in the lead. It helped me to focus more on delivery.

"Get ready to push, Erin," the doctor said with a smile on her face. It was a way better experience. I felt safe there. I gave two good pushes, and our daughter was born. It was so easy. As I held her for the first time, I cried out, "This is my best friend!" I had just given birth to my best friend.

"Let's call her Henrietta, after my great aunt," Mark said as I looked at her sweet face and replied, "Autumn Rain is better!" We argued for a bit until we settled on the name, Molly Elizabeth. It was a name that started with an "M" like Miles and Elizabeth after my mom and his grandmother. Little Miles came to the hospital with his Nana and Bumpa (my parents), and he loved seeing her. It was so sweet to see him hold her and look at her the way he did.

Our family was growing. Having a baby girl was meaningful to me, knowing I had a daughter to pass on the skills of keeping the home and motherhood.

God had kept us safe thus far, and we were thankful to bring home another baby. Another precious gift from God.

I had to make a choice. It was between my new baby and my husband. Here I was with a desperate need to have surgery to correct the mess from the first delivery and a beautiful baby that I wanted to nourish. The doctor said she would not operate if I were either pregnant or nursing. The reason being, the tissues would not heal properly. On the other hand, I had a desperate husband that could not be with his wife properly until the issue was fixed.

What would I do? Should I not nurse my baby and just feed her formula so that I could be there for my husband in the ways he needs me to be? I wanted to nurse her for at least a full year, but that would put my husband out. He had already been deprived for over a year and a half save that one occasion in which I conceived Molly. I know it sounds crazy, but even using the bathroom was painful. Showering was painful. But a man has needs. In a way, I was relieved because, for some reason, I had slipped into a rut from my past abuse. The shame of it all had held me back in so many ways. The act of intimacy was altogether dirty to me in my mind. If I had an excuse to be inactive, I would take it. My body was as cold as ice when it came right down to it.

A bargain was made. I wanted to nurse for a year, but he couldn't hold out that long. So I offered a compromise. "Six months. I will get the surgery when Molly is six months." He could see that there was no convincing this mother or bargaining for less time nourishing her child. I remember crying because I knew I had to commence the act I hated and stop feeding my fat and beautiful baby girl. She loved nursing, and I couldn't imagine taking that away from her, but something had to be done. As much as I hated the act, I loved God and knew it was wrong to withhold myself from my husband.

I had everything going for me, yet I couldn't take hold of the joy it bestowed. The most patient, adoring husband, the beautiful purpose of motherhood, gorgeous little children staring back at me, and all I could do was look back. I was like the wife of Lot, who looked back at Sodom, frozen in a pillar of salt. As a prisoner to my past, I opened the door to the devil and his destruction.

Many days I remained in bed wondering how I could escape the shame. My poor husband would come home to me as I was crying and wishing I was dead because my mind could not bear the burdens I placed on it. The sad thing about depression was I felt that it was a choice. I chose it, and it grieves me now that I could not see past myself.

I stopped cleaning and cooking. I did what most moms do. I bought instant foods and gave myself the easy way of mothering. Set your children in front of the television, give them cereal to munch on to keep them busy, nurse the baby when needed, change diapers, do what you have to do, but it's essentially survival mode. You don't take pleasure in mothering when you resort to the bare minimum and putting out fires when they spring. It was the point when you leave the messes to pile up because you don't have the energy to sort things. The more days that you neglect the housework, the worse you feel. The little messes form into mountains, and the feeling a mother gets was overwhelming. My "all or nothing" resolve was quite apparent as I shifted from doing everything with gusto to the bare minimum. Closing out the world was easy with the television.

By this stage, I was so far gone that I could only think of ending my life. Somehow God felt a million miles away. When we attended church, I would sit in the back and hope to hide from people, but the people would find me, and they would smile at me. Out of sheer habit, I would smile back, but I was just pretending. There was not a shred of happiness or thankfulness in my heart. How can you have everything, yet feel like you have nothing?

I went to Mike, our pastor, and told him that I was in such a state of perpetual grief. He remembered when I was on medications for my mental problems back in college. He went on to say, "Mental illness is a real thing, Erin. Your mind has a chemical imbalance. Taking medication is not admitting defeat. If you get an infection, you take pills. This is just like that. You take pills that will help your brain make more of the chemical it is unable to produce." He made perfect sense. It wasn't my fault. I could see that it was a simple fix, and that gave me hope when I told my husband. We had geared ourselves up for making an appointment with a psychologist to get me back on my medications.

The Slob & The Demon

For whatever reason, I failed to make that appointment, and things progressively became worse. I was now cursing and trashing my home, which was the opposite of who I was. The following Sunday, as I was behind the glass in the nursery, holding my daughter, I said in a gruff voice that I could hear with my ears, "You have no idea there is a demon among you." My lips moved, yet my mind could not understand the voice that came from them. My daughter looked at me and started to cry. She was such a good baby, and she barely cried. I was scared. Would the pills take that voice away?

I couldn't tell anyone that this had happened because it was too crazy. Each day I held on for dear life, wondering if that voice would come back. By the end of the next week, I could not bear another day of worry, and I told my husband that I could only think of death. "Should I get on the pills?" I stammered and shook like I was on the edge of a cliff, just waiting for him to pull me where it was safe. I knew I was on the brink of losing everything if I took one more step in that direction.

He said with perfect calm calculation, "No. That won't work. It's not a mental illness." I stared up at him in complete shock, "It is demonic. You have a demon."

"How could that be? I am saved," I said with bewilderment.

"You know back in the day of Jesus when he was healing people? He recognized two kinds of things: one was lunacy, which was mental illness, and the other was demonic possession or oppression," Mark continued with his point.

"Yes. I do know about this," I said as I scrolled through the recesses of my mind searching for the exact places I read that in the Bible.

"There were no pills to cover things like this. Jesus just cast out the demons. Yours is not a mental illness. You have a demon." You have to understand; my husband is as strait-laced as they come. He doesn't talk much, nor is he given into crazy ideas. When he speaks, I listen. His heart is so steady and pure that what comes out of his mouth has to be true. I know my husband, and anything but facts and figures will proceed from his mouth. If he can't back it up, he won't even say it.

"Shall we call the pastor and tell him?" In contrast, I was the type to pursue all of his ideas or proclamations aggressively.

"We won't have to," he said with a surety I have never seen until that day. "God knows. He will deliver you tomorrow." What? That was even crazier than the voice I heard coming out of my mouth. God was just going to know about this without us telling anyone, mysteriously. Oh, you have no idea what was going through my mind.

The very next morning was cold and frozen. It was bitter, and the wind pierced us as we marched into the doors of that little church on the corner. I didn't say a word. My lips were sealed. I wondered how this was all going to play out or if my husband was actually off his rocker now. Maybe I was sick, and he caught whatever I had.

There we were standing in the very last pew behind a row of very tall people. I was glad for it. I wanted to hide. As Mike picked up his guitar that morning, the same guy I sang with dozens of times started the worship. At this point, I could not sing, which was unusual for me. Generally, I am the loudest one in the room singing my heart out for Jesus, but the devil had stolen that joy as well, and I was suffering in silence.

All at once, I froze. There was no reason for my body to become so rigid, and as my heart started pounding out of my chest, I thought I would be swallowed up in it. No one knew. I felt like I might die right then and there behind the wall of people where no one could see. I don't even think Mark was paying attention, but I could not move my arms. They were stuck and started to crunch inward slowly.

The song stopped in the middle. There was a complete interruption as Mike set the guitar down, "There is someone here that needs deliverance. God just told me I needed to stop singing." Mike never did that. He was a pretty stable person, too. Was the whole world going mad? Or was this for me? Mark knew it was for me. It was my deliverance that he foretold. He grabbed my rigid body, which by this time was folded inward like a form of rigor mortis as he dragged my body toward the front, practically carrying me the entire way. Just my feet were scraping the carpet as I was hauled. Still, I could not move, and while we passed all the others on the way up, I could see the look of horror on their faces. Especially the pastor. He looked like he saw a ghost, yet he didn't allow himself to break the call of God to deliver such a one as me.

"I don't know what the situation is," Mike said like he was trying to appease the onlookers who begged for a reason for this madness. "In the name of Jesus, I rebuke any spirit that might be on her and ask you to deliver my sister." In a flash, I was limp, my heart calmed, and I felt so much peace at that moment. "Take her home, Mark," Mike whispered. It was silent. Not another word was uttered as my husband gathered up our two little ones, and, linking his arm with mine, we made our way out the doors and into the bright white of the freezing air. The sky was pure crisp blue, and the gleam of the snow on the ground blinded us. I had never felt such peace. It was like I could have jumped across an ocean and floated upon a cloud. The presence of God was with me again. I felt the life come back into my body every step I took.

Not a word was exchanged. I was speechless. I just got into the car, and we started to roll to the end of the street, trying to process what just went down minutes before. "Stop!" I said as I grabbed his arm. "I have to go back into the church and share my testimony with what God just delivered me from." The suburban came to a screeching halt because he knew it was what I needed to do. He turned the big rig around, and we marched right back through those doors. I never stopped. I kept walking straight to the front as I abandoned my family at the back.

Mike moved over and gave me complete control over the pulpit. Until that day, I had never spoken at a pulpit, but it was time. I lowered the microphone about seven inches until it was right in front of my lips. "I had a demon, my husband told me. He said God would deliver me today, and as you have witnessed, He did. I came in here a mess, wanting to die. I had no hope, and the devil was after my life." I paused, "I can't explain it; all I know is that I have hope again, and I feel God's presence. God is real!"

I walked down among the crowd who had just been on a rollercoaster ride with emotion, and they too must have been trying to process it all. I smiled, and it was a real smile again.

Later Mike told me that he knew it was a demon because he could see a manifestation of some sort on my face that told him. I had white skin with dark circles around my eyes, but at the moment he touched me, he said my face was changed, and the demon was released. It frightened him.

You would not believe how controversial such an event is among the Christian people. Some say it was a demon. Others say it is not possible. For years I have wrestled with the understanding of what happened to me. Was I even saved? Some would argue that a saved person cannot have demonic activity in their life. They believe a person can be afflicted outwardly with sickness or disease. I have learned there are two forms of human demonic activity: demonic oppression and demonic possession. Demonic oppression is defined as mild to massive demonic harassment or influence.

Meanwhile, demonic possession is characterized as full inhibition and control of evil spirits over the human body. They are both said to happen internally. The possession form is not possible for the believer because they have permitted the Holy Spirit to dwell within, thus making their body a temple. Full demonic possession only comes with permission in the same way. You can't have full control of both; it must be one or the other. The demonic spirits come in through doors, and I do remember a few entries I left open.

Sexual abuse is a door, especially if it is opened or allowed by a parent. The evil that is put on the victim is mental in the long run because the evil penetrates the mind. The worst of my sexual abuse was mental. Pornography is another door. When I was growing up, I was surrounded by porn and viewed more than I care to admit. The visions of immorality burn images into your mind and create pathways. Practicing in the occult is another door. As a child, I would practice with Ouija boards and tarot cards for fun with my mother or other kids in my school. I had many frightening occurrences in the paranormal. The Halloween Witch festival that I so ignorantly attended was another sure door.

You have to permit demonic spirits, and they gain permission when you open such doors. I am confident that I was not wholly possessed because I still could use my body and had some control. However, the gruff voice taking over my mouth was freaky, and I can't explain that. I know that I was born again when I was only 15 years old and had an intense experience walking with God for many years. Over those few months of darkness, I still knew that God was there. I was shaky in my faith and gave into the seducing spirits that sought to take control. The demons just clouded me for a time, and they were not finished, as you will find out.

This was a changing point in my life. I was free to push past the darkness into the light. I began to take possession of my calling with all my heart. The mountains of messes were cleaned up, and the television went off. I was able to enjoy every piece of my growing babies. Just like when I was a child, I had to go along with whatever the atmosphere was and bounce from one thing to the next. My little ones never seemed to be affected by the months of despair. They were as happy as ever, and we were a happy family again.

Memoirs of a Keeper: Angels & Demons

Chapter Nine

THE FALL & THE FARM

The six months came too soon. I had to start weaning Molly. Every time I nursed her, I cried, knowing those days were numbered. She took the bottle fine but preferred nursing. When she consumed her last drop, my heart broke. Each time I held her, she would grasp for her comfort and nuzzle her face to my breast with nothing I could offer but cuddles and kisses.

Soon after, I went in for the reconstructive surgery. Everything went well, and I was off to heal at home for several weeks. There was no pain. It was such a relief to be able to have that area fixed up again. Mark and I scheduled a honeymoon overnight in Marionette, WI. Mom and Dad gave us money to enjoy ourselves. We never had any extra money, so this was such a blessing and a gift. I booked a turn-of-the-century, Victorian bed, and breakfast to celebrate my new body. The place was on beautiful Lake Michigan, the same lake that Mark asked for my hand in marriage several years before. We enjoyed peaceful walks beside the water and fine French dining in this little French tourist village. It was perfect in every way. My husband had his wife back. It was there that we conceived our third child.

Deep in the night, one early spring night, I heard the still small voice of God in the form of a poem. It was of His love toward us in sending His son as our gift. I awoke with a pen and paper to record each word. The more I wrote, the more I saw the vision set before me. Each poem was rolled like a scroll and placed into colored plastic eggs. The eggs were tossed into people's lawns for them to pick up and read. It was like planting seeds. These little colored eggs were the seeds.

I brought forth this vision and idea to our little corner church, and all the people were delighted. We bought plastic eggs, and I had hundreds of poems printed. One morning we all gathered together to roll the lyrics and stuff the eggs. I brought eggs everywhere I went and planted them in bushes, on car windows, in people's yards, gas pumps, and even right into people's hands. They were delivered by the hundreds of people in our church to get the love of Christ out. Years later, a blind man made a wooden sign with the message on it, the same poem, because it was what God used to bring him into the fold. I never knew how far-reaching it would be. There was no church number on there. It was just signed with the red letters, With love, Jesus Christ.

A small family, who loved evangelism, started coming to the church. They were encouraged by the egg project and also drawn to our family. They started inviting us over for meals and fellowship. We were given a King James Bible and told it was the only accurate way to read God's word. I jump when someone gives me something deeper to know my God, so I replaced all the copies of our Bibles with the KJV. Today, I still use the KJV, but I know God uses all versions to tell his story. For years I had the New International Version, and I came into a profound understanding of God with it. To me, God is bigger than words on a page, or versions of this Bible and that. He is a Living God. He can transcend language, the boxes people put him into, and reach people right where they are at.

"Owe no man anything, but to love one another," Doris said with conviction. Doris and Derby were one of the newest families to come to our church. Doris was taller than I was physically but also spiritually. She had a very thick head of dark brown hair and was a competent woman. This woman could do anything a man could do, but she was learning to be a keeper of the home as well, so we started on the same page. She and her husband were very righteous. They had everything paid for. We, on the other hand, were in debt up to our eyeballs and on government assistance. I was signed up for a program that gives food to young women with children. The program gave cereal, milk, cheese, and juice. We had a lot of bills and a tiny extra for groceries. I never thought I was doing anything wrong to take advantage of this program. Doris had a differing opinion. She proclaimed, "It's not right to have this home and take from the government. You need to scale back and live with less."

I wasn't ready for this kind of rebuke, and it sent me into a state of embarrassment every time I went to the grocery store. People everywhere must have thought I was taking advantage of taxpayers' money, or so it seemed in my mind filled with shame. I felt like a failure and a leech to the system. The words fell on my ears like condemnation. How could I sell everything? How do we start over? Should we live in a shack? So many probing questions ran through my mind as guilt permeated every thought. My husband worked for a building company, working long hours, and I didn't have the heart to tell him that he was terrible at getting us into that debt.

I thought so long and so hard on this that I eventually realized that we could start fresh. We could sell our home. The answer in my mind was not a shack or trailer park, but a farm. Buy an old junky farm and grow all our food, so we never had to beg for money again. This was the thing that caused me to consider the paths of old, the road less traveled today, for it was the way that leads back to the land.

Mark had fixed up the home we were in so beautifully that it sold the first day on the market for $50,000 more than we bought it, which gave us a nice down payment on the new property. We were simple folk, the kind that was practical in a lot of ways. Being as young and inexperienced in the ways of the land, our little family only dreamed of owning our small farm in the country. Out on the land, we could grow a big garden, the kids could run and play, and perhaps we'd have some chickens to lay eggs. Most nights I would just dream of farms as fairytales.

Later that fall as I was dreaming of cows and chickens, something shook the world. It was September 11, 2001, and I remember lying in bed the morning the Twin Trade Towers were destroyed by hijacked airplanes. I kept watching after they showed the first tower in flames with smoke pouring out, and then the other plane came to hit the other tower. People were falling or jumping out the windows to their death, and soon, both tall buildings just free-fell to the ground with one sweep and a cloud of smoke. It shook everyone's faith, as I recall. Everyone was terrified, and I just knew it was odd. I wondered how the third building, building number 7, also fell and didn't get hit by a plane. I told Dad that I thought it could be controlled demolition, maybe an inside job, and he started to think I was crazy. First, the cults and the Bible thumping, now I had all these conspiracy theories.

I used Dad's computer to join it all together as I created some graphic tracts to hand out. I showed evidence of the inside job and targeted the fear part and how people shouldn't trust the government but rather God. Needless to say, I was kicked out of a few grocery stores and other places as I tried to warn people. No one listened. I started to become weary, trying to help others see Jesus and convince them that they needed him. A tragedy like this one seemed like a good time to preach when everyone was fearful. After being ridiculed and reviled for trying to convert everyone in sight, I gave up trying. Dad was right; if I kept carrying on like that, I would be alone with my Bible.

One day, after I was busy handing out tracts, Mark came home from work and said he saw a little farm for sale on three acres of land. Excitedly, we jumped into the truck, and off we went to see this new property. It took a lot of imagination for us to see what it could be. The farm was dirty and messy and falling all apart. It was not a dream, but there was a twinkle in my husband's eyes, and a smile on my face, for we knew that we could make it perfect. Of course, it would take some dedication and determination, which is just the type of grit we had.

First things first, the house in town was sold, and we closed on the farm on my birthday. "This is your birthday present," Mark said with a grin stretched across his face encircled with a short black beard. We packed up our things and moved to my parents' home while he tore into that mess of a house. It was winter, so Mark's construction work was slower, which gave him the time to work more hours on the house. He would take our little boy with him, and they would pound out the walls and tear off the carpets. There were dust and grime on every surface, plaster pieces, and wood chips scattered all about.

One cold December evening, I came to see how things were shaping up. I waddled into the main room with Molly at my hip. My belly was pretty big as I was nearly eight months pregnant. I climbed up the old wooden staircase to see the upstairs rooms. I smiled with excitement thinking about what room would be Miles, which one was Molly's, and the other one would be for the new baby and us very soon. You could see clear through the house because Mark and his little two-year-old sidekick took out all the walls and windows.

"Mama, I'm a big helper. I work hard," Miles said proudly as

The Fall & The Farm

he started pounding another crooked nail into a board lying across the floor.

"I'm sure glad Daddy has you to help him. This place is a mess, so he needs a good helper like you," I said as I watched my boy hit his finger with a swat of the hammer and shake his hand like it didn't hurt that much. I glowed with pride while Molly sucked her thumb and held tightly to my hip. Molly wasn't walking yet, so I wouldn't dare put her on that dirty floor.

Just as I'd finished looking and started to walk down the staircase carefully, my foot slipped on a chunk of plaster, and down I went, baby and all. Molly was still fastened to my hip, so when Mark heard that loud bang and scream, he dashed down to help us back up. As he tried to pick Molly up, he noticed her leg was broken in half! I limped out of the house, while he carried the broken child, and we drove straight to the hospital.

I never left my small girl's side, as I prayed for healing or ease of pain. By morning, little Molly girl was put in a body cast from chest to toe. No more visits to that farm for us. We instead had a visit from the CPS. They wanted to make sure our daughter's leg was not broken from an act of domestic violence. I was terrified, thinking that if I said the wrong thing, they might take our children from us. Children do have this type of injury in cases of physical abuse. It is hard to imagine anyone using that much force on such a beautiful creature as a little child. We had to go through a series of visits and learn how they want you to discipline your children.

We were back at Mom and Dad's home. We started calling them Nana and Bumpa. Good thing Nana was a nurse, for she cared for me while I had been laid up from the fall and for Molly, who was in the body cast. I had already potty trained her, so we had to retrain her to go in a diaper. There was no way around it. Nana kept her so clean under that cast and fixed us home-cooked meals each day. I lived like a queen there as Mom waited on us hand and foot. Molly learned how to scoot on a little cart with wheels. There she would go from one end of the house to the other, pushing off the floor with her hands.

Doris had been telling me about giving birth to the baby at home. She said the doctors give vaccinations that can cause many health issues because of all the toxic additives, along with all the other intervention. I knew nothing. She taught me so many controversial things in such a small amount of time. I wanted the very best for my children, so I took every word to heart. If she said no vaccines, I made sure they never had another. Everything she told me made sense.

I had been a good student of hers and hired a midwife to come to our home. Her name was Mrs. Graham. She was a tall, slender middle-aged woman who had an assistant named Pam. They were lovely Christian ladies who wanted to make my first home birth a beautiful experience. After the fall, the midwife did not feel comfortable delivering my baby at home because of the broken pelvis and the varicose veins that blocked the opening. The surgery fixed the tissue but not the issue with the varicose veins. Nothing fixes that, and from what they told me, it only gets worse with each pregnancy. The veins were prominent at this time, and I could understand her concern.

Pam still wanted to help assist at my birth, which had to be induced. I had another doctor who was attending. He could tell my pelvis was broken, and induction was safest, so they could be there to assist with any difficulties. With my history, problems were inevitable. I sat on the big birthing ball while Pam braided my hair, singing hymns, and reading the bible to me. It almost felt like I was in the presence of the angelic host. Every contraction was beautiful, and I breathed through with the sound of an angel's voice. They gave me the epidural, which numbed any pain of a contraction.

As I pushed a few times, my daughter's head was crowning. The first thing she heard as her ears were born was "Great is Thy Faithfulness." Pam kept singing her into the world, and it was altogether glorious. So peaceful. They scooped the tiny girl and placed her on my chest. Megan was the smallest of my babies, weighing only 6 pounds 10 ounces. My little peanut. I held her high above my head as I looked into her brand new baby eyes, and I proclaimed, "You are my best friend!" Nana brought our other two small children up to the hospital to see Megan. Molly was out of the cast and already begging to hold her new baby sister.

"Meet your new best friend," I said as I cherished the thought of a future for the girls being sisters. I never grew up with a sister, and I had always wished for it. I was sure they would be lifelong friends.

"Baby! Baby!" Was all Molly could say as she poked her finger into her eye or nose. Poor Megan would cry. Miles was the proud big brother of two beautiful little sisters. He was a bit of a sass by this time.

Anytime I would tell him what to do, he would stomp his foot and protest. Just recovering from my broken pelvis, helping Molly learn to walk, a brand new baby, I had my hands full. If he would have only listened, it would have been much easier.

One day as I took Miles and Molly outside for some fresh air, he was nearing Bumpa's fishponds. I lunged toward him in fear he would fall straight in when he pulled his arm away and said, "Let me go!" That was not going to fly with me. I immediately demanded, "If you do not come away from that pond this instant, I will bring you inside to give you a spanking!" The neighborhood boy was standing beside me, and when Miles decided not to cooperate, I grabbed him and headed for the house just as I had promised.

I grabbed a wooden spoon and gave him a few swift swats to the behind, so he knew I meant business. We went about the day as usual in happy spirits when I heard sirens going off. They got louder and louder until I saw the police car pulled right to the back door of my parents' home. My heart started pounding. What could be an emergency? Every doom and gloom thought passed through my mind. Was my husband okay? I walked toward the door to greet the police officer.

"Ma'am. We got a 911 call that you were beating your child in this house," he said in an assertive tone. I was shaking and wondering how anyone knew. I knew I would never beat my child, but who would make such an accusation? Oh, yes, the neighborhood boy. He was the only one who overheard my threat. "I am going to need to examine your child," Mr. Policeman demanded.

"Okay," I stammered in fear, hoping my manner didn't tell the wrong story to make me look guilty for a crime I did not commit. I brought Miles out to the policeman, where he pulled his drawers down and looked at his butt. There were no marks, of course, but I was worried about what he would say.

"Did your mommy hurt you?" What a question to ask. A spanking should hurt, but this was like a nail that would seal the coffin.

He looked down and said, "Oh, yes. Mommy spanks me, and it hurts." There it was. My mind found a picture of me behind bars with a vision of him packing up my three in the back of his car, never to see them again.

He ordered the CPS to come and start revisiting us. This time, they were not messing around. Spanking put us on the radar, yet it was not illegal in the state of Wisconsin. The rule was that you must use your open hand, not a wooden spoon, I learned. With every meeting and appointment we had with the CPS; I felt more and more bullied and scared for our future.

Soon the upstairs was made ready for our homecoming. I was glad to flee the confines of a city where neighbors waited for good stories they could use as ammunition. The thought of moving into our country farm was beyond words. There was a bathroom with an old claw-foot tub and three bedrooms. What more did we need? Well, there was no kitchen, but that would come along the way. To our little family, everything was perfect. I happily cooked meals on electric skillets and a microwave oven in the same room that Molly slept. I boiled water in a fryer and washed dishes in the same tub we all bathed in. The nights were long, as Megan howled and screamed. During the day, Molly would push the baby in a doll stroller around the upstairs bedrooms. Back and forth and back and forth.

As Molly had learned how to walk correctly without help, she toddled along the hardwood floors. This was the first time we had ever heated a house with wood that we chopped outside. Mark had just started to learn how to keep the fire hot enough to heat the home, yet he often did not realize how hot it could become. One morning as Molly marched across the living room floor, she stepped onto the floor grate that was made of iron. I came running when I heard her scream and the searing of her little feet. Quickly I whisked her into my arms, but the damage had been done. I didn't know what to do. Should I bring her to the hospital? If I did, they might think this was abuse. In Wisconsin, you have three strikes and then out. We were already in the system twice, so another suspicious occurrence, and we could lose the children for further inquiry.

I called Dad, and he told me not to call or bring her in. "They can't do much for burns anyhow," he said as he made arrangements to come out to help me fix our little Molly up. She was fine. I kept her feet guarded and held her in my arms so she could feel comfortable while we waited. Bumpa came in the back door with gauze and burn creams. He lovingly tended her feet while I prayed for quick healing of her skin. Within a few short days, she was back on her feet, and you couldn't tell she was ever burned.

Outside, the snow covered all the dirt, garbage, and rubble, so it was starting to look somewhat like a dream. The homestead came with fifteen geese, eighteen guinea fowl, twenty-five ducks, eight turkeys, ten cats, two rabbits, and one black hen.

"They pecked me in the eye!" cried Miles. "Those naughty turkeys!"

"Let me see," I said as I looked around his normal looking eye. "Oh, my. This is serious. What are we to do?"

"We gotta shoot them turkeys, that's what we gotta do!" Miles said excitedly.

"Really? Oh, well, I guess you're right." I said because I knew already that these animals were not friendly, and somehow, they had to be dealt with. This was a whole new adventure for our family. We never killed livestock before, so we weren't too sure how to go about it.

First off, the geese were much more of a problem than the ducks or turkeys. Those geese were bossy and temperamental. Bumpa was more experienced in the way of birds, so Mark let Bumpa catch the sassy geese. They cornered them into the top part of the barn so they could not escape. Mark used his body as a roadblock so that they couldn't fly out of the barn door. Bumpa walked toward what he thought was a cowering bunch of birds when all at once, the entire group turned toward him and started to beat him with their wings. They flapped their wings so much that they threw his glasses clear across the barn. My husband looked on in sheer disbelief.

"Let me at em!" cried Miles.

"Get back, little one. Bumpa knows what to do," Mark laughed as he saw the poor man wrestle with fifteen angry geese that were determined to win. Bumpa grabbed the bold birds by the neck. He got them where they could not defend themselves. Mark grabbed the ornery geese from Bumpa and put them into the back of the truck one by one. They shipped them out to the local butcher, who wrapped them in nice little packages for the family to store in the freezer. I never made goose before but figured it was close to chicken, which was easy, so I put it in the roasting pan one day.

"This tastes like roast beef," I said while I pulled another piece off the cooked goose.

"Just a little greasy," Mark exclaimed, but we all enjoyed the new experience of roasted goose. Miles couldn't stop eating it because he knew it was our home-raised geese, but deep down, he was still yearning to see his daddy shoot those turkeys.

The next thing that had to go were the ducks because they were domesticated, which is a big word that means they had to be fed. When you have twenty-five ducks lined up at the back door looking for food besides the ten whining cats, it becomes a big problem when a person tries to escape to the outdoors. You get mobbed by a whole group of hungry animals. When you're holding small children like we were, it was no small job. I would dread leaving home at times for fear of facing that challenge. So, I called a friend who had a husband who was a duck hunter. He came out with his big truck and his big gun, which was an exciting situation for Miles. He got his outdoor gear on and was ready for the hunt to begin. Blast, bam, pop, bang! Soon there was silence and off went the guy in his truck filled with 25 ducks.

No sooner did the truck disappear between the forest trees that Miles already wished for more.

"Daddy, can you get your gun? We have five more to shoot. Those turkeys will get away if we don't get em now!" Miles stammered with thrill.

"I think we had enough shooting for one day," replied Daddy while they saw the whole flock of guinea hens scramble past with their loud shrieks and cackles. Nothing could be louder than that, but the guineas are useful. They feed on ticks and other bugs.

One day, Mark started to saw some boards for the house when his hand got pulled into the blade. Off went two of his fingertips. We were spending the day at Nana and Bumpa's home while he was sawing the boards. I heard a loud bang outside. I peered out the window to see what happened when I saw my tall husband kicking the trash can clean across their driveway. Blood was streaming down his arm as he held his arm high. I think he was angrier than in pain. He was mad that he was so close to getting the kitchen finished that he knew it would surely stop the progress. He had to go to the ER, and later he told me that he stood there with his hand in the air throbbing in pain for over an hour because they didn't know it was that serious. He was so quiet and calm that they must've imagined he only had a superficial wound.

They had to cut his wedding ring off because the finger had swelled to the point of cutting off the circulation. We never did get the ring fixed. He was laid up and could do no more work on the house. We did what most people only dreamed of and nestled into our home in the country with all the peace and quiet. We stayed in the upstairs of our house a few weeks that winter waiting for the bandages to come off. No more sounds of pounding nails or sawing boards.

We enjoyed looking out the window to the snow-covered ground and seeing the migration of the sandhill crane. Sometimes the big birds would peck around in the field looking for a morsel of corn, but when they took off from the ground, it was a sight to see. The wingspan was about six feet long, and their call was just so beautiful. Sandhill cranes migrate to the country every year to have their young. Now that the guineas were nesting and spring was just around the corner, we waited for a new adventure. Most of all, we enjoyed the smell of the old wood-burning stove that heated the little farmhouse all winter long. It was cozy and quaint in the upstairs rooms.

One night as we cuddled close on the mattress on the floor to stay warm, I detected the smell of smoke. I nudged him awake. Megan was coiled up beside me, nursing away as Mark jolted out of bed, taking big puffs into his nose. He hurried over to the chimney, which was roaring with fire. We called 911 and begged them to hurry over before the entire home would be ablaze. We gathered the three little ones into our arms, covered in blankets and coats, and headed out to the suburban to sit and wait in safety.

Our breaths were visible in the freezing air as we shivered in the middle of the night, watching flames rise from the chimney. The engine was taking its sweet time to heat and warm us.

The big firetruck rolled in with lights and sirens blaring. They got their long hoses hooked up and started spraying water down the chimney to put out the flames, and thankfully the fires were contained, and we could reclaim our home in the dark of the night.

With the burn and the chimney fire in the past, my husband became an expert quickly, and we never had a fire grow out of control again. He is one to learn from such experiences. Heating with wood is lovely when you know what you are doing. The heat from wood is much cozier than electric or gas heat.

Memoirs of a Keeper: Angels & Demons

Chapter Ten
THE GARDEN & THE AMISH BONNET

Soon enough, Mark was back to work on the old house, with Miles at his side, pounding and sawing more dust. When the drywall started to go in, the dust-covered the entire second floor, and I wasn't the least bit happy. The children had fun drawing pictures with their fingers in the dust on the floor.

"Molly, look! I drew a dinosaur," Miles yelled as I rolled my eyes, thinking that was just what I wanted, enough dust to do an art lesson on the floor. But, sure enough, since I was practical, I started to give that art lesson. I sat down on the floor as my skirt got covered in white dust, and I began to draw.

"Here is a sandhill crane and, watch, here is one flying," I said in a happy tone. The children watched on with smiles as the floor shook with every pound of the hammer, causing the dust to swirl. We always tried to make the most out of every situation.

One glorious day, Mark yelled upstairs and said, "Everyone, come! I have a surprise for you." Off we all went down the staircase. I fell to my knees and started to cry as I watched their daddy turn the water on in the new kitchen sink.

"My very own kitchen! Thank you, Lord! Thank you, my darling husband! What a special day it is!" I yelled as I twirled and skipped across the new kitchen floor. Right then, I imagined the bread that would be baked in the oven that would soon go in that space between the cupboards. I dreamed of the day I could wash dishes in a real sink, for my back was aching from bending over the clawfoot tub to wash the dishes for so long.

"Mamma, I could help you bake!" Miles jumped for joy.

Mark smiled a very long time until he opened his mouth. "Well, it is not finished yet..."

"But that's okay, it won't be long now," I said with anticipation.

It was not long before the entire first floor was ready for furniture and family dinners around the table; what a blessing and just in time for planning our first garden. Mark got a rotor tiller and broke the ground out the back of the kitchen window. He toiled and toiled until the land was made ready for seed. Oh, this would be a great big garden. It was no small job for our little family. There were rows and rows of green beans, green peppers, tomatoes, potatoes, sweet corn, zucchini, beets, broccoli, cauliflower, squash, pumpkins, and more. All planted in the rich black soil. He picked that spot because the farmer before had his cows out there for years, so the soil was good and rich. Whenever planning a garden, we learned that it is best to pick the spot with the most nutrients in the soil. The blacker the earth, the richer the nutrients will be.

In the meantime, life was springing up all around, and messes were unveiled. There was insulation as well as boards and glass and nails everywhere in sight. It was no place for a child to run and play, but since they had nowhere else to go, the children found their way around the rubble. They found the kittens that were just born right outside the back door under some boards and insulation.

"Spuk, spuk-ee," Molly said while she squeezed the little kitten that she claimed for her own. It was a tabby kitten covered in gray and white stripes. She walked around everywhere that spring with that kitty hanging down from her tiny elbow.

Miles grabbed the little orange kitten with force, saying, "Butterscotch is my kitty. He likes to go hunting with me." And off he went with his toy gun, straw hat, and a kitty on his shoulder. He started hiding around the corner of the barn, spying out those turkeys. Miles was bound and determined that those turkeys had to go. The day finally came where Mark got his gun out and followed the big white turkey tom. Bang! Miles ran over to the big hill of white feathers and poked it with his toy gun.

"Yup! He's dead, Daddy," Miles said with a proud look on his face. The two of them dragged that forty-pound monster of a turkey to the shed where they tried to figure out what to do next. Bumpa was a phone call away, so he and Nana stopped by to help. Soon enough, the group managed to skin him and cut the meat so it could run through the old metal hand crank grinder. After Mark ground and ground and ground and then ground some more, the meat was stuffed into freezer bags and stacked into the freezer. Now, since the tom was gone, the four female turkeys had no protection. One by one, the coyotes came for them.

The early mornings were rude as ever before, as the guineas would shriek across the front of the house under the window where we slept. Sleep was precious to a mamma who was up during the night with a crying baby, and rude alarms were of no appreciation even if they ate ticks. So out, Mark went to see what he could do. Miles was right alongside as usual. Oh, but they had a whole bunch of babies now that they scurried close to the flock. They scared the flock back to the woods and over a fence to a neighbor's land. Mark had already called the neighbor, Farmer Phil. Farmer Phil was more than happy to take the tick-eating fowl since he was nestled into the forest where ticks weren't in short supply. The guineas never came back since they knew that they were well fed where they were.

Later that spring, we met another neighbor who gave us a little banty rooster. I was so pleased. For now, I thought that dream of having chickens that laid eggs would soon be a reality. Well, we only had one black hen, so little did we know that one hen would only provide, at most, one egg per day. That would not be enough to feed this growing family, but it was an amusing prospect.

One early morning as Miles was out checking the barn for adventure, he found a special surprise. His legs could not run any faster as he dashed into the house, mud and all.

"Mamma, Mamma, you have to see..." Miles stammered with excitement. "The chicken..." taking breaths in between, "laid eggs!!!!"

So off our group ran to the barn. Jibity, our faithful dog, galloped not so far behind and always wanted to be a part of everything going on. I was running ahead of them all since it was the moment I had been waiting for my whole life. I rushed into the messy barn, and Miles pointed out the exact spot. Jibity put her nose up to the edge, sniffing and sniffing. It was an old box filled with about twenty eggs in a nest.

"Oh, we shall have eggs for breakfast today!" I shouted. Miles jumped up and down a few times and screeched with joy.

"See, see!" Molly said, pulling at my skirt. So, up I lifted her to peek into the box.

Carefully, I lifted out four eggs into my apron and gently carried them to the house. As I warmed up the frying pan on my new stove, the children slid two chairs on either side of me so they could watch while I cooked those eggs. I smiled with enthusiasm as I started to tap the egg on the counter—tap, tap, tap. I carefully held the egg above the pan while the children moved in a little closer. Megan was sitting in the infant seat, looking around the room. The table was set, and they were hungry. I put a little butter in the pan in preparation. Miles and Molly still leaned in an inch closer, waiting to see what a real farm-fresh egg looked like. Carefully, I pressed my fingernails into the shell and opened ever so slowly. Plop! Out came a fully-formed, black chick onto the frying pan. We all gasped in disbelief.

"That's what a real farm-fresh egg looks like?" Miles asked in wonderment. "Well, I'm not eating it!" He said with his face snarled up.

"Baby, chick!" Molly squealed in amazement.

"Well, kids, this is terrible. I think I ruined breakfast today. This poor chick!" I said as I lifted the lifeless creature from the pan and turned the burner off. We returned the other eggs to the nest and hoped they would hatch soon. That morning we ate oatmeal because there were no fresh farm eggs to eat, but we learned something about chickens. Chickens lay one egg every day, and if you have a rooster, those eggs will get fertilized and can grow into chicks if you leave her set on them. After twenty-eight days, the eggs will hatch one by one.

The first spring on the homestead was filled with new life and a new adventure. The most exciting thing of all was when the chicks finally hatched, and the children could hear the peeping and see the little black puffballs follow their mother hen all over the barnyard.

The garden was planted, and our little family waited to see signs of growth. Every day the children would run out to check for green beans to pick. Daddy was out every evening tending and weeding that big garden. Living next to low land, the mosquitoes would swarm out as the sun went down. It was a hum that was so distinct and forceful.

The Garden & The Amish Bonnet

Daddy was brave to work so hard as he was eaten alive. He would hoe and prop the ever-growing vines up so they would bring forth fruits to harvest. Soon came the day they had what they waited for.

"Daddy! I picked a bean, and I ate it," Smiled Miles. "There are tons of beans out there! Come on, let's pick em!"

It's funny how a child can find one bean and say there are tons when in reality, there was a handful or so. But all the same, it was exciting. Our little family had officially grown some hearty green beans, and it was a thrill. I knew that soon there would be too many just to eat fresh. Once you see that first bean, well, before you know it, there are tons, and you better be ready to pick them. They will keep producing more, the more you harvest. Within a week, the bushes and poles were full of beans.

One hot summer day, I took my children out to the garden to pick green beans. I just hated going out early in the morning or late in the evening when the mosquitoes were out. The only other option was to go in the heat of the day. It was so hot and humid that it was making their hair curl in a hundred different directions. The children had tiny wet curls all over their little heads as they helped me in the garden, pulling beans from the vine. I stuck baby Megan in her pram, so the rest of them could work hard. A baby can only appreciate so much as they peer out a non-moving seat. As you can imagine, there was only so much time that a mamma has before the inanimate stroller becomes a wild frenzy of screams from boredom. Sitting in the dirt with their arms stuck in between the thorny vines, the children pulled and pulled. Snap, snap, snap. Molly and Miles soon got distracted with baby chicks and kittens, so I was left to myself in that big web of vines. I knew that the few minutes of picking would have to be enough for the little ones, and soon the contented baby would begin her fuss unless I came up with a game that would cause the children to regain more interest.

"Children," I hollered since they were already out of sight. I crawled out of the cluster of vines, brushing the dirt from my long dress, to take a look across the barnyard for clues to where they could be. As I took in a deep breath from the overwhelming heat, I bent down to pull off a vine. Out of habit, I shook the green leafy tendril in front of the baby, for I knew that a baby needs something to touch and experience if they were to remain contented. As her mouth opened wide, Megan's tiny hands trembled with excitement grabbing for the vine. Since the baby was busy again, I turned my focus back to the barnyard, "Children!" As Miles and Molly came running toward, I said with a twinkle in my eye, "Would you like to play a game?"

"Yes, Mamma!" Miles said with enthusiasm.

"Okay...let's see who can pick the most beans. Here is a bucket for you, Miles," I handed him an empty bucket, "And one for you, little girl."

That was that. The game began, and whole vines were being yanked off in a whirlwind of competition. Of course, Miles was a bit more motivated because boys like to win. I sat there with a smile on my face and a giggle in my breath as I watched the children enjoy the garden game.

Days passed, and beans were cut up and put in freezer bags to be kept frozen. There was still a longing in my heart, a yearning to have a family cow. I didn't know how or where to find one, but I knew that I wanted a small one. As I drove across the countryside, I would see big black and white cows. Holstein cows were in no shortage there in Wisconsin. The country was peppered with big dairy farms filled with hundreds of Holstein cows that weighed over a thousand pounds. I figured I would be crushed by one bump from a cow that size if I were to milk by hand.

One sunshiny day, as I gathered the children into the van for a country ride looking at cows, I noticed it was time to fuel up. All the children had to be hauled into the small gas station to pay at the counter, which can be a project in itself. As we piled into the shop, there was a man, a tall, lanky man standing off in a corner. He had a beard, a straw hat, and he looked to be Amish. That was the first time I saw a real Amish person, for I had no idea they lived in Wisconsin, much less that they would be in a shop near our home. My heart was racing as I approached the unsuspecting man.

"Are you Amish?" I asked as quickly as I tapped him on the shoulder.

"Yes, I am," he said as he grabbed his long beard and looked at me standing there.

"Where can I find a family cow? A Jersey cow?" I stammered, "You know, for hand, milking?"

"I don't know, but if you drive about fifteen miles north of here, there is an Amish store. Follow the signs. You can't miss it. They just might know where to find one," he said in a hurry as he rushed out the door to get back to his job.

An Amish store? Really? I could hardly believe it. That was the most wonderful news. I packed the children back into their seats and followed the signs to the Amish store. Well, there were two Amish stores at the time, and the first sign said, "Miller's Bulk Foods." That had to be the one he was talking about. I unloaded the children and walked into the store. The sound of the little bell ringing brought a thrill to my heart. I looked across the tiny store to see bags of flour, beans, stacks of rice, noodles, and candy. Aisle after glorious aisle, I touched the sacks of food, hoping I had enough money to buy a couple of things to make this trip worth our time. Thoughts swirled around in my mind as the children started pulling stuff off the shelves and I was busy correcting them to stop touching everything in sight. The bell rang again, announcing someone's entrance to the store. I peered through the bags of flour to see the most beautiful sight. It was an Amish woman! She had a blue dress with a white apron tied around her not-so-slender waist, a white bonnet covering her wispy gray hair, and a pair of glasses fixed on her round, cheerful face.

"Well, hello! My name is Katie! Katie Miller," the woman said with utter joy.

"So nice to meet you, Katie! My name is Erin, and I have three children," I said as I gathered them proudly at my side while adjusting the baby higher on my hip. "I just love your store. I have waited my whole life to see a store like this!"

"Welcome to our store. Do you wear dresses all the time?" Katie asked as she noticed my long, drab jumper, just an old thrift store rag of a dress.

"Yes, I do. I guess I try to dress more like a lady," I continued, "I used to wear pants all the time, but I kinda thought it would be fun to wear dresses as the women used to a hundred years ago. I like old-fashioned things!" I said it with a sense of pride since most people I knew thought I was over-the-top for dressing that way. It was not a popular way to dress in those days.

Katie smiled, "Do you do it to please the Lord?"

"Well, I guess so..." I tried to figure out what to say as Katie grabbed my arm and pulled me into her home this time. The children hurried close behind. The house was dark and drab, paneling on the

153

walls with linoleum flooring. Not what I pictured an Amish home to be. In my mind, I saw hardwood floors, wooden rockers, kerosene lamps, and white walls. Instead, there were big, fake leather chairs and sofas covered in big blankets and towels, plastic toys strewn all over the floor, and piles of books. We sat and visited for hours until Katie convinced me that I should wear a head covering if I wanted to please the Lord even more. As teachable as I was, I embraced the idea that very minute. Katie fetched her youngest daughter Rosie to find her a covering. Rosie was about seventeen years old with dark brown hair and rosy cheeks to match the name. Quickly they fitted me with the white bonnet, and because it was so stiff, it slipped off soon after.

"Oh, my!" Katie said, "Rosie, gep mich und schpel funs Erin." (In Pennsylvania Dutch, this means: Rosie, get me a pin for Erin.) Half the time, the Amish will speak in English and the other half talk in PA Dutch. Some words sound like our words that have been "Dutchified." Like the word snack, for instance. They would say, "snacka." Rosie pulled two pins from her dress, as they used them to close their dresses instead of buttons. Buttons were only for little girls who couldn't handle the sharpness of the pins. Rosie grabbed my head with the bonnet on and shoved a pin on both sides, quilting it into my hair. Now that the bonnet was fastened to my head, Katie started to jump and cry for joy, "Oh, how the angels in heaven rejoice! For what was lost is now found!"

I saw the tears stream down Katie's glowing cheeks, and it thrilled my heart to know I would be one of them from now on. It was like a new beginning. I had a place to call home, a new family to visit, and a whole new world to discover. Even though I knew that the bonnet on my head did not save my soul, I sure enjoyed every minute of the new friendship and the acceptance it brought.

Oh, the cow? Well, that will come later. For now, we drove back home, bonnet and all. When Mark walked up the stairs after a long day of work, he had to look twice at me, for he never saw anything like that before.

"Why do you have an ice cream pail on your head?" He asked with sincerity and a halfhearted smile.

"It's a head covering! 1 Corinthians chapter 11 talks about it," I went on. "By the way, I met the Amish today!"

He giggled at me and said, "Take off that pail and give me a kiss!"

The Garden & The Amish Bonnet

That would not be the end of that "pail," for I had found something that would bridge the gap between two worlds: the modern world and the world of the plain folk. And the rest of the world would see that strange enough.

Chapter Eleven
THE APRON & THE COMMUNITY

The kitchen was finished, and I was able to set up grandma's old kitchen drop-leaf table. I remembered sitting at that old table as a little girl with my legs dangling off, waiting for whatever Grandma had prepared for me. I could now put my three around the same wooden table. They would wait for whatever I prepared, and I was happy to cook hearty meals. Most times, the children would help me cook or bake, and it would be something we just did for fun. Everything was a game. They followed me everywhere, and we did practically everything together.

One day as I was making my way down the treacherous steps to the basement, Miles wanted to follow. Well, the steps were just waiting to break through, and I didn't want him to get hurt, so I commanded, "Miles, you must stay in the kitchen. I'll be right back."

As I was loading the dirty laundry into the old washing machine, I wished I had either the steps fixed or the laundry hooked upstairs. The dirty stone walls of the dark basement were haunting. Being down there was damp, cold, and a bit creepy. The floor was concrete and brittle. When I did my laundry down there, I prayed that I did not drop a clean shirt on the floor because it had to be rewashed. It was that sort of situation that wasn't practical at all.

While I was complaining about my laundry in my mind, I heard a loud crack. Turning my head to see what had happened, I saw Miles laying there at the top of the steps screaming his head off. I dropped the basket and ran up the broken wood stairs to find his arm hanging there broken in half. No bone was protruding, but the forearm was hanging, making it look like he had another elbow joint hinged right in the middle.

"Mark!" I yelled at the top of my voice in complete desperation. He came running to see Miles sitting in my lap with the arm dangling halfway. "They will take our children!" I cried with fear. "This will be the end of us, another broken bone." I took deep breaths as I held my child and considered the worst-case scenario. "It's the third strike." We couldn't doctor this one at home. We knew that we would have to take him in. We knew they would be suspicious of us even more. I stared into my husband's eyes with complete dread. Miles was still crying in pain, wincing his eyes and kicking his legs.

Mark shoved me aside with tears in his eyes. They weren't the kind of tears that flowed, but his eyes welled up with shaking lids knowing we only had one plea, "Oh, God!!" He said, quivering with all his might, "I beg you." A short pause, then he held his little boy's floppy arm in his hand, "Heal my son in the name of Jesus!"

We both sat amazed as the arm instantly zipped back into place, and Miles relaxed as if nothing had happened. "Daddy, my arm is fixed," Miles said as he moved his little hand around a bit. "Jesus healed me!" My tears turned from fear to the greatest joy in that small but enormous moment.

We all brushed the dirt from us, as Miles explained, "Mama, I thought I was a bird. I was trying to fly off the gate, but it didn't work." We all started to giggle at that story. The silly little boy didn't realize staying in the kitchen meant staying in the kitchen. He must have figured flying wasn't a part of the deal. "Next time, Miles, you need to listen to Mamma," I warned.

I never saw anything like this happen before; a complete, instant, physical miracle. It was a good thing Mark was there because who would believe me if I told them? God always made sure Mark was around to confirm the stories. Using a man with factual precision is essential. Having this miracle was so critical. God knows when He needs to intervene because there was no other way. I am sure He knew that we would've had our children ripped from us that day if He hadn't stepped in. God is good. That miracle also strengthened my faith that God is real. Seeing an arm magically move and fuse is something we would never be able to forget.

The children and I made our way to the Amish quite often or as often as they would invite me. The phone rang, "Hello, this is Katie."

"Hi, Katie, it is so good to hear your voice," I gripped the phone with excitement.

"We were wondering if you would like to drive us to pick strawberries," she inquired.

"Absolutely!" I said as I started dressing my children for the day and whisking them out to the van to drive to Amish Land. Giddy, with a child-like thrill, I hopped into the driver's seat, and away we went, not a minute to lose over hills, blue clouded skies, framed in by farm fields and edged with trees.

I picked up Katie and Rosie from the store, and then we drove to her other three daughters' homes to pick them up. First, there was Mary. Mary was a short, little Amish young mother, slender with a gentle stare. Her hair was dark. She loaded her babies onto her lap, and we drove down the road to pick up Elsie. The Amish do not use seat belts nor car seats. I guess it is because they ride around in buggies that are void of both. Elsie only had two little boys along. Her other children were at the little white schoolhouse in the center of the community on an old one-lane road. Elsie had wispy brown hair trying to escape her cap and a charming but confident look about her. She was a little taller than Mary and of a medium build. The last stop was for Verna. Verna was a little thicker, and she waddled out, expecting another baby with a little one fastened to her hip.

I had a jumper on with my white Amish cap pinned to my hair, and they all had black ominous looking capes with big, black-hooded bonnets to almost entirely cover up the white caps that were beneath. This black bonnet hid their face as it overshadowed it. I didn't want to tell them, but they looked a bit on the dreary side. Almost like something I saw on Halloween with the circle of witches. It was nothing like that, of course, and when they explained that it was to make them look more meek and humble, I erased the evil from my mind in a flash. At any rate, it also seemed much too hot to wear such things on this day that we went picking in the hot sun. When I asked, they told me that they were required to wear them by the law in Amish Land. It was in what they called "The Ordnung."

Memoirs of a Keeper: Angels & Demons

Once we arrived at the strawberry patch, they all unveiled the black capes and bonnets and rolled up their sleeves. I saw them rush out into the patch, and before you could even think, they had a whole flat already picked. I could see that they knew how to work, and they did fast. When I saw them in motion, I immediately wanted to join in. They talked in their language, and half the time, I wondered if they were asking questions about me. When you speak another language that others can't understand, it was easy to talk about them, and they would never know. Every time they would chuckle out loud, I would smile and giggle with them. If I was going to be among them, learning their language was a must. I wanted to know what they were talking about.

"I want to learn your language," I said with eagerness. It drew them closer to me somehow because they had this English woman looking at them, wanting to know all that they know. Everything I observed and everything I heard them say was like living water to me. I tried to drink it all in and fill my longing heart. They instantly agreed to teach me the language starting with the small greeting phrases.

"Say, vee beesh du," Katie recited. I repeated the phrase trusting it meant something nice. She continued, "That means, 'How are you?' in Dutch."

I said it over and over to each of the sisters, and they all responded, "Eek bin aww rat." That meant, "I am all right." They giggled at how I would say things at first, but Katie kept encouraging me by telling me I was doing great. Each of the ladies had about eight to ten flats overflowing with strawberries. I have never seen a person walk off with that many. We piled the strawberries in the back of my van and met at Mary's place to 'work them up.'

Mary's home looked like a shed, the kind of sheds my husband built regularly. It was part shed with dirt floors and part shop where her husband Dennis had his horse harness business. The last part on the end closest to the country road was their dwelling place. It had linoleum floors with some old recycled cabinets along the side facing the street. With a little window over the sink and a table stretched across the length of the cabinets, it had the feeling of home. When you walked through the kitchen, it opened up to a living room area with old thrift store couches and chairs covered with blankets and towels. On the other side of the furniture were long sheets or curtains hanging down, separating the living room from the bedroom. I was beginning to think the Amish have no taste for decorating with all the ruffled polyester hearts and pictures of horses gracing the plain white or peach walls, which reminded me of something I would've put in my closet to decorate back in the 80s. It was not what I had imagined, but it was perfect. They actually could do no wrong in my eyes. The taste was of no matter to me anymore.

We made our way through the home and the shop beside it, to the open part of the shed where the horse buggies were. I was transfixed on those empty buggies and longed for a ride. There was much work to be done, so I refrained from asking for a ride. My children were full of dust, and red strawberry smears on their clothing and faces. Miles was playing with Elsie's boys while Molly stayed at my side. The Amish children didn't know English at all, but when you have little children playing, they figure out how to communicate. The great thing about children is there's no cultural divide nor language barrier. They don't care about what color your skin is or what kind of clothing you are wearing; they just play.

Megan was sitting in her car seat while she watched us work. We started by cutting off the green stems on the end and plopping the strawberries into a clean bowl. With six ladies cutting, the strawberries were finished quickly, and as we worked, we talked. I saw community for the first time in my life: good, wholesome, productive activity. They took a potato masher and began to crush and sugar the strawberries before cooking them on the stove for jam. To my surprise, they were making freezer jam. I had no idea that they had freezers. They had a community freezer run on a diesel engine that looked like a semi-trailer. Once the jam was set up, I helped haul the containers off to the trailer. I could walk right down the middle and set them on shelves. We had placed these on the shelf marked, "' Dennis." I learned that everyone refers to the woman in Amish Land by her husband's first name. She was "Dennis Mary." I was, "Mark Erin." I also heard them refer to an entire family as just the plural form of the husband's first name. In that case, Mary's family would be "Dennis's." They called my family "Mark's."

It was so kind of them to help me make my jam and put it into some old cool whip, mayonnaise, and sour cream containers. They used such products in their cooking, and here I thought they made everything from scratch. I figured they never went to the grocery store because they had their Amish bulk food stores and what they could grow on their farms. Boy, was I mistaken. They had the staple items that they keep on hand for baking and cooking. In their pantry, you'll see boxed breakfast cereals, fake mayo called salad dressing, marshmallows, corn syrup, peanut butter, crackers, and chips. They do use fresh milk and get that at the nearest Amish dairy farm in the community. Some things they get at the bulk food store, but they pay drivers to bring them to the grocery stores in town several times each month. "The English," who was anyone white and non-Amish, are paid taxi drivers. They tried to pay me, but I didn't want to be just an English to them; I wanted to be grafted in as one of them.

One by one, I dropped each lady off to their homes. My last stop was Katie, and she invited me in again. As she sat in the torn-up leather recliner with a bunched-up towel trying to cover the holes, I could see she had the same black socks and shoes that all the other ladies had on that day. I asked, "Do all Amish women wear black socks and shoes?"

She returned, "Oh, yes. It's more humble. We try to keep ourselves less flashy for God." There was a hint of pride under her breath, and I felt ashamed as she glanced down at my brown leather shoes with white socks. I ashamedly pulled them under my skirt and thought I better try to find black stockings and shoes when I was around them. I didn't want to offend them or cause them to think less of me.

Every dress they wore was fitted with an apron. I didn't own an apron, so I asked how I could get one. "Rosie can make you one!" They made all their clothes. The dresses, the coats, the aprons were all made on a treadle sewing machine.

Rosie came bouncing into the room with a smile on her face as she asked me to stand while she measured my waist. Was she going to make me an apron right then and there? As fast as she bounded into the room, she raced up the steps across where we sat only to return minutes later with a folded piece of white fabric under her arm. "What would you like your apron to look like?" Not only was she making it right then, but it was also going to be "made to order."

Images of Ma of the TV show Little House on the Prairie swirled through my mind. I wanted to look like her and as a pioneer woman. With excitement, I asked, "Can you make the apron like a pioneer woman?" She looked a bit confused. Then I remembered she would have no television and no way of ever seeing what they looked

The Apron & The Community

like. I went on to paint a picture in her mind. "You know, with a square piece above the bottom like this." I motioned my hands over my chest right where the square would rest as I continued. "And then it would have a strap that would go around my neck like this."

Rosie had a very confident look about her as she smiled, "I can do that. I know exactly what you're talking about!" She sat at the treadle machine with that cloth and whipped out the most beautiful apron. It was exactly what I dreamt up and something I always wished for since I was a little girl. I always wanted to be Laura on the Prairie, and this apron made me that much closer. I quickly pulled it over my head, and she tied it around my waist. It was perfect, and I was in heaven. The children had become restless, and I needed to get back home to cook a meal for my hardworking husband, who would wonder where I was. This was the time before we had cell phones.

At home, Mark was standing there in the driveway, picking up more rubble around the farm when we rolled in. He stared as I drove past him with that white cap over my head, and as I sprung out of the van, he could see I had the matching white apron. The look on his face was a crinkled up, sarcastic sort of "you've got to be kidding me" look. I didn't care, because I was still dancing in the clouds of my dream.

The next day I made some fresh bread in my stove. The aroma filled every corner of our little farmhouse. I pulled it out of the oven and knocked the crust with my fist to hear the hollow thud as I put my nose over to smell it. The scent transported me to Grandma's kitchen again, where she would give me a slice of bread slathered with a thick layer of her homemade strawberry freezer jam. I wanted that same memory for my little ones.

As the bread cooled on the countertop, I skipped across the kitchen to reach into my freezer for a container of jam. Even better than jam was to add a layer of homemade peanut butter. I pulled out the processor and dumped some peanuts in the top until they came out creamy. The children were happily playing in the other room with boxes making forts. This moment had to be perfect. I gently sliced the crusted fresh bread and placed them on a beautiful plate. The bread was set right there in the middle of that old wooden table along with a little dish of jam and peanut butter; all made with my own hands.

I gleefully called, "Children, come! It's time for lunch!" I brushed my apron off as I went into the other room to pick up Megan off the floor and set her into the highchair. Everyone was quiet as they watched me ever so slowly slather the pieces of bread with jam and then with peanut butter. Molly licked her lips in anticipation. With excitement, I proclaimed, "Today, you will get to have a sandwich completely from scratch!"

Miles took a bite, and his eyes broadened, "This is tasty!" After swallowing, he wrinkled up his forehead in deep thought. I could see him scanning a list around in his memory as he inquired, "Who's Scratch? We should thank her!" I almost choked on my sandwich as I laughed.

Trying to get my breath and still laughing, I replied, "No. Scratch is not a lady. Scratch means that everything is made by hand or homemade." Pointing my fingers toward the dishes on the table, I continued, "You see here. I made the bread and jam and the peanut butter all by hand, so it's all made from scratch." He smiled and continued chomping off big bites of his sandwich. It was understood that simple. The quiet from that moment on around the table was because we were all too busy enjoying the delicious sandwiches to talk.

I pinned the cap on and tied the apron about my waist, and made another trip to Amish Land. Each Amish farm we passed, we saw laundry snapping in the wind, horses grazing, and buggies parked out front. Sometimes I drove past a horse-drawn buggy, and I saw little faces peeking out of the tiny windows. They all seemed similar, so I'd never know if I saw someone I knew. Rolling down the gravel drive of Miller's Bulk Foods, I found Katie standing next to her smiling husband, Melvin. Melvin had a long black and gray beard that hung past the start of his shoulders down the middle of his chest. His teeth were sparse, but his cheer was real. He liked having us come around. Often he would talk about the history of the Amish. I was fascinated. Tales of their ancestors being burned at the stake for their beliefs haunted my mind.

I found out that they were all Roman Catholic to start. This was back in the 1500s as he recalled, "A German by the name of Menno Simmons got a hold of an outlawed Bible. It was back in the time of the Reformation where Martin Luther translated Latin to German so the people could understand in their language what the Bible said. Menno became a convert by reading the Bible and learned that baptizing a baby was a crazy notion. In a time where you could pay for your sins with repetitive religious activities or with money, he could see that babies were not full of sin," Melvin paused to stare deeper into my searching eyes. He continued, "The more he read, the more he saw, and the more he wanted to break out of a vain and lifeless church. He wanted to know God and be baptized into the family of God when he chose to follow Christ." I was following Melvin with every ounce of my attention because I was raised in a Catholic church. Some of the things I had grown up seeing in the Church made more sense, and it seemed altogether senseless the more I heard him say. Of course, why would a baby be baptized? They are entirely innocent.

The more Melvin talked, the more passionate his tone became. "Menno found others, and they formed their sect. You get the name 'Mennonite' from his first name. They would all become baptized, and when they were found out, the Latin Church would torture them to try to get them to renounce their new belief. Give up their faith on pain of death." His face became sullen and full of sorrow as he bowed his head that was thinning on the top, "They were burned at the stake. They even had tongue screws placed in their mouths to shut them up because while burning, they would be singing songs to worship God and to try to tell the onlookers about Jesus and the love of God." Wow, I felt broken for these people. I could see this all playing in my mind, families torn apart for their faith. "Later, they came to America, and the Mennonites had some progressive ideas, and they split. The other sect was led by a man named Jacob Ammon. He wanted to keep closer to the old ways." He looked back and gave a halfhearted smile, "That's where we get the name 'Amish.' It's an offshoot of the Mennonites and named after Jacob Ammon. The Amish pride themselves at being closer to the old ways, but they lost the fire they had."

He pulled me out the door of the store, which had the bell, and into the back door of his home. We passed the kitchen where Rosie was kneading bread dough on the table. She looked up and smiled, "Hello, Erin! Vi Beesh Du?" I remembered just how to answer as I beamed with pride, "Eek Bin Aww Rat!" Melvin was impressed. He had no idea I was learning the language. He brought us through the living room to an old bookshelf where he pulled a very thick book out.

"This is the Martyrs Mirror. Every Amish home owns one or should," he said as he opened it and skimmed his finger over the page. "In here, you will read about our forefathers, who shed their blood for the sake of their faith in God. These are true accounts and some letters written to loved ones. They would often write to their loved ones when they awaited their executions." The book was giant. Must have been over 600 pages, and I wanted to read it one day. Just then, someone drove in. It was a customer, an English person. Melvin rushed out to take care of them while the children and I sat down in the dark living room.

"Katie, is that why you all wear the same dresses that look like they are from the 14th century?" I wondered.

"Yes. We Amish tried to stay with what we were taught. We do as our forefathers did." She added, "We have to keep our ways, or else they will be lost forever. We try to be a 'Peculiar' people who are unblemished from the world." I could see that. It made sense. It was so primitive, so primal in a lot of ways. They were so different. I wanted to be a part of this tradition somehow. I wanted to be a peculiar person for God and wanted to be so committed to Jesus that I would abandon all sense of fashion and the world. Katie looked at my jumper, and she knew that I was ready to jump into a new separated lifestyle. It must have been written all over my face.

"Elsie can teach you how to sew dresses," Katie said as she leaned in with a smile that pushed her round cheeks toward her ears, which were covered by the white cap. I never knew people made their clothing. My whole life, mom always brought me to the store to buy clothes. Sometimes I had sacks of hand-me-downs to find what I liked or used thrift stores. It finally dawned on me that clothing was not always mass-produced in factories in foreign countries who often use slave labor. I learned that the Plain Folk makes their clothing on a sewing machine. "Elsie makes her patterns so she will be able to figure out something that will suit your size," She said, looking at my smaller frame.

"That would be amazing!" I said with all my heart. All my dreams were coming true. Now I didn't have to make skirts and shirts look like a pioneer-style; I could make something that would be before that era, even. Soon I found the perfect time to pick up Elsie and bring her down to my home. I wanted to make it worth her while, so I suggested, "If you have laundry, you can bring it to my place, and we can wash it and dry it." That was a big help for her since she had just found out she was expecting, and she was quite tired. She brought her patterns and her mounds of dirty laundry. Thankfully, I was prepared because I had run to the store to buy a piece of a muted, slate-blue fabric that we could use. I also found some cream-colored lace and buttons. Elsie was so kind as she lovingly laid out the material with her patterns at the top. We both cut piece after piece, and she began to sew them on my electric machine.

Within a few short hours, I had a real dress of my own. It was not precisely Amish because I didn't have a rule that dictated the exact pattern. In fact, my dress had lace around the collar and waist with white buttons up the bodice. Nothing like they could wear. It was much too fancy for them, but for me, it was perfect. I wanted a dress I could wear out in public, something that would make me peculiar, yet people would know it wasn't Amish. They would think I was old-fashioned. She even made me a head covering with a little of the white fabric and a band of lace all the way around. It looked more like a skullcap of sorts.

Elsie gleamed as I stretched the dress over my shoulders for the first time, buttoning every last button. Twirling and prancing over the beautiful hardwood floors of my dining room, I imagined how everyone would think I was old-fashioned and stunningly unique. Everyone in my mind would embrace the new me as if I had finally found my true nature, in like fashion to how all my relatives celebrated their Native American heritage with dream catchers, beads, and Indian fried bread. We come from the Mohican tribe. People in the world celebrate differences and culture. I was now representing my old-fashioned heritage. My great-grandmothers would've sewn a dress that looked much the same. Grandma told me stories of how they all wore head coverings to the church in the old days. All women did. Why not reclaim some of these valuable traditions?

Molly followed me around the room with every twirl, twirling the little checkered dress that was passed down to her from her cousins in Chicago. Michelle, my brother's wife, is Dominican. Her grandmother sewed a whole line of the most beautiful Dominican dresses for her daughters, and when they outgrew them, my girls got them which was such a delight.

After I brought Elsie home in that dress, I tried to show it off to my husband, who was working all day in the junkyard, covered in grease. When his construction jobs dried up each winter, he wasn't too proud to take a dirty job, such as a junkyard sorter. He had to make money to support his ever-growing family. The second he laid eyes on me, he was smitten. Just kidding. He rolled his eyes a little and wondered if this was just a phase or if I was going to dress this way forever.

"I made this dress!" I said with my chin held high. I twirled around like a little girl so he could see the entire dress. "Now, I look old-fashioned like women used to dress." He wouldn't dare steal my joy nor burst my bubble. Instead, he nodded and said, "It's really nice." I took that halfhearted compliment and ran with it. Soon I was making clothing for the entire family. Dress after dress for the little girls and I, pants for Miles, and even little black denim coats with alining.

Everywhere I went, people would stare and wonder if I were Amish. I stopped putting lace on because I wanted to fit in. I only wore my lacy dress if I was with the 'English' people who happened to be our relatives. Mom was horrified and embarrassed to go out in public with me by that point, and I couldn't understand why. I thought she would think it was amazing because I was creating clothing that would save money. I was like Grandma more and more, and I looked more like Grandmother Hubbard than anything, yet I was lost in the bliss of it all. When you're passionate about something, there is a strange thing that happens. You abandon reason, and as you stand on principle, you ignore the naysayers that pop up along the way. For me, it made me want to do it all the more like I was some elevated spiritual genius.

Miles started translating my stance as a measuring stick to every woman who would come in our midst. "You wear pants. Oh, no. You're going to hell!" he would say with sincere dismay. It was like he got on a soapbox to preach that woman should only wear dresses. That wasn't my intent, and I often had to take the uninformed soul aside to tell him that dresses do not save a woman. There were times I felt so ashamed when he would open his mouth because it made it look like I had proselytized him that way, which was far from the truth. In short, I didn't much care at the time what anyone else was doing because I couldn't see past the Amish and becoming one of them.

Meanwhile, at our little Baptist church, the speculations of us joining a cult mounted. Doris warned it was not at all necessary for us to be this way to enter heaven and I knew full well. She was good at calling me out on things. Mark had been working at her husband's junk yard for a low wage and had I not said a word to anyone else, I could have been all the wiser. Yet my mouth has a tendency to get itself in trouble. The Bible says out of the mouth the heart speaks, so I had to have a seed of vindictive bitterness hiding in there someplace.

The Apron & The Community

I must have resented her for the times she said that my affection toward my husband was like a woman on a bar fly. They didn't show affection and she was pious so I knew my ways irritated her. I opened my big sepulcher of a mouth in the nursery one day to the itching ears of nursing mothers who were wanting to know why I was dressing like a pilgrim and how come I was sad. It always starts like that. You sit in a corner with a frown. Truth be told, I was frowning because I wanted to be sitting in an Amish church, not in a Baptist one. And everyone wants to know why your sad. So I told them things about Doris that I could not take back. The gun of my mouth was loaded and those bullets went out to assassinate her character.

A day or two later, when my phone rang and I saw her number flashing, I knew I was in deep trouble. I owned it. As she told me what a slanderer I was, I agreed with tears streaming down my cheeks flushed from embarrassment. My heart was pounding and I felt like a deserved to die for what I did. I asked her to forgive me yet she said she already did and that she would never trust me again, nor did she really ever wish to see me again. I was marked. Here I was dressed from head to toe in what looked like a religious lady, but on fire from hell itself after that moment. I could not breathe and the weight of shame closed in on my chest. I felt the consuming fires of condemnation upon me as I wrote a four page letter to every lady in the nursery that day, including a copy of that letter to Doris. I admitted my guilt and that I knew that I was one to be marked as a slanderer and a busybody. I also told them never to trust me and I realized I did not deserve their forgiveness.

We stopped going to the church and I confessed this sin to all my Amish friends at the time. They told me that I did what was right before God to confess and to bring my sins into an open shame before the lady's I offended. Essentially, I crucified myself and this act became a pattern for me when I wronged someone. Deep down I knew it was a bigger problem. I was giving myself the punishment that I wished others would have gotten for the crimes against me as a child. It was like I was righting these wrongs by paying for all current and future wrongs, yet only Christ was pure enough to take that shame and pay for it in full. I had to come face to face with this charade I entangled myself into eventually and realize I was not able to make such payments on a cross of my own making.

The turbine of life kept turning and I needed to get back to work as the Amish said, "There's not enough time in the day to sit around feeling sorry for yourself!" All us Amish "Fraws," or wives, would go from one house to the next to help in butcherings that winter. Many hands make light work in the community. Everyone pulls together to help one another out. It is marvelous. My ancestors would have done similar in the good old days. It wasn't just partial to the Amish or Plain folk. Especially when they don't rely on modern conveniences as much; they rely instead on numbers. People in number, more hands, and happy helpers. "You scratch my back, and I scratch yours." They reciprocated that help, and that was where I was led this frigid November morning in 2002.

We met at Allen and Elsie's farm that morning. The sun was barely up, and we were all catching forty-pound turkeys to slaughter. Thanksgiving was around the corner, and they were going to have quite the turkey to feed the families that would soon gather to feast. Allen was a slender man in his early thirties with a flaming red beard and beady eyes. His beard furled with curl under his turned-up nose. He had a black 'sipple cap' pulled over his ears, hiding the rest of his thinning red hair. The Amish men do not have a mustache. They keep that shaven. The hair on their head looks as if you placed a bowl over it to cut around. Allen was unusually cheerful that morning. "Hi, my name is Allen. Glad you could come today to learn!" his smile was revealing his mouth full of straight, white teeth.

Allen went off into the darkness of the barn to grab another turkey to chop its head off. The ladies were dressed in our plain drab dresses with black coats and scarves pulled around our heads like babushkas. We looked like old Russian ladies as we launched into full swing. I stood there with Allen's mom, Rosa. By this time, she was taking an interest in me. His sister Maybel was the most talkative besides Martha. They all wanted to know who I was. Elvesta was his youngest sister of fourteen children. We all were pulling the thick, white-feathered skin from those turkeys that seemed twice the size of any turkey I had ever seen. They were snitching into the cows' grain and fattened up off of that corn.

We had our arms up to our elbows, drawing out the insides and pulling them out of each carcass. It was my first butchering experience, so I wasn't at all accustomed to the smell, the heat of their bodies when you put your hands in. I just abandoned all my senses as I plunged my hands into one bird and then the next. They wouldn't be able to say I didn't know what I was doing or that I was slow and clumsy. I learned to work hard and fast while talking. The adage "When in Rome do as the Romans do" became a saying I fixed into my muscles that morning. When in Amish Land, do as the Amish do. Just do it. No questions. Just work. Don't think about the blood and guts; just push through it. There's no room for repulsion.

I was so glad to work elbow to elbow with Allen's family. They asked me all sorts of questions, and I began to fill them in on my whole life story. The children were all upstairs where it was warm, and one of the Amish lady's daughters was making sure they all played nice. You could hear the stampede over the basement rafters above our heads. Lots of thuds meant they were having fun.

Rosa was snapping the spines on the turkey bones to have more manageable pieces to work with. By lunch, we had cut all the 'hingle flaysh' or chicken meat off the bones. I learned a lot of new words that day.

We all rose from the dark, damp basement with blood on our faces and a job well done. One by one, we washed our hands and stood in the room, waiting for the next step. When the clock struck noon, the prayer commenced. The Amish men from the farm fields came in and lined up around the room by the food. They didn't pray out loud, but one announcement of the father of the home, "Purdy Saya," and all became utterly silent. All we could hear was the ticking of the old wind-up clock on the wall. Even the children were in utter silence. "Purdy Saya" means "Sit Pretty," which does not make any bit of sense. They even said so, but it was just what they do. It meant that they were starting their silent prayers together before eating. As I stared around the room, I saw everyone bowing their heads, and with every tick of the clock, my heart pounded with thankfulness. How do they know when to stop, I wondered as the quiet time carried on. Suddenly, Allen cleared his throat, and then the others cleared their throats in unison while picking their lowly heads up from prayer. They released the little children from their grasp to play.

The long table was lined with cakes of all sorts, Jell-O, pudding, noodles, and a little of the turkey meat ground up and formed into patties. The patties were pan-fried, and Elsie opened a jar of applesauce and homemade catsup. I sat back and observed the order of operations.

All the women had brought a dessert to pass, and I had brought nothing. That was the first thing I noticed. The Amish used a hard plastic bowl, and the bowls are stacked high for each person to make their plate filled with food. I watched as the Amish women made plates for their small children, followed by the men. The men piled noodles, patties, canned beans high on their plates and then poured "Apple Sass'" over everything. They said the food's too dry without it. I couldn't see mixing apple sauce into all the hot food; it made the food look like slop. After the men made their way around the table, whatever was left was for the women. We all scraped the last bits from the pans, but mostly the women eat whatever their little ones leave on their plates. "Waste not, want not," I guess was the motto. Or you could look at it like this... maybe they know they won't get as much of the good food if they don't fill their children's plates first before the men go. That way, they get something in the end. I hated the idea of eating after my children, so I made small portions for them, so I did not have to scrape it into slop for my belly. There is a silent rule that you NEVER leave food on the plates. You scrape them clean with a spoon.

The men came up for dessert first. They loaded high like haystack cakes and puddings and Jell-O only to pour milk over the whole lot. They called it "Cake Soup." I called it sweeter slop. The sound of spoons scraping in every direction told us that they were finished, and we would be back to work in short order. We women went through to gather up all the soup plates and spoons to rinse them. They have a system for this as well. They put a small amount of water in the first bowl, scraped it clean, dumped the dirty water into the next dish, and so on. This conserved the water. One woman washed, and another rinsed and placed the dishes into the drying rack. No sooner did it hit the dry rack than another woman grabbed the dish to wipe it dry, which another will put away. It was like a fine-tuned assembly line. I worked myself into the job of washing dishes that day. I could see that this job had to be done with precision and speed, or the entire operation would be delayed. Right then and there, I learned how to move my hands in and out of the water in a frenzy.

After the floors were swept clean and the house in order, we made our way down to the dark and cold basement to find all the strips of meat ready to grind. The meat was seasoned. Rosa dumped this spice and that spice over the meat to make turkey bologna. Her ice-

The Apron & The Community

cold hands worked the spices into the strips of meat until it was evenly distributed. Martha was ready with the tubs filled with meat to send outside to the men for grinding. Once the meat was ground, it was packed into glass jars to can. They sliced the meat right out of the jar to make bologna sandwiches for the husband and children's lunches each day. There were stoves and burners in various areas with pressure canners blowing steam. I bet they canned up a hundred jars that day in a few short hours. All the bones were put in iron cauldrons over a fire outside to boil. The men kept the fires going while taking long wooden poles to stir. Beards, straw hats, and denim were all I could make out through the smoke surrounding them.

I went home tired. I worked from morning till night, but I wanted that life. The work didn't scare me away. It etched community on my heart that would last a lifetime. I found a community, and it was home. I could see that this was what God created us for. When we work together for a greater good, for the good of our neighbor, we are keeping the law of his love.

"Love your neighbor as yourself."

Chapter Twelve
PORK PATTIES & CHICKEN LICE

*T*hanksgiving arrived, and Mark's family came to celebrate with us. His sister Anne and her husband Scott, his mother, brother Matt, and his Grandma Betty all walked into our little farmhouse filled with the scent of the holidays. They all brought their unique dishes to pass. Candles were burning, the turkey was roasting, the gravy was bubbling over the stove, and fresh bread and pies. That year I made a pumpkin custard pie. Katie taught me how to make one and how to make the flakiest crust. The secret was lard; pig lard. By this time, Maybel had donated bags of her families' rigid white caps, and baby girl dresses to my size dresses, which were her young teen dresses. All with pins. I learned how to pin myself up in a dress.

As they walked into the room, they all tried not to stare and act like nothing was amiss. None of them had seen me during my transition, so they were a bit shocked to see us decked out in full Amish. No one dared say a word. They just focused their attention toward the three little Amish amigos on the floor, who I dressed to be as authentic Amish as I could. I even cut Miles's hair in the bowl shape down to the denim pants with suspenders built-in. I learned how to fix Molly's hair with tight braids and a little white bonnet to cover them. Having braids hanging down was vulgar to them. I just did everything they told me.

Memoirs of a Keeper: Angels & Demons

Nothing had to make sense.

The gleaming white tablecloth was over the old wooden table that stretched across the hutch that Mark's grandfather had made forty years before. He was a woodworker. All of the photos of Jerry looked just like Mark, and they even had the same talent with their hands. Grandma Betty was getting frail. She had a head full of little gray curls and round glasses to push up her little nose. The table was set with my grandma's rose china, and everything looked beautiful. After mashing the potatoes and pouring the gravy into a serving dish, we placed all the glorious food upon the table. Mark said a prayer, and we all began to fill our plates. Steaming turkey sliced with a layer of gravy, Anne's beautiful cranberry bread, Grandma Karen's corn pudding, and Grandma Betty's famous creamy mashed potatoes filled our stomachs.

After filling our bellies with the delicious food, we talked and enjoyed our time together. I filled them all in on my Amish adventures and all that I had learned. They nodded their heads just like Mark always did, but you never really ever know exactly what they were thinking. His family has always been more private. They were guarded, not given to much deep conversation as I always was. They were great listeners. I could just talk and talk, and they would all just sit there and listen. Occasionally, they would ask questions. While listening to my stories, the children hurried from one lap to the other, giggling and playing. Miles was nearly as talkative as I was. He would tell his versions of the stories, and they would all laugh. It was much cuter coming out of a three-year-old's mouth. Uncle Scott gave piggyback rides and wrestled Miles down until he needed another sip of some 'strong water' as he would call it. Just plain well water from our farm, but it was a game he always played with Miles. When he took the sip, he would get stronger and throw Miles up into the air and twirl him down to the floor in play. Miles always wanted to give him more of that strong water until he was loud with laughter.

We got to hear some stories from Grandma Betty over the weekend. She told us about when she used to ride in horse-drawn carriages at the beginning of the last century. In the winter, they had sleighs. I loved Grandma Betty. She always accepted me and loved seeing the children. She only had one child. Mark's mother was all she was able to have. An only child. She and Grandma Karen always stayed for a long weekend. There was something different about this time.

Pork Patties & Chicken Lice

She seemed slower than usual, and I even gave her a nice shower. Her frail frame stood in the water, and I took care of her as I took care of my grandmother, with a gentle touch like Florence Nightingale. There was nothing she and Grandma Karen loved more than to be with the children. It brought them so much joy. Even though I suffered the pains of rejection before we were married, somehow, it was gone, and all the love for the children was what I chose to celebrate. I loved seeing her happy.

A few short days after they had left, we found out Grandma Betty was in the hospital. She seemed so happy there, and they all thought she would pull through. She was a tough woman her whole life, a hardworking keeper of the home and a nurse. But her heart was winding down, and she died happy, in her sleep, that night. She peacefully drifted to Jesus. She was in her 90's, had a good life, and it was her time. We packed up our crew and headed down to Milwaukee for her funeral. Miles sang "Amazing Grace," just as she had asked. The family celebrated her life and legacy that day as her body was put to rest. It was hard on her daughter, Grandma Karen, because she had moved in with her a few years before, and now she was alone. I hated the thought of that. No one wants to be alone. As much as she was able, I wanted her to come and stay with us.

We continued to make many visits to Amish Land. Now that I got acquainted with Allen's side of the family, I went up for every butchering day I could. From house to house. First, we were at his sister Orpha's for pig butchering. She called me up and asked me if I wanted some meat. They would slaughter another young hog if I wanted. Oh, yes, I wanted to have my own canned meat. Orpha's big, light-green farmhouse was right there by the highway that passed over. They had a long driveway leading into the big red shed that looked more like a false front from a western film. I met Lee. Lee was one of the funniest Amish men I ever met. He was always tricking and joking around. His voice was strangely a combination of Danny DeVito and Moe from the Three Stooges. His humor was like one of the Three Stooges except for the fact that he was full Amish. His long beard tussled with every chuckle.

Orpha had the voice of a dove, so gentle and sweet. Her beautiful, slender face had eyes that smiled. The edges of her eyes naturally turned up like a little bit of a smile. Dressed in the drab butchering dresses, with our heads wrapped in woven headscarves, we all got right to the job. Orpha, Rosa, Martha, Elvesta, and their brother Harry's wife Edna Mae gathered around the plastic table out in the shed where the pig carcass laid. We all had knives in our hands, and we started slicing off strips of meat. It was much easier cutting meat off the pig than it was the turkeys. We only had the big bones to worry about, not all the small slivery ones like the turkeys have in their legs. They were like spines and challenging to work around. While we worked, we laughed at the occasion jokes from Lee or when they tried teaching me more Dutch. I always had a funny way of reciting phrases. "Eek moose di schlake gayva!" I would say, and they would roar with laughter. Lee taught me that one. It meant, "I am going to give you a spanking!" That is what you say to your naughty children if they get out of line. I would say it a dozen times, and a dozen times, they would ask me to repeat it. Each time the laughter got louder.

Orpha taught me, "Say un deesh spay duh." That meant, "See you later." She wanted to give me some other 'nicer' phrases. Orpha leaned in like an old friend with a whisper, "Oh, don't mind Lee, he's a bit of a jokester. He's always teasing us." Maybe she thought I would be offended from all his teasing about things that weren't true. Thankfully, I grew up with a few jokesters in my family, and I knew that tone of sarcasm and wit. I could play along and milk out the story with them. That made Lee like me all the more. The more I played along, the more he had to come up with. They knew we were somehow cut off the same cloth. Different worlds, but we were instantly family.

Before lunch, we had cut every last strip off of three hogs, seasoned it for pork sausage, and Lee ground it all up. They had this industrial-sized grinder. It was from a butchering shop, and the hopper could fit about 25 pounds of meat at one time. The place where the ground meat came out was five inches in diameter. It didn't take long to process meat. The fat was put through there to grind up for making lard. We all gathered round in silence for the prayer and then the food. All the other dishes were the same. The noodles, the cakes, the pies, the Jell-O, the jam and bread, applesauce, and pudding, but the meat was fresh, seasoned pork patties. Wow, those were amazing. I was so glad I paid them for one hog so I could have sausage at our home. This time I brought a dessert. I knew all the women pitched in, and I wanted to make sure I did not come empty-handed.

Pork Patties & Chicken Lice

Soup plates loaded down, as usual, to end in the fast sea of clanking and scraping of spoons at the end. The afternoon was filled with canning. Us fraws were at Orpha's table, forming balls of meat with our hands and pressing them into the shape of patties. We would line them into baking pans like rows of sardines, one after the other. Orpha kept the ovens full of sausage patty pans to brown up the meat. When the patties came out, they were much smaller, and we started shoving them into glass jars to can. The pressure canners were ticking and steaming all afternoon. Up to that point, the thought of eating meat from a jar was revolting to me. It seemed like canned dog food to my mind. I spent much of my lifetime in the kennel, and I remember digging the meat out of the jars for the dogs. To my surprise, it was terrific when heated up because it was seasoned. So handy. I learned that one of the most extraordinary things the Amish do was to can meat. It may be a lot of work the day you butcher, but every day for the rest of the year, you don't have to thaw meat or worry that it would get freezer burnt. If the power goes out, the meat is safe in the cellar for years. I once opened a jar that was shoved to the back of the cellar shelf that had to have been there for six or seven years. It looked the same. I opened it, and it smelled fresh. We cooked it up, and it tasted the same as the first day it was in the jar. Marvelous, indeed.

Making meals became a snap for me. I could be gone all day long gallivanting with the Amish helping them work, come home and cook a meal in less than fifteen minutes. I would just dump the meat and vegetables into one pot, heat to a boil, season, and a delicious stew would cook up. I refuse to do it any other way, even today. Besides the satisfaction of looking at shelves lined with home-canned foods, I've always loved the convenience of it.

No sooner did I get home, I got another call, this time from Rosa. "Hi, Erin. This is Rosa," she said in a sad tone (which I learned was her telephone voice). I wasn't sure if it was just that she wasn't fond of the phone or if it was due to the fact she was standing in the subzero weather, in a hurry to get back to the barn chores. In a way, that sounded like she was saying it because she thought she should speak out of duty, "Well, we are butchering some chickens today. I thought I would let you know in case you want to come help, but you don't have to."

"Yes, I would love to help," I returned with all the enthusiasm of my heart. "Do you want me to bring a knife?"

"Yah. Yah. That's okay." Then and awkward pause, "Okay. Well, I have to get back to the barn."

"Say un deesh shpedul!" I said, hoping that would trigger some camaraderie. She giggled a little and repeated the same phrase before we hung up the phone. That gave me some hope that she welcomed me. The most old-fashioned of all the Amish invited me over. Was it a dream? I didn't want to spoil it. Every ounce of my body felt tired, but I just ignored it so I could be one of them. You can't be one of them if you were sitting on the couch at home doing nothing. You have to love working and pushing yourself in the presence of fatigue. Smack yourself awake at the break of dawn, jump out of bed, put on the drabbest 14th-century peasant dress, a dirty apron full of blood from the day before, roll up your sleeves, and get ready for some more blood and guts, or you'll miss the mark every time. I wasn't about to miss the mark. I pulled up my black socks and laced up the ugliest black shoes and walked over to the closet to find only dark, ominous-looking, polyester dresses hanging for I had since gotten rid of my English clothing. It was between dark brown, navy blue, dark wine, or green. I threw the dress over my head with some thick leggings under to keep my legs warm. My husband tried to look away every time because he was now married to what seemed to him a Russian peasant from the refugee camp. I wrapped my head with the black woven scarf, and out I plunged into the cool of the morning with a baby on one hip, knife in the other with a dessert pan under my arm, and two toddlers following close behind, ready for adventure on the farm.

As the van rolled into her gravel driveway, I passed her big, white farmhouse that was across an even larger red barn. There were sheds and building all around and lots of horses. Big draft horses were hitched up at the end of the lane, and buggies were coming in after me. One by one, the ladies would stop their black buggies and step out with big black capes and bonnets over their butchering attire. Ezra was Rosa's husband. He was juggling the team of horses but dropped the lines to help hitch each of the girls' horses to the hitching post. I went to greet him. He had the typical very long gray beard and dressed in navy-blue denim. The pants were patched up in many different spots. His hands were thick farmer's hands. Strong with years of holding back the team of eight draft horses to plow over the farm fields. That day he was getting ready to spread manure. Ezra walked toward me with a big smile, "I heard a lot about you!"

"I bet," I chuckled. There was a kindness about that man that seemed fatherly to me. Miles bounded toward the horses and wanted to be on the cart with him. Ezra went off as the ground thundered with the mighty hooves of the eight drafts. We stood in awe as we could see him disappear over the field behind their barn. I followed the women into Rosa's kitchen, where the table was set tight against the paneled wall with benches to sit on. It was right under a fancy clock that would play songs every hour. Rosa was hunched over the sink finishing the rest of the breakfast dishes. She was never idle. She was about my height with rounded shoulders from years of bending over working always. Her cap was a bit different, not as stiff, and her eyes were almond shape. As we all placed our desserts on the counter facing the table, she was already tying a tight bandana around her head after taking the cap off. I did not know they wore bandanas. She said it was for the lice. "Lice?!" I said as I started to wonder what I was getting myself into. I agreed to the blood and guts but not lice! No one told me I would have to deal with that too.

"It's just chicken lice," Maybel leaned into me with a slight giggle as if that was going to make it better. "The chicken lice don't like humans. They just jump on you and crawl around for a bit, and then they die," she continued trying to console me because my face was probably exposing my revulsion. Rosa looked a bit impatient but motherly at the same time as she handed me a cloth, "Ya. It's no big deal. Here put this scarf on your head; it might help." In her posture, it communicated to me the silent rule of "Buck up. Don't be a wimp." I followed the entourage of Amish women out into the cold again. They hung the chickens, one by one, by their feet from a laundry post. Rosa did not waste a lick of time as she chased them down and handed them to us.

What were we going to do next? Oh my! Yes, with a knife in hand, I swallowed hard as I watched them abandon their femininity as they started grabbing one head at a time and sawing the heads clear off. I thought that was the man's job. Nope. And they pushed me ahead to claim a bird. I grabbed the head as it was trying to save its life. "Pull the head down hard so that neck is tight. It will chop off easier when you do that," Martha said as she smiled. It was just another thing they do. I had to do it, too. I hated it, but I was there. Again, I grabbed the moving head for fear of it pecking me, and I just closed my eyes and hacked it off as fast as I could.

I took a deep breath of relief as the head was off, and the bird started jerking and spraying blood and lice all over me. I couldn't get away from the dread. More and more chickens. Hundreds. And after hacking off heads, you have to yank the feathered skin off their lifeless bodies; all the while, your head is crawling with lice. I was so miserable. My head is itching just thinking about it. The only consolation was the laughter and conversation we were having. Half the time, they talked in Dutch, which made it worse for my itching head as I would scratch it in confusion from time to time, wondering if I caught what they were saying.

It was a cross I bore that day. I felt like I had been in a war wrestling chickens in the barnyard, hacking heads, and warring the skin off one by one. All at once, I could take it no longer, and I didn't even care if they thought less of me, "How do I get the lice off? They won't die!" They all stared at me, knowing I was at the end of my rope by that point.

Ophra said in her soft tone, "Well, it will only last a few hours, probably." They probably were used to it. What on earth did those chickens do to get lice? I vowed that day that if I raise chickens, I will find a way to make sure they don't get it. Rose showed me mercy as she led me to the shower in her basement. She turned into mother hen, "If you wash with hot soapy water, they all will die!" I couldn't thank her enough for having pity on me and loving me so much. She and I became so close after that. Rosa was my Amish "Mem" or mom. She took me under her wing, and I spent hundreds of hours under her training. She was a true keeper of the home, and I could learn a million things from her. A virtuous woman in every way!

The word quit was not in my vocabulary, so I put on the bloody clothes, shook off any other lice, and since there were no more chickens to kill or skin, I knew I was out of danger for more lice exposure. I went right back out to the barn to help gut the chickens and then take their bodies apart. We cut the legs from the thighs and stuffed those into the jars to can with the bones on. All the breasts were gently sliced off and put into the freezer. The breast bones were boiled for broth.

The men came in from the field, and they went right to the sink in the mudroom and washed their hands and faces. They all carry a comb in their pocket, so you see them all combing their hair after taking their hats off. The hair is all combed straight forward and down in a perfect bowl form like Friar Tuck. This time I met a few new faces. There was Harry, Willis, and Milo, their sons. Harry had an auburn-colored beard. He was a father of nine or ten children and had a farm down the road. He was married to Edna Mae, who I had worked with another time. Edna Mae, Lee, and Mary were siblings. It was confusing. Lots of them were related somehow. There were the Bontragers, the Yoders, and the Millers mainly. Willis was married, and I had worked alongside his wife Mary all morning. They had a little one and one on the way. Willis and Mary ran the dairy farm and lived in the big part of the old, white house. Ezra and Rosa lived there in an attached part of the house they call the "Dawdy Haus" or what we would call a Grandparent's suite. They didn't send their old to homes. They didn't have health care plans. They just took care of each other.

Ezra told me that day the cycle of life for the Amish, "This is how it goes…You get married, you have children. You take care of the children while they are young. You change their diapers and feed them. It's a cost. A considerable cost. When they are old enough, they go to the community school where they learn some English." He continued to declare, "They finish school around fourteen years old. They finish in the 8th grade, and that is when the girls work with their mothers, and the boys go off to work full-time. The money they make goes to their parents until they are twenty years old. The parents use the money to pay off the farm and get ahead. The youngest son usually gets the farm because he will put the Dawdy Haus on and take care of the parents until they die. You took care of them, and now they take care of you. And the cycle continues." I saw a lot of wisdom in their ways. It seemed to make sense. I liked the thought of people taking care of each other.

While we ate our lunch, the spoons were scraping again as I saw a room full of men staring into their bowls to make sure they found every last remnant of their lunch. The pots were steaming, and the smell of broth filled the air. After the bones came out, all of the women gathered around the table and picked the bones of any remaining meat, making sure to get every last little bone that might have stuck in there. No one wants to have soup and accidentally chomp on a tiny bone. The broth was poured into each jar with a handful of the bone meat. Later, when they make noodles for their noon meals, they cook them with a jar of this bone broth.

I couldn't get enough of this life that I plunged myself headfirst into.

Chapter Thirteen
THE CHRISTMAS BAN & THE NIGHT TERROR

*C*hristmas was around the corner, and the days were filled with butchering and canning with my Amish Community. Martha invited me by for apple butter, making one winter day that December. I arrived to find her, Rosa, her mother, and her sisters out in the shed cutting or "schnitzing" the apples. All you could see was the tops of their white caps as they hunched over their bowls of apples with knives in their hands. Pulling up a chair and shifting my cap on straight, I began to schnitz alongside my new sisters. Martha dumped all the cut apples into a big hopper and started to run them through the applesauce mill. Slowly you could hear the soft sauce drizzling through, and the smell of apples hung in the air.

"What is apple butter?" I asked as I had never heard of anything like that. I imagined butter melted into the apples, and somehow it was buttery. Martha looked at me with her slanted, beady eyes fixed on her oblong face. She was short, fair-skinned, and freckle-faced. Her hair was a bit reddish, slicked back into a large bun under her cap. Her legs were strong and thick, and she was a worker. I was so thankful for the invite into her home to work and learn how to make apple butter. As she kept turning the crank, she squinted her eyes in my direction, "It's like apple sauce, with a whole lot more sugar in it. We will cook it down about halfway over the fire outside in the big black pot." That sounded so old-fashioned and fun, something they had been doing for hundreds of years, no doubt. The apple butter was smeared on your bread like jam. It was spiced with cinnamon and tasted festive.

After all the sauce was ready, we dumped big metal bowls into the black cauldron along with bags and bags of sugar. Her husband, Eli, started the fire beneath it. He was tall, thin, and had a very sparse, scraggly black beard. He was a jovial man who loved to smile and laugh while he worked. We all huddled around the open fire as we took turns scraping the bottom so the apples would not burn. It was a lovely smell of fire, sugar, apple, and spice. There was nothing like it, and smelled like Christmas.

Eli was a minister in the church. I found out that they pick the ministers by casting lots. You don't have to study to be approved. All the men on the day of the lot pick up an Amish hymnal call the Ausbund, and if theirs had a slip of paper in it, they were the chosen one, chosen by God Himself, or so they believed. Most of the men who got picked found it a burden from what I have learned. They hoped not to pick the book with the paper, but they went along with it because it is God's will.

We all gathered for lunch in the same as we always do, with the silent prayer and the sound of the clock ticking. My heart was beginning to embrace the silence as a way we all communed with God in one quiet, powerful force, thankful in our own ways. A beautiful way. I found out that they said to pray out loud was to go on like the pagans for want of being heard. To them, it was an act of pride, for God knows the heart and knows what we want before we even utter a word. I can see it from both sides now. I loved my silent conversations with God, but with my mouth, I have never been ashamed to shout at the top of my voice, His praises. It was Christmas, but there wasn't one decoration for Christmas. No tree, no lights, no tinsel, nor angels on their shelves, and I was left to wonder, "Do the Amish celebrate Christmas?"

Eli answered with confidence, "Yes, we Amish do celebrate Christmas as the birth of Jesus, but we do not want to be as the world adorning our homes with fancy things." Martha continued, "Ya, we don't have trees, but we like to exchange gifts, and the children have a special Christmas program at their school. You should come!" All the sisters agreed.

By this time, my eyes started to smile, "Ya, I would love to

The Christmas Ban & The Night Terror

come! Thank you for inviting me." I wondered if I should have a tree or decorate my home. After I arrived home with about twelve pints of home-canned "Apul buddl," I discussed the whole Christmas decorating with my husband. I had already made him ditch the television. To my surprise, he hated Christmas decorations anyhow. He was glad not to have a tree. To him, it was too commercialized and an added bunch of work. Mom came out to help with the children, as she often did. She was the most amazing grandma who was always bearing gifts and treats for the children. I never had to buy a single pair of shoes or socks as she always brought those and little coats and hats. Although we were relatively poor, Mom always made sure her grandbabies were warm. She hated the Amish look, so she often bought the children cute pajamas and jogging outfits that they could wear at her house. Mom tried to be supportive, but I could tell it was difficult for her.

"When are you putting up the tree?" Mom asked with a little fear under her breath. I think she knew we weren't going to do that either, and it riled her up. It was sacrilegious. How could we bring up little children without Santa, much less a tree? We had told her several years before that we would not lie to the children about Santa, and that was enough to make her mad.

"Well, we weren't going to decorate this year," I said in a quiet, cowardly fashion. Her face started to look a bit annoyed.

"What? Is that too worldly now?" She said with sarcasm, "You are getting really weird, Erin. Whatever you want. I will take back all the Christmas presents then." It was a punishment of sorts, I suppose. Hit me where I would concede. I could see the children nearly crying, and I didn't want to do away with that part for them. The Amish had gifts. I had already dug myself into a hole. Well, she was right! I was thinking more Amish by the minute, and the thought of having anything like the world would jeopardize my standing in the Amish Community. I would be far less committed if I would do ANYTHING other than what they did. She could tell my allegiance was with them.

"Mom, they have gift-giving. We can do that!" I said, to try to make peace with her in some way and to appease the children. I was caught between two hard places: Family tradition and the Amish culture. How would I pick and make everyone happy? I began to put it off on Mark as the scapegoat, "Mark doesn't like trees. He hates them, so I have to honor his wishes, too. It's not just the Amish." Mom rolled her eyes once again and started playing with the children. That brought her the most joy of all.

It was a ban of sorts. That year we put Christmas in the ban, I guess you could say! The Amish put people in the ban, and I found out from all my little chats with the ladies during our working that Melvin was in the ban. He may have been on fire for God, but he did not like to follow man-made rules. Or some of them, I should say. It was over an outlawed fax machine to help him with his orders and for business. That winter, I spent so much time with each of the ladies. I got to know all the town gossip. This lady was cutting her dresses too short, while this lady's cap was getting stiffer and more pointy in the back, one person was caught with a tape recorder listening to music, and other stories of people misaligning their rules a bit. There were a lot of little things that seemed to ebb at their core and cause division. Melvin had lots of skeletons in the closet that I found out over time. There was a bit of a mystery with the man.

He introduced me to some other plain folk who was also once a part of the world and decided, like us, to try to live the separated life; The Pear Family. They had about ten children or so and gathered in their homes to worship God and have fellowship with other believers. The women wore scarves on their heads as their so-called coverings and long-outdated floral or plaid dresses. Mary Pear was tall and talked like her nose was forever plugged. Her glasses were pushed at the top of her turned-up nose that revealed her gleaming white teeth. Melvin showed us the way to their home one Sunday morning. We gathered in their living room on couches and chairs. Most of her children were grown. Her husband's name was James. He was around the same height as her with a full beard.

These plain people didn't believe in shaving the mustache off as the Amish do. The Amish used to have beards hundreds of years ago, but around the time of the Civil war, as I remember hearing, the fashion of the day was men sporting mustaches. One man, in particular, was the trendsetter. His name was General Custer. Because of their nonresistant stance, which means they do not fight or shed blood but turn the other cheek, and their cause against dressing in the fashion of the world, the mustaches had to go. For the past 150 years, the Amish require the mustache to be shaven. The Amish men, I found out, are never allowed to take a clipper or scissors to the rest of the beard for trimming. They

The Christmas Ban & The Night Terror

started growing the lower beard when they married, and by the length of the beard, one could tell how old a man was, or sometimes how long he was married. These plain men, instead, have the shorter clipped hair and trimmed beards.

Mary had homemade dresses and made them with each of her lovely daughters. In her sewing room beside the kitchen, you could see about six working sewing machines, one for each of the girls to practice on. She wanted to train her girls to make everything from clothing to bread. Her children worked like well-oiled machines. Mary would rattle off a dozen instructions while they all zipped back and forth, making sure everything was done right. These plain people were much more severe about God than the Amish were. There were no jokes and no Christmas either. They completely ban Christmas in every form. No tree, no nativity, and no presents. It was all evil and pagan to them. The Kuddle family also gathered in the home fellowship, Carol and Billy, and their eight or ten children.

When it came time for singing, the voices broke through my heart like a heavenly chorus. Every part of harmony was there; the high voices to mid-range ladies and the deep full sounds of the young men singing bass. It was terrific, and I just wanted to be with them forever, just for the singing. The service lasted about three hours, and each of the grown men would go up and preach a sermon with much emphasis on modesty, purity, humility, and separation from the world. I got this message loud and clear from every angle and found myself even more convinced than ever. They started to tell us about all the things that are pagan. Even the children's stories had pagan images. Pagan influences were all around me, and since I was a little girl, I could see that my whole existence was pagan. It all must have been a lie or a trap of the devil, everything I knew. My mind was forming lots of conclusions about my life and what I wanted to take a stand against. The pendulum of my heart wanted to abandon everything and to swing to the opposite extreme in every way. Mary told me my life was all of the occult, and when someone practiced paganism, and they became a friend to the world, they were opening the door to the devil. She told me about idol worship, how people put statues in their yards or on shelves, and prayed to them just like they did from the beginning of time. I remembered Grandma having statues of the Virgin Mary on her shelves, or crucifixes of Jesus, or how many other Catholic people

Memoirs of a Keeper: Angels & Demons

I knew wearing medallions with the saints on them, praying to them as if they were gods. Everything I knew was idolatry, according to her. I almost felt utterly hopeless. What had we done in life that wasn't of the world? Everyone must be on a path to hell somehow, according to her. How could a person get to heaven when so many things in life happened to be vain or had no spiritual meaning? Life started to become hard as I began to work on the things that were revealed to me as evil. The more I did, the more I felt the weight of the world pressing on my very heart. I think the more I condemned myself and judged myself, the more I allowed myself to sink into self-pity and shame.

Every Sunday, we were visiting their homes and sometimes even the Kuddle's Bakery. For months, I had kept in the fact that our son, Miles, who was only about three years old, was having night terrors. I didn't want to admit we were dealing with this because it would be the smoking gun; they would all know we dappled into something evil. He would wake, screaming his head off, and when we would find him, he would be sweating and shaking. What he said was what scared us the most.

"The witches are telling me that they want to take me in a canoe to hell," Miles said with his eyes opened wide with fear.

I would ask him, "What do these witches look like?" I could not find anything in my home or anything he would have even watched since we did not own television for most of his years. Since Mary's firm stance on paganism and idolatry, I removed anything from our home that could be an idol. I tried to cleanse the evil out, but where did he get this dream of witches from? Maybe there was a book I didn't know about on the shelf.

"They are tall," he continued, "They have black-hooded capes on. I can't see their faces, but they stand around me and the fire in a circle." Night after night, the same dream. Oh no. I knew what this was. It was a familiar scene, the scene I witnessed several years before when I was pregnant with him, the Halloween witch meeting. He was there in the womb, and whatever those witches said over my womb was coming back to haunt him. Nothing could calm the little boy's fear. He was afraid they would take him down to hell. We prayed with him each time and pulled him into our bed to help him feel safer, only to find out he laid awake watching for them. I had to tell the others. We were at the bakery, the Kuddle's Bakery, that Sunday morning.

The Christmas Ban & The Night Terror

"Can we please pray for my son," I said in full assurance of their prayers because they knew how to stand against the devil. As they all stared in my direction to hear the story, I continued, "He wakes at night with visions of witches that want to take him to hell." They all gasped simultaneously and leaned in closer as I finished the story with the Halloween scene we went to those years ago. It was a sure open door to the devil. I had the experience a couple of years before with the demonic oppression, and we just didn't know that it may have also touched the mind of our dear son. They told me that the devil was always after the firstborn, and he was in hot pursuit of our son. They demanded we repent of our sins, the sin of leading ourselves into that meeting and opening the door. After we repented, they put the child on a chair and asked him about his dreams. Miles told them everything. He was so scared to go to sleep at night, he told them. Soon, they all poured oil over his head and prayed for him. They commanded that Satan leave him and all his witches and demons never to hurt our son again. They yelled at the devil and told him that he couldn't have Miles.

It might sound farfetched, but he stopped having these bad dreams about the witches for quite some time. They had to go. Our little boy felt safe once again. It is a scary thing to play around with the occult and put yourself in danger. Many things in life have more profound consequences. The devil was not done troubling our son or me. He knew our buttons, and he found many ways to try to destroy us. I held fast to the scripture, "For we wrestle not against flesh and blood, but against principalities, against powers, against the rulers of the darkness of this world, against spiritual wickedness in high places." Ephesians 6:12

We went on to celebrate Christmas at Nana and Bumpa's place. My Grandma was there in her wheelchair sitting next to Uncle Jimmy. Uncle Jimmy didn't ever say much, but I could always tell he was happy to see the children. Mom picked Grandma up from the nursing home. Mom was like an angel in so many ways. Always rescuing, tending to others' needs, Mom always put everyone before herself. This year Mark's mom came to visit, so she also came with us. It was still a bit awkward to have both our mothers in the same room because they were so different. So opposite. My mom was the height of selflessness, taking care of me, my children, Grandma, Uncle Jimmy, and all the other relatives.

Memoirs of a Keeper: Angels & Demons

It was a sweet time to gather together. Miles was off playing, then asking when he could open his presents that were stacked under the tree. Molly was pushing her new baby doll in a buggy and running it right into Grandma Great's legs in her wheelchair with a stern scowl on her face saying, "Grandma, move!" We all laughed. My brother and his wife enjoyed giving special gifts to all of the children. Michelle was loud but had a big heart. Every Christmas, she would buy loads of gifts beyond her means because her way of showing love was to give gifts. At times I felt so badly about not returning the intensity and value of her gifts because we were too poor. When I asked her not to buy for us because we wouldn't reciprocate, it broke her heart. She said it was her Dominican culture. They don't expect anything in return. There were colliding cultures, and I had to choose to accept her love even when I could do nothing in return. It was hard to get gifts, knowing you couldn't give back. Humbling. Michelle was so beautiful, and she looked like a teenager.

Here I was, wholly dressed 100% Amish, along with our children. I couldn't even imagine what Mom was thinking. We looked so opposite in every way that it was rather humorous. Megan was on the floor, eating the paper that the other children were flinging in her direction, unaware. Molly started to sing to her baby while she paged through her new Bible. It was heavenly. Mom was having the time of her life, seeing the joy that the children had with opening their new presents one after the other. That was the essence of Christmas for her. I loved seeing her happiness. It was like the joy of a child coming out in her eyes.

Soon after, we did travel up to the Amish schoolhouse for the Christmas show. It was the first time I saw how they do things corporally. The schoolhouse is a long room with windows up each side. They have wooden benches facing forward situated into two separate sides, and the men are on one side and the woman on the other. Wow, that was such a shock for me. I was used to always sitting beside my husband during a church event, so this was quite odd, but we didn't want to upset the order of things. The children were dressed in dark blues, grays, greens, and browns. Nothing fancy. Nothing Christmassy. No tree. Just a lot of heart. It was little school children play-acting and singing songs. When they finished, we all joined in the chorus and watched the children open their gifts on the stage in front. It was simple and charming. In

The Christmas Ban & The Night Terror

the basement, we all joined for silent prayer and a whole lot of Amish goodies—sugar to the max. The joy of Christmas comes in so many different packages. Theirs was just a little plain.

    I couldn't have felt more at peace that year as we snuggled together in our old farmhouse heated with wood, watching the snow fall outside the paned windows. The best gift of all was being loved and loving those things that were right there in front of me.

Memoirs of a Keeper: Angels & Demons

Chapter Fourteen
The Secret Meetings & the Holy Kiss

*T*hat winter was spent mostly in Amish Land. I saw the beautiful life they lived, and the cycle of life, the community at its finest. I remember the first time I was invited to church. It was in Ezra's basement. We pulled up in the van and parked near the schoolhouse where they couldn't see the van. I did not want them to notice we were English by our van. Mark thought it was all ridiculous. That head covering I wore, which they tell you represents submission from a wife to her husband, was altogether void. I symbolically wore the pants when it came to the Amish but in the form of dresses and bonnets. I could be quite miserable when I did not get my way. Mark just kept his mouth shut and went along for the ride most days. This day was no exception. As far as the eye could see, there were horses and buggies. Men were putting horses into the pasture, and the buggies were all there lined up like black dominoes.

Maybel had given us everything we needed to fit in for this big occasion the week before, so we were suited up. She made Mark the pants and vest, which she laughed were the largest she had ever sewn. She gave us girls our black shawls and black bonnets. I had since learned to sew the girls' caps, and we had our suit dresses on. The suit dresses are exceedingly plain by nature but elaborately complex due to all the pins. Maybel showed me the way to pin-up. First, the dress went over the head. Then the stick pins were quilted across the front where buttons would generally be. Then we grabbed the two sides of the opened bodice and stuck the pin in and weaved it in and out so that we only saw little dots of metal, but the opening was thus closed. It took about ten stick pins to close the front of the dress properly.

Next, the cape went on. It came to a "V" in the back, pinned to the belt in the center, and the front was crisscrossed over your chest loosely to act as a double cover. They said this was to hide the womanly figure. It covered the shape of the breasts, and women could nurse discreetly under the folds. It was like a built-in nursing cloth. This was also heavily pinned into the waistline belt, which was sewn into the dress. I bet there are another six to ten pins that had to be shoved into that area. The final addition was the apron. For church, the women pinned up the white capes and aprons, so the white apron over the top of the cape wrapped around and pinned in place. I must have had about fifty pins all together and being poked by a pin now and again presented a possible annoyance.

One might think that I was annoyed or allowed that to hinder my Amish progress. Not a chance. I think Mark was hoping I could see how stupid that part was. He was wrestling with his new sleek pants. When he had to go to the bathroom, he had to try to figure out how to open the broad fall pants. There were about three buttons under the flap and four buttons across the belt-line to open for any emergency, which would become an emergency just by the fact that he had to go through so many buttons just to pee. Later, he told me he was mad. I didn't know since I wasn't there in the bathroom. He passed the line of men. They were all kissing each other. A line of men, about 100 feet long, standing in black Amish suits with the black hats, kissing. Mark was glad he was not Amish at that point. It is customary when meeting for church to kiss each member—on the lips! The men only kiss the men on the lips, and the women only kiss the women on the lips. They call it the "Holy Kiss." It is mentioned in the Bible, and they treat that as proof enough that it needed to be religiously practiced. I didn't get kissed that day. The women just shook my hand.

About nine o'clock in the morning, all the Amish quietly walked toward the basement after the kissing had commenced. We were led to the basement (where I had showered off my chicken lice a month before), but this time it looked completely different. There were wooden benches lined up tight like sardines with one aisle down the middle.

The Secret Meetings & The Holy Kiss

Like the schoolhouse, there were men on one side while the women and children were on the other side. They said it made it less temptation for sin. What? Seriously? I was thinking, how do you sin if you sit next to your husband? I figured it made more sense to sit with my husband because of the little children. He could help me manage them. Our children were thankfully already trained to sit still. I brought little quiet things for them to touch and play with in their hands, or they fell asleep in my arms.

It was three hours of sitting straight up on a hard, wooden bench listening to ministers that didn't speak a word of English. The songs, in the beginning, were drawn out as long as they could and sounded like an ancient Gregorian Chant. One Amish man started the phrase, and each syllable of the German was brought up and down with the voice at different pitches that sound very melancholy and sad. But I was right into it and could mimic it perfectly. It was still the most amazing dream for me. Lost in the not-so-harmonious nor enchanting voices, I was in a trance. I thought half of the people were tone-deaf. Mark was sitting over there with his eyes wide as saucers, staring around, and I could read his mind. He was thinking, "If this isn't a cult, I don't know what is!" In his mind, not only did he have to be looked at as some sort of weirdo to them, but he also had to endure the tortures of listening to a language he couldn't understand. What could be worse in his mind? But for me, I loved the vintage culture. And this was the height of old-timey culture.

When the people became thirsty, they walked to a sink and used the same tin cup. Young and old, sick and well, they all had that lone cup. I thought I would sooner die of thirst than ask for sickness by sharing with the entire church of the same cup. It was there that I realized I was a germaphobe, and kissing on the lips and sharing cups was not the way of a germaphobe. After long sermons of three different ministers, they announced something. In a flash, everyone turned entirely around in the opposite direction and immediately dropped to their knees on the concrete floor. It was a long prayer, and my knees weren't used to the cold concrete. That was the first time I had heard a prayer out loud, but it was only done out loud in the church by an Amish ordained minister from the casted lot. When they all stood up at the end, and the service was concluded with another ancient song, we all filed out of there. It was claustrophobic too. There on those benches, we were squeezed into each other so tightly, we could smell our neighbor. Some of the Amish I knew were pretty cleanly. They showered regularly, but there were those that I don't think ever knew about deodorant. I smelled many armpits that day, mainly because I was so short and at the eye level of most armpits. Because of my height, I have also been tucked into many people's armpits for a hug. Thankfully, the Amish women I didn't know wouldn't hug me.

I was a bit foreign to them. Many of them stared down their nose at me like I was some piece of trash. It was there that I realized fitting into the Amish wasn't going to be all cake and pie. It was going to be a challenge to win the church's favor. And the church still had to decide together on a vote if Mark and I could even join. I knew Mark did not want to join, but I never told them that. I wanted them to all believe it was our sincerest hope that we could join the church and raise our family as tried and true Amish. What I figured was that I could somehow convince Mark as time went on.

The men started loading the benches on top of each other to make these long picnic tables. These benches served a two-fold, innovative purpose. The women were busy slicing the homemade bread we were silently required to bring. On went the fake cheese spread in big tubs, sugary peanut butter in another tub, pickles, jams, and plates full of sliced bread. This was our lunch. One announcement in German and every head bowed in unison for silent prayer. The people started shuffling into the benches at the table, squeezing in as many as they could. There were about fifty people at one time smearing different stuff on their bread before cramming it into their mouths. I bet they were all so hungry and bread with these nasty-looking spreadables hit the spot. When it came time for us to sit at the table, they proceeded to add more water to each of the cups.

You didn't get new cups nor fresh water. You had to drink from the same cup as the shift before. I wanted to be on the first shift, but since I wasn't, I just decided that I was not thirsty. The cheese spread seemed like the only viable option because peanut butter didn't seem right to have Karo syrup and marshmallow fluff in it. I put a thick layer of this plastic-looking cheese onto my slice of bread, and to my surprise, it was pretty good. One portion of that was enough for me.

As I walked away from the table with my three little ones searching for my husband, I saw a few children holding puke bowls and looking very sickly. Images of the lone cup, the kissing, and the shared drinking glasses at the table flooded my mind, and I was a bit concerned. Whatever was going around; I found out, goes around. In community life, everyone shares in the work, the companionship in joy, and all the sickness taking the good with the bad.

In the afternoon, we did what the Amish always do. All the families branch off into their closer-knit family groups to relax and have fellowship. They pop popcorn and have a slow afternoon gathering together. We were invited to the Bontragers' home, which happened to be the same place that day. Rosa was off making some mint tea that she freshly picked from her garden beside the house, while we all huddled around the warm-fired air that rose from the massive iron floor grate. The popcorn was sprinkled with sour cream and onion powder, and everyone reached into the same bowl. Only thoughts of germs plagued my mind, yet I reached in because there was trust between us.

In the corner sat a little older, but still a strong man named Ivan. Ivan was what they all called the ape-man. His arms were longer than his body, his fingers short and fat, his teeth spaced like a chimpanzee, with hair growing over his face except for his eyes. His beard was one of the longest-furled beards of all the men, mostly gray with strands of black running through it. Those ears pushed straight out. His brow was longer than his nose, and it loomed over his sunken eyes, and the hair of his brow was thick, and hairs went in every direction. When they all asked him to do the chimpanzee, he sprung to the floor with his arms hanging in front of him. Curling his lips under so all we could see his spaced teeth, he made monkey sounds as we all rolled in laughter. I had tears because, strangely enough, I had learned about all the false cavemen the textbooks made to look half-ape and half-man was now staring at me from the middle of the floor. He must have been the missing link for the proof of evolution. Only the evidence would have to be millions of years old to be accurate; otherwise, it could not support the theory of when we started to walk upright and go from ape to man.

Then Harry started to pull up Ivan's pants leg to show us his abnormal growth. Harry, laughing, said, "Oh, look, Ivan's bagging up!" He said this as he began to demonstrate milking that thing hanging from his leg. It did look like a teat of an animal, but they just called it a straight-up "pig's tit." These Amish farmers were crude in a lot of ways. They said the "s" word for poop like it was normal. I laughed half the time because I just couldn't believe how they talked. In the hilarity of it all, I felt like I was with family. My relatives growing up would have been just as crude because they were the old-fashioned farmers, and that must have been a part of the culture of yesteryear. My belly hurt from laughing so hard, and I glanced over at my husband, who I had never seen laugh so intensely. He was doubled over, staring at Ivan when Ivan came to formally introduce himself, "So, I hear about you. You must be Mark." He looked up because he was shorter than I was. He stroked his long beard and held it there with his round stumpy hand. "I'm Ivan, Ezra's brother. Do you work construction?" Mark responded with a nod, and soon he was given a job. Ivan needed a driver, and his last English driver was a drunk, so Mark fit the bill. He could have a good worker and a ride. Milo also worked on the crew with another young guy named Danny Ray.

Trying to keep my husband from embarrassing himself, I pulled Milo aside with us and asked about that holy kiss and how it weirded us out. Milo laughed, saying, "Ya. You'll have to do that when you join. Man, today, this old guy was visiting from Indiana, and he wrapped his greasy lips around mine!" As he giggled and shook his body with a bit of disdain, I glanced over to find my husband looking more like he swallowed a ghost. Forget any chance of joining after that story. My husband was not up for that dreaded holy kiss, much less greasy lips of men he didn't know.

Later was the evening singing. The singing was for the "young folks." The young folks consist of the young unmarried adults and teens. They all line up at a table to play cards and then sing, facing those of the opposite sex. I imagined this was one way they got to know their future mates. This time all the woman sat on one side on benches and the guys on the other side facing the table line with the young folks. They first had a full-scale Amish meal with all the fixings and desserts. Large casserole pans filled with potatoes, meat, and cheese, bowls filled with salads, pies, and puddings, cakes of all sorts. This meal was like a lavished royal feast. Everyone filled their plates. The young men first, then the men, then the young ladies and children. Lastly, we old fraws, which was the natural order of things among the Amish. The songs were sung in English, which surprised me. They were hymns and other spiritual themes. It was quite lovely. Anytime it was quiet, we could hear the loud hiss of the gas lights. They stood over propane tanks with tall metal posts. These lights lit a room far brighter than a standard light bulb. The only drawback was that they gave off a lot of heat. If a fire was roaring and those lights were blazing, we'd be sure to sweat. A room full of sweaty Amish was not always the best situation. Of course, I was in love with all of it.

We started getting invited for such winter activities as skating and even the ice cream suppers. Beyond the field, they flooded the valley, so the ground became a thick, smooth layer of ice. Perfect for ice skating. Mostly the young folks got together for the skating about one night a week. It was their social time. One particular evening, Mark and I drove to Ezra's for supper. Mark stayed there with the children, and I rode in the buggy with Milo and Elvesta, their youngest two. I strapped on my skates and went out there trying to keep up with the rest of them. A tall skinny kid named Enos Lee came swooping, weaving in and out of all the girls and boys forming the line in the middle. It was the caught line. I got caught, and as I started making my way to the line, Enos Lee ripped past, and before I could think, I was face-up on the ice staring at Milo trying to rescue me. He lifted me, and I brushed off the snow, tried to toughen up, and carry on with the skating. You read old stories of these sorts of things, these positive things people used to do in the good old days. It was the life that I always dreamed of. Taffy pulls, ice cream socials, ice skating, hot chocolate, soup, sleigh rides, and building snowmen were all the things that make winter cozier.

Allen and Elsie invited us over for fellowship more and more. They were becoming very disillusioned by their Amish heritage. Elsie had a tape recorder. She made a black coat with buttons to cover her pregnant belly, and they had some outlawed photos of their family that they tucked in the top drawer of the dresser. Allen told us with tears in his eyes that he had trusted Jesus for his savior. He told us about the horse idolatry he had that brought him to the desire for repentance. God struck some of his prized horses down dead, or so he said. He said God was trying to get his attention.

One horse was struck dead in the field by lightning. The other was his buggy horse. That one got off of the hitching post one evening while he and his family were visiting another family. The horse and the buggy raced out to the highway and into an unsuspecting couple who were driving, and it killed them all. I knew the passion they had for Christ. I could see it in their eyes. They didn't want a vain and empty list of rules; they wanted to be ruled by God. It wasn't long before they were in the ban, too. I tried to convince them not to do things against their church to start with because the way the Amish see it is disobedience. They weren't getting banned for Christ. They were getting banned for the little things that they did that were against the rules. It wasn't right for the case of Christ. We heard stories of other families that left the Amish, and they told me it was all starting with faith in Jesus alone. They got this spiritual connection to God, and they saw it as a vice that pulled them closer to the world.

I could see it both ways. To be an excellent testimony to their people, they should abide by the things they were accustomed to until they were cut off. It just clouded over their faith choice and made it look altogether rebellious. The other Amish thought when you started going on about your deeper faith in Christ, they just knew it would lead to rebellion in the end. They said that their people who started that way ended up in divorce, the women chopped their hair, the men shaved their faces, got vehicles, and soon the future generations weren't even practicing Christianity. Allen and Elsie were so upset about the rules that had no biblical origin. I could also see that. They would argue, "The Bible does not tell us what pattern of clothing. It doesn't say we can't drive a car. God does not tell us to use buttons or pins." We saw them get into heated debates over these rules, and it always brought more and more division. Here we were trying to find community in a place where people were going their ways.

Soon we came to find out, Freeman, one of the Amish ministers, was also having these ideas of a deeper faith in Christ. We began to meet in their homes secretly. It was a very unorthodox thing to meet privately about Jesus. It made us all feel like we were hiding away and sneaking around with our outlawed faith. No one was supposed to know. We had Allen's, Melvin's, Freeman's, and us all gathering in the name of Jesus, and I was caught in a fierce battle between families. I was hearing gossip on both sides and felt like I was a spy. I could report or not report those things I was hearing. Who could I trust? Would I blow their cover and get us all put in the ban? Discussing such weighty matters was just what I loved doing, but I wasn't taking sides at that stage. Mark was leaning farther away from joining the Amish as the others told us NEVER to join and that our faith would be silenced the second we got sworn into their church as a full-fledged member, even if we even could.

The Secret Meetings & The Holy Kiss

We had various guests coming to our secret meetings. One, in particular, was a very tall African man who was named some kind of prophet. Miles had never seen a black man, and the Amish called him colored, which was kind of strange and seemed prejudice. Were the Amish against the people of a different color? I aimed to find out. Miles marched ahead of us, and he stared at the man with dark skin. As Miles furrowed his brow, we all thought he was going to comment on his darker skin, the color of skin he had never seen until that day, but he instead asked, "How come your teeth are so white?" Our nerves settled as we all burst into laughter at his question that was so innocent and true. Against the darkness of his skin, the teeth shone so brilliantly white. He came to all of our homes, and we had many secret meetings until he had to return for his family in Africa.

At one particular meeting that brought us over a hundred miles away, we met other Amish families fleeing their churches for similar reasons. Now, I must tell you; this family was unaware that we were never actually Amish. When we walked in, the man of the house walked up to my dear husband and kissed him right upon his lips. Mark didn't see this coming, so his head jolted back with fright, and his eyes widened more than I'd ever seen them go. The man was just being polite and still accustomed to the Amish way of doing things. He likely never knew that Mark was against such a practice, as it weirded him out completely. We still laugh about that story where Mark got kissed by a man, an ex-Amish man at that. I was sure Mark would take his stand against me now.

I admit that I sure was not an inviting bride. I remember how frumpy ugly I looked and how he had to drag me off to Walmart looking the way I did even as I held my head high, thinking that I was the most beautifully dressed creature in the world. He would always take another cart because to be with me would be to admit he had stolen the Amish wife off of some other man, and he was just the driver. He claimed I had a disease. He called it Amish-Mennonites. He no longer found me attractive. That was my goal. I wanted to be less attractive to men, so I would not be hurt any longer.

The long, drab nightgowns were another deterrent. One morning he was practically crying. Why did I not want him? Why was I so stubborn to dress in a way that he would have a hard time enjoying me? My past crept in again, and I needed to work harder to be a better wife to him. He said with sorrow in his breath, "I feel like you treat me like I am the pervert. Like I am the one who hurt you when I would never hurt you. I just want to be with my wife and wish that she wanted to be with me." It broke my heart. How could I make him feel this way? He had never hurt me, but he paid a lot less attention to me since I dressed so unfashionably Amish. His lack of awareness made me mad, and I felt I could only feel wanted if I was with the Amish. That was where I thought I belonged. But it was all wrong. I just needed to be the love of his life. It took me some time to break out of some of these things, but I had to start somewhere. I knew I needed a revival.

In between the secret meetings, I was still venturing to Amishland to help butcher and can meat with all my Amish sisters. Rosa invited me to help butcher a few hogs one frigid February morning. I was hovered over the carcass, stripping the flesh off the bone while talking about all the ways some of the people were rebelling against tradition. Maybel and I were taking trusted glances toward each other, not to reveal the secrets. All at once, I felt a jolt in my gut so severe; I had dropped to the floor. It felt like I had been kicked. Rosa told me to stay upstairs and rest and wait until Mark could get off work with the guys to come and pick the children and me up. I didn't want to stop working, but the pains were getting worse. By the morning, my eyes were matted shut with pink eye; I was vomiting and having massive cramping with bleeding. When I could take the pain no more, I asked my mom to come and get the children and me. She was always there at the drop of a hat.

Mark picked me up from her house, and we went straight to the ER. They said I needed emergency surgery. I had an ectopic pregnancy from what the ultrasound showed. I had to sign a paper to tell them where I wanted my baby's remains to be put. It seemed like we were going to kill my baby. Was this an abortion? What was going on? I never thought I would have my life in the balance where I had to choose between life and death. I heard people saying that abortion was only okay in the presence of a medical emergency to save the life of the mother. I had never understood what that meant until that moment, and it hit me hard. I said in desperation, both in pain and the pain of my pending decision, "Can't you just cut the baby out and implant him into my uterus?"

"No, that's impossible," they told me. I had to sign off on this surgery, knowing I would wake up not pregnant. Well, I didn't know

The Secret Meetings & The Holy Kiss

I was pregnant until that day, so all the news was sudden and hard to swallow. "Do you want to have the baby's remains sent to the funeral home? Or put into the public burial? Or would you just like to donate the fetus to science?" All of those options sounded impossible in my brain.

I grabbed the nurse's hand that was holding the clipboard with the paperwork. "Can I have my baby's remains to take home with me?" She rolled her eyes as if this was the first time anyone asked such a strange question, and she ran out to ask pathology.

"Um, well, I guess that will work," she returned. I was glad I could give my baby a proper burial just with our little family, who did not even know at that time. I hated it all. It all seemed grossly unfair. I had to choose my life because, in a matter of days, I would be dead along with the baby that would never survive outside the womb. I was only about eight weeks or less pregnant. They counted back as my eyes rolled back to sleep. In recovery, I laid there a bit out of it and waited to find out what happened. Strangely, they went in and found I had a grapefruit-sized cyst on my ovary, and it was not an ectopic pregnancy. They did a D&C and claimed I had passed all the remains of my baby at home. All that pain I was having was due to having a miscarriage. I was a bit relieved that I didn't have to be the deciding factor for my child's life and that God, in His infinite grace, worked it all out.

Soon after, I became pregnant with my fourth child. I was still struggling with inner shame, but I was crying out to God for some deliverance once again.

Chapter Fifteen
The Black Socks & the Angel

*A*t home, the feelings of loneliness prevailed. There I was pregnant and with three little ones, three and under. When I was home, I was alone in my heart. Those days when the Amish didn't invite me up for work were long. I didn't want to live fifteen miles from the nearest Amish. My husband was working from morning until night, and by the time he was home, he would work on our home. That spring, the butchering was through, and the gardens weren't even started. It was a slow time on the homesteads everywhere. I became restless.

I barely saw my husband. He rarely took notice of me. He was probably frustrated. What had his life become? I had no idea the thoughts going through his mind as he worked harder and seemed to ignore me altogether. He did not want the Amish life. I knew it, and it started to draw the life out of me. I put every inch of my soul into learning to become Amish, and I knew deep down that it might not happen. I became bitter toward the thing that kept me from the Amish—my husband. I wished him dead so I could just go and marry an Amish man. That thought started to haunt me each day as I became wicked in my imaginations. If I sat and tried to reason with him, Mark just stared over my head and wouldn't look at me.

One day, I asked him to get me a pair of socks because he was upstairs. He yelled downstairs in a very sarcastic tone, "You want

BLACK SOCKS or BLACK SOCKS, or how about some BLACK SOCKS?"

I fearfully answered, "Black socks are fine." I knew this was the turning point. He had bottled his hatred for too long, and it was bubbling over by this point.

"How did I guess????" He kept yelling, "I mean, who in their right mind would want to wear white socks? For heaven's sake, that would be a sin!" His voice kept increasing in decibel as he fumed every word, "Black socks are more HOLY. Of course. Yes, they are more humble, RIGHT????" He pounded down the steps and threw a wad of rolled-up black socks at me with all his might. I thought he was going to kill me first. Finally, the silence was broken. It was official. He hated how I was dressed. He walked towards me and said, "And those ridiculous dresses! They are butt ugly! But, of course, you think you are doing this for God!" I could tell my Amish days were numbered when all I wanted to do was be Amish. I prayed an Amish knight in shining buggy would come to rescue me so I could live my fairytale.

By this point, I had sold my soul to the devil. Every day I could, I would pack up the van and head off to Amishland for the day and stay until dark, just doing what I wanted to do. My marriage seemed in utter chaos, and I didn't care. There were such deep-seated bitter memories I was pulling to the forefront of my mind. Mark never protected me. When his mom or step-mom or anyone would attack me, which happened more often than I like to admit, he would just sit there and watch. You would think he would've stood up for me, would've helped fight any non-physical battles that would leave me wounded for days. I could hardly handle the darts, but I wanted a hero. My past came up like it always had of coming up in my mind. I was a prisoner to it once again, shackled in shame. The old tapes of vial pornography kept replaying in my mind. I would even hit myself in the head, trying to get rid of those visions. I hated my mind. It seemed to be flooded with impure thoughts, and I felt like I was on the road to hell.

"I will find an Amish man to run away with!" I blurted out one day as we were brushing shoulders, ignoring each other in the laundry room. I waited for a look of jealousy. I waited for anger; for something!

Instead, he stared at me with this expression, I will never forget. "Oh, that's stupid. You shouldn't do that, Erin." It was like a father to a daughter or a schoolmaster to the pupil. Oddly enough, I listened. I just obeyed, and the feelings I once had gone away in that instant. I'm not sure why I sobered up so fast. No one ever knew, and I never told anyone, so my sin could stay hidden.

We moved up to this little camper for the summer while Mark built a cabin for my parents in Goodman, WI. Our family and Ivan's crew were there. Elvesta came to help be the camp cook. They worked all day, and we planned breakfast, lunch, and dinner over a tiny camper stove. It was fun as long as I was with the Amish. We took the children to swim each day, and as hard as I tried to hold on to the simple Amish lifestyle, I knew it was slipping away. My heart was broken. Elvesta could not understand because she was raised Amish. I didn't choose where I was born, and my obsession with being Amish was the one thing that the devil used to try to destroy me.

One week when it was just the guys, I was crying and took Mark aside, "Please. Please. Please," I begged on my knees, pregnant and desperate, as I continued sobbing. "I will die if I can't become Amish. It's the perfect way to raise a family, and we are a testimony to them for Christ." Right there, I was grasping for straws. Christ wasn't in it at all. My heart was so far from Him. The Amish were like a cruel addiction, like the alcoholic begging for another drink from the bottle or they will die, I was begging for the thing that would slowly kill me spiritually.

His head was facing down by this time, and as he drew his heavy head up, he said, "I can't. I can't. If I join the Amish, I would be giving up my faith in Jesus. I can't do that." There were wells of tears in his saddened eyes. I could see that this wasn't just about me. His honesty was so sharp; it was like a sword that pierced through my heart. Forcing this humble creature to submit to my dreams was not at all what I wanted. Deep down, I knew that I would have to give up. I couldn't just then, but everything at that moment seemed to me like I wasted thousands of hours learning something that I will never live, which was a lie. I just needed to find Jesus again in the mire I was wallowing in.

As time rolled on, I became numb, just staring blankly ahead as I had already died. I was only in a shell of my body, and that body was vexed with the pains of a growing womb. Since the fall two years before when I was pregnant with Megan, my broken pelvis started to feel like it was drawing apart, and the pain had made it hard for me to walk.

It was winter, and the cold of the outdoors could not compare to the coldness of my heart. Death was something I coveted, for I thought

Memoirs of a Keeper: Angels & Demons

I was worthless again. I thought the world would be happier without me in it. How could I forget all that God did to save me? Why was I so blind to all that I had to be thankful for?

One cold evening, when I could hardly walk, I went outside to die! I jumped into a snowbank and offered my body to the subzero temperatures. My husband came searching for his wife, calling desperately for me. And when he found me there, he sat there nearly crying, begging me to live. I screamed, "NOOOO, leave me; let me die!!!!" And he picked me up in his strong arms and carried me kicking and screaming back into the warmth of our home. He held me in his arms and said how much he loved me, how he would die to protect me, how he would lay there all night outside if he had to keep me from freezing to death, that my purpose in this life was not over. He was able to see me as something I was not: a pure and precious gem.

Later, I met this man who was working with Mark on a job. Something drew me to him. He looked at me and told me, even as I smiled, that there was a sadness in my eyes. It was like a gift. I opened up to this person I didn't even know, and he told me how sinful I was. ME, sinful? I was sinned against as an innocent child. I was rejected by nasty people. I was hurt and in pain. How could I be blamed for this? I was so mad at first. He told me that I was so focused on "ME" that I put "MYSELF" over everything and on the throne.

He said this because I was telling him, "I'm home all day taking care of these kids, and my husband comes home and is too tired to help. What about me? I am tired! I want to raise my kids Amish; my husband won't allow me to do this. What about my dreams? What about how I feel; they are my kids! I have been through so much. I, I, I, and what about ME? ME, me, I, me, ME, ME, ME!!!!!!" That was my sin. Depression is selfish. When you are depressed, you can only think about yourself – about poor and unfortunate – you. I was seeking my way. He forced me to look at my heart. I hated him for it, but I realized later, as I thought about it, that as a Christian, I am not here for ME. I am here for a purpose. Christ did not come to die so that I could worry about ME. The scars were deep. I needed a miracle. I felt like when I got rid of the one demon a couple of years before, and I had made room for a whole pack of them. It was far more profound than a realization. It was demonic.

I had gone to a big event at a local church. There was a man

The Black Socks & The Angel

there who was a witch doctor, a shaman from Venezuela, who had gotten saved. He had a special gift to see into the spiritual. He gave his life to Jesus, and he could tell just by looking at a cartoon for kids if the devil inspired it. Chief Shoe-foot was his name. He was nearly seventy years old at the time, and he could speak no English. As he shared his testimony in front of thousands, the interpreter would tell us in English what he was saying.

I was broken. I looked Amish. I was a mental case. I was a mess. I just nearly killed myself because I was so depressed that I realized I needed this man to see me and to look into my eyes and tell me what he saw. Would he see past my smile and my plain dress? Would he see my heart, the cold and desperate heart that needed hope again? I waited until all the others left the building until he was standing alone beside his interpreter. I had grievous sins and bondage of selfishness and lust, secrets from things I had seen in my youth that I could not get out of my mind, and it was killing me. I was a prisoner. I was stuck, and I needed to move on from that point. My family depended on it. The chief took one look at my smile, and he searched beyond my eyes.

"Your heart is a heart bound in darkness like a cloud covers the light," he said without hesitation through the interpreter, "God shall deliver you and your heart will be free, and the light will one day shine for all to see." As quickly as he spoke those words, he left the room, and I stood there searching my heart for any possible way of finding my freedom. In my desperation to find my cure, I wrote a letter to a Miss Donna Glee who was the wife to David Glee. They wrote articles and books for a family ministry. It was an ugly letter. I told her about all I had stored up in my mind. I told her there was no excuse, and even though my innocence was taken from me at such a tender age, I couldn't live like that any longer. She didn't know me at the time, but she said that she wrote with tears in her eyes because she grieved for me. She gave me her husband's preaching CD to listen to called "Sin No More" and that I should listen to them three times over. I did. But nothing yet. I knew that I was redeemed. I knew that I could have power. All my realizations became more apparent to me that I was a child of God. I wanted to be free.

Still, the pain from my shattered pelvis worsened that I felt was unbearable. The injury from falling down the steps with my previous pregnancy was coming unglued with the growth of my newest child. I held my hands over my enormous belly, my dear husband trying to figure out a way to carry the load of three little ones, a bedridden wife, and a child on the way. The weight of everything was on him. He had to put food on the table. He could see the mounting bills, the wind and cold blowing outside, and a wife that couldn't get out of bed.

He cried out for reinforcement. With three children under four, he needed someone to help. Two Amish girls came to stay at the house and care for the things of the home. I felt so bad to put this all on his shoulders, but as the baby grew in my womb, the bones were pulling apart again, causing a high level of pain. I couldn't shift weight on my feet at all. It was just one of those impossible situations. I had a hospital bed in my living room because I could not climb the steps to our bedroom. There I sat for months waiting for my baby to deliver me from that pain. The Amish girls would cook and clean and take care of the little ones. I sat in the bed since I could not lie down. I had a toilet beside the bed and a walker. Many people came to pray for me.

As I lay in that hospital bed in my pain, and in my desperation, I cried out to God. I begged Him to free me, not from my pain, but my dark-covered heart. I wanted to have joy. I wanted to lead my children in joy and bring the new one into the world with peace, gratefulness, and thanksgiving. It was a struggle for me ever to be happy. I just couldn't let go of my past.

One day, Molly, my little girl who was barely three years old, who could barely speak in complete sentences, toddled over to my bedside. Mark was sitting on the edge of the bed as this came forth from her lips, "Mommy, Jesus told me that you are going to die this Thursday!" She said with such clarity of speech. It was creepy. She shuffled off like she didn't say one word to us. With a tear-stained face, I looked up to my weary husband, and as our eyes met, we blinked a few times from the shock of those words. What did our little girl just say? It freaked us out. Here I was in that hospital bed only a week away from my due date. And she doesn't even speak in sentences and especially not with such gravity about death. Molly was just a little girl.

I called my mother, a nurse at the time, and told her about what Molly said and she was just as freaked out because she went to see a palm reader. She knew I disagreed with consulting palm readers, so she didn't tell me. Later she said to me that the palm reader could find information on her life and my brothers, but when asked about my life, the palm reader said, "I'm sorry, I cannot see anything on your daughter, for she is covered in blood." Well, my mother assumed I was going to hemorrhage and die from losing blood. But because obviously, that did not happen, the blood was seen in the spiritual realms as a covering, the blood of Christ. It was literal blood on my account. No evil could touch me because I was under that blood. I was excited that she said that, because it was a pretty cool validation for the reality of the protection I had in Christ, under His shed blood.

Around the same time, my help dried up. It was early January, and I had no one who could keep helping. Mark had to stay home from work to care for me because I couldn't be left alone with the little ones.

BUT that was not the end. I did get scared, of course. And my mother thought I was a goner, in a blood bath. Wednesday night, I sat in my bed with tears streaming down my face, and I begged God for a miracle. I had no idea what Thursday would bring or if I would even live to tell this story today. I had no promise of another day and a foreboding feeling that something would happen the next morning. I proclaimed, "Jesus, I know You are my healer, I know You are my deliverer and my redeemer. I trust that you can do all things. My life is in Your hands, and I pray for Your will to be done." I remember the feeling of God whispering in my heart that He would make His power known. And that it had to come through my head, my husband.

That long night rolled on. I lay there completely awake. Thinking. Praying. Wondering. While it was still dark, I heard the creak of the steps as my husband started to descend. I turned my head to see him standing there on the steps with his arm stretched out. His finger was pointed right at me. His eyebrows were furled, and he looked mad. In a voice like thunder, he said, "GET UP AND WALK!!!!"

I felt a surge run through me, and I did get up that same instant. I got up, and I walked for the first time. No pain. No nothing! I had varicose veins the size of a golf ball in a very intimate spot, and they were also gone in that instant. I walked to the bathroom shaking. My husband followed me, and he started crying and fell to his knees, praising God. My husband typically shows zero emotion. He doesn't get giddy or mad quickly; he just sits like a statue. So this was out of character. We both held each other and cried tears of joy.

Not only did God heal my body, but He also healed my mind! It was like everything was washed clean. I was able to feel the darkness flee, and instead, the LIGHT, the glorious light of Jesus, rush through. I started to clean my house and immediately burned all the poetry and painting and writings I did in that state of depression. I burned it all. Mark gladly took each article from my hand and brought it out to the burning barrel. No more. No more of the bondage. I was finally FREE. That was the first of the wave of miracles.

I went up to the Amish and was leaping for joy, and some fell to the ground praising God. They could see that God healed me. Others stood there with their arms folded, and they said, "Maybe you were never in pain to start with!" Some said, "Why did God heal you, when others out there, like mothers dying from cancer, don't get healed? Why you? Why wouldn't God heal them? Your thing wasn't that bad!" Yet others stood in disbelief because the alternative would be to realize and perhaps admit that all the motions they went through and the stubborn pride of their culture could be in vain. If Jesus is real, then we could know Him personally, and there would be no need to try to earn our way in. His payment was enough to settle the debt we owed. We could trust in the finished work of the cross! A gift! Nothing we could do to earn it! It was a testimony of the greatness and realness of God.

I went to the health club with the kids to play with them. I felt so good even though I was nine months pregnant. I jumped on a giant trampoline in my Amish dress! When God heals, He heals.

A few short days later, I felt the pressure of birth coming on. Mark whisked me away to the hospital. I had wanted a home-birth, but no midwife would touch me. I was too much of a risk. There was a reason why this all happened just as it did. I wanted to be like all the other moms I knew and birthed at home. There was a rite of passage for those who did this. It was like a club. They all shared about their home births, and I just sat back, shrunk down in my chair as I admitted my lack of faith and said, "I had mine at the hospital!" God had a reason He protected me from my home-birth dreams. I still think home-births are fantastic if you can have them, but sometimes God has another plan and instead cancels our plans.

"Be Thou My Vision," I sang as I rolled my body upon the birthing ball in my little dark hospital room. I sang hymns with all my heart. I sang so loud that I wanted the entire floor to hear my praises. I was healed. God was–and is–real! They must've thought, "Who is that crazy lady down there?" God just miraculously healed me, and I could

The Black Socks & The Angel

not contain myself. If God can fuse bones and take varicose veins away in an instant, that's a miracle. Even my doctor said it was a medical miracle.

The time was at hand. I usually had to have all the drugs to help with the birth pain because each of the other births posed complications. This time I was going ALL NATURAL. No drugs. My water broke on its own for the first time, and I was finally put into the bed to prep for delivery. The nurse told me, "Stop pushing! The doctor is on his way!" Stop pushing? NO. I was ready; that baby was coming with or without the doctor. Mark held me around my shoulders, trying to help comfort me as I pushed out the baby. All wet and slippery, I saw him and grabbed him up in my arms. I sat there cuddling the slimy, little, precious one. The doctor came in to make sure all was well and said, "Looks like you had two miracles this week. Congratulations on a perfect little boy!"

I held the little boy, and we named him Michael Stephen Harrison. He was perfect in every way. I gazed into his little eyes, and he was just so peaceful. Wrapped in a little blanket, I clutched him close as I nursed him. It was around six p.m., and my mother was anxious to bring the little ones out to see their new baby brother. Miles was so concerned for his baby brother. He told the nurses, "Don't suffer him. Be careful with him!" Suffer meant, to Miles, to suffocate.

After the three little proud siblings made their way back home, Mark and I remained in the dimly-lit hospital room. All at once, a nurse came in and stood at the foot of the bed. She was all drill sergeant-like with her clipboard in hand peeking at us over her bifocals. Her hair was really short and curled close to her head. She was plump and had to have been in her fifties.

"Listen to me. Do not place the baby in bed with you. Do not feed him after eight p.m., either. When you're done feeding him, you must wrap him in a blanket and place him in the cart beside the bed." She was not through with her instructions. "Right at midnight, you need to ring the nurse's station because they will need to take an "Empty-stomach-weight."

What was this? I never heard of this empty-stomach-weight test. I snuggled with the baby, just thinking that I better listen to this nurse. I was afraid that if I did something against the rules, I would have my kids taken from me. So I fed him at eight p.m. and wrapped him gently in his blanket and placed him softly into the carrier beside my bed. Usually, I would have had the baby in bed with me at all times. I wanted the baby close to me and to feel warm. I couldn't take a chance. I sat, waiting for that clock to strike midnight so I could call them in, and I could hold him again. It was all so strange. Mark was just lying on the cot on the other side of my bed, sound asleep at the time. The room was dark. But the light that shone from the clock was dim.

I dozed off for a minute and awoke with a jolt. I was afraid I missed the clock. I peered through the darkness and saw the hand click into place—it was midnight. I immediately pushed the nurse button. "Can I help you?" came over the loudspeaker of my room. "Yes. It is time. You wanted to do that empty stomach weight on my baby at midnight so you may come and get him." Then silence for a moment.

"What? I never heard of this order," exclaimed the nurse in surprise, and I followed sharply, "The nurse told us!" She quickly responded to keep the peace, "Okay, we will be right down to get him!" I looked over my baby. The room was still dark. He appeared to be sleeping to me and was so peaceful. The nurse came into the room and grabbed the handle of the cart that contained my son, and she wheeled him out into the hall.

Time passed, and I became unsettled. Fifteen minutes later, I rang the button again, wondering what the holdup was. "Can I help you?"

I returned, "Yes. Is my baby done getting weighed. I would like to feed him," thinking he was half-starved to death. "We will be right down," the voice said. A nurse came in looking half startled, half under control as she very seriously told us, "Ma'am, we're doing everything we can." Those were the words that communicated to a person that things were pretty bad. My heart started to race as I continued to listen to her. "When we got him, he wasn't breathing. You need to come out here right now."

Mark helped me into a wheelchair and wheeled me down the hall to a glass window that revealed a team of doctors surrounding my lifeless son. There he lay, white as dust and dead as could be. Electric paddles were being applied to his little chest. With every thud, his small body would jerk. I couldn't stop the tears pouring down my face. I could see the tiny coffin that we would put him in; I lived through the funeral in my mind. I could've sat there wondering why I was healed for this? Why would God show His power to give a miracle to bring death to our home? How come I came through the fire unscathed to be burned by the dart of death's cold sting? How could I have tasted of the grace of God to have it ripped from under me? BUT I did not. Instead, I knew, I just knew that if God healed me, He also had a plan. I uttered in a feeble voice, "The Lord gives, and the Lord takes away; Blessed be the Name of the Lord!"

I asked Mark for my Bible. As they worked tirelessly for what seemed a long time, I read the 23rd Psalm, "Yea though I walk through the valley of the shadow of death, I will fear no evil…" I started to sing a hymn. How could I sing when everything was good but not still sing in my most resonant moment of loss? I sang, "Be Still My Soul." Over and over, as every tear dried from my face, I was filled with hope.

Just then, I heard it through that peace from Jesus, that beep. And then another beep. Beep. Beep. Beep. He was raised from the dead. My little boy was alive!!!! We didn't know if he would stay alive, but his heart was beating softly again, and he was now on life support. We didn't know if the twenty to thirty minutes, his heart was not beating, or longer if he would have brain damage. No one knew but God. We just knew, for sure, that God had a plan.

They took him in an ambulance to another, much larger hospital. Mark and I followed in our car. When we found him, he was lying there with heart scans being pulled up on screens overhead. The woman specialist told us at that moment, "Your son has an exceedingly rare heart defect. It is called Transposition of the Greater Arteries, or TGA. In short, his heart is hooked up backward. The arteries that are supposed to be crossed lie parallel and the blood is circulating from the heart and only back to the lungs instead of to the rest of the body, including the brain. It is the most fatal of heart defects, and until recently, it has been undetected. Most babies would just simply die, and the cause of death was unknown. 99% of the time, this condition is caught on ultrasound. All babies have a hole in their heart while they are in their mother's womb that naturally closes after six hours (which would have been midnight the night Michael stopped breathing). He was born at 6 p.m. That hole is meant for blood circulation through the placenta and umbilical cord to exchange oxygen to the baby from the mother. When that closes, the heart of the baby needs to take over that process. If the arteries of the heart are backward, as was in Michael's situation and which is the cause of TGA, when the hole closes, the heart continues to pump the blood in the wrong direction. So that is why the blood pumps to the lungs and not to the rest of their bodies. Do you understand?" I was dumbfounded, to be honest, but I listened. I deferred to her level of understanding. I answered, "Can it be fixed?" The doctor smiled, "Yes! I'm glad you asked. We just need to get him to a surgeon who has performed the arterial switch and have the procedure done." Michael was placed on a gurney, still on life support, into a helicopter traveling high in the air hundreds of miles away. Mark and I needed to drive down to Milwaukee Children's Hospital to meet him down there. As I looked up into the clouds, I prayed that they would safely guide the pilots to the destination and carry my precious cargo. Such a little one so far in the sky, like a star in the night. My little one was in the hands of God.

At the hospital, I sat by his side and kissed his precious little head. Wrapped in a web of wires to keep him alive those short days, God worked an even bigger hope in all of our hearts. We knew that this was not by chance like so many would like to say. This story was a miracle that cannot be refuted.

Now here is a humbling question; how did the nurse know? Later, when I asked the hospital to thank that nurse for alerting us, they did not have a nurse of that age or description. She didn't exist, according to the hospital staff. Nor did they ever hear of anyone giving those strict orders. For one, if I would've had my way, I would've had a home birth and been snuggled in my bed with the baby. Six hours later, he would have been swept peacefully to Jesus, and I would've had to live with the idea that I smothered my child. No one would have known. If the nurse didn't tell me to keep him out of my bed, the same end would've happened. I would have woken up in the night with a cold, lifeless baby! Only God knew!

We believe God sent an ANGEL or messenger to alert us. We believe there is no other explanation. All those stories of angels who look like baby cupids, with little wings to hold them in the air, have vanished from our reality as we saw this one that looked like an older lady. And only God knew the beginning from the end. He knew what we could handle and that I may not have been strong enough to take such a fate as that. Besides that, God has a unique plan for Michael's life.

The Black Socks & The Angel

There was a reason that Mikey did not have brain damage. His heart was fixed four days later by one of the best heart surgeons in the country. He came home four days after that. And now my son lives a normal life. This verse came to life for me, "The Spirit of the Lord is upon me, because he hath anointed me to preach the gospel to the poor; he hath sent me to heal the brokenhearted, to preach deliverance to the captives, and recovering of sight to the blind, to set at liberty them that are bruised." Luke 4:18

Memoirs of a Keeper: Angels & Demons

Chapter Sixteen
THE NEW BEGINNING

This is when I really felt my life begin again. It was a definite turning point. Everything before this time was dark, with rays of hope shining through to keep me from becoming completely lost. A candle was all I had within my grasp to light the way in a dark cavern. Now I felt that I walked out of the cavern and into the glorious light of the day. Everything seemed new, and it was there that I started to take hold of all that Christ had died to give me.

My past was like a corpse that I dragged around with me. I didn't have to. I chose to. The stinking, rotting poison of my past used to be there. Like a rotten piece of meat that you leave out, it doesn't take long to cause the entire house to wreak of it. It was something I was always reminded of everywhere I turned. God was there all along, loving me, protecting me, and ready to heal me. I just didn't want to trust Him enough to let Him carry the dead away. He gathered up the brokenness and shame that day and washed it away. I was new.

Was this the day that I actually got saved? No. I believe with all my heart that God saved me when I was only fifteen years old in my bedroom crying out. I may have been saved, but I was still allowing myself to be a prisoner to my past. This was the day I took hold of my salvation and lived in that redemption.

There I had these four beautiful little children, and I never really enjoyed them thoroughly. That morning I woke up, and I found an old bag of clothing from my time before the Amish phase took over my mind. It was like a switch went off. All the passion and purpose I had to be Amish vanished, and I wanted to be normal again. God fixed my mind. He rewired it to desire what I had instead of what was on the other side of the fence. I grabbed up a skirt and a shirt and slid them on. My husband woke up to see me standing there with white socks on, my long hair brushed and hanging over my back. The smile he gave me was my vote of approval. I hadn't seen that kind of smile for a couple of years. He pulled me toward him, and something happened inside me. I wanted him. I truly desired my husband for the first time, and we were a truly married couple. That feeling was altogether new and miraculous. There was no more shame or dirty feelings. No more tapes of disgusting pornographic images playing in the background; it was like a new mind. It was the mind of Christ.

Motherhood and being the keeper of the home became something that day. I danced through the house with true joy. My new baby was so good. He never cried. He had to be quite tough for all he had endured through those weeks before. My children's memories of a sad, distracted mother were wiped away. They danced with me, and we made our way to the kitchen to make breakfast. The life I had right around that table was finally what I wanted. Real joy comes when you enjoy what you already have. Each day seemed to be bursting with possibility.

That spring was altogether new. Adventure seemed to be around every corner on our little homestead. My art came back in the form of taking pictures of my children. We would spend hours playing outside, and I wanted to remember every inch of it. I started sewing prairie dresses for the girls with bands of lace over soft calicos and lots of beautiful fancy ruffles. Their lovely, soft blond curls were allowed to blow in the breeze. All the caps and tight braids, black socks, and drab dresses went out to the storage barn. We were free. Picking flowers in the field and just gazing at clouds was our dream together. I took photos of everything. Then I painted the pictures and hung them all over the walls.

My creative energies ran wildly. Together with my children, we wrote stories. One story we wrote was called "Broken Hearts." It was a story from Miles' perspective of his baby brother's heart surgery. I had documented the entire event in the hospital with my old 35-millimeter

The New Beginning

camera and the video recorder. My dad made a beautiful video, and I ended up donating a copy of my illustrated book to the children's hospital where it still is today. The newspaper came out and interviewed me, writing a story about our experience to help others going through similar things. They took a photo of me reading the book with my children huddled around me on the couch. A man who used to be one of dad's band students from long ago asked for a copy of my book. I couldn't believe he would want one of our books. I quickly printed off the photos of the pages and put them in a little photo album for him. He wanted to get to know us and hear our story. I invited him to our small homestead and made him a meal. As he sat at our table, he smiled so much that we lovingly called him our Uncle Smiley. He would come by and read stories to the children whenever he could take a ride out to our farm.

God always has a way that when one door closes, He opens others. We lost a lot of our Amish friends when they finally found out about our secret meetings. They had to put us all in the ban. I couldn't be around them anyway because I was different but a good different. When we lost a few friends, we found new ones. Uncle Smiley was a true friend, and he encouraged me to keep taking pictures. I found a new way to express myself and to share my gift with others.

Mark loved the new me. He also knew that I was the type of woman who needed to use my gifts. He bought me my first digital camera, and I started a photography business. Taking pictures of children, then families, graduation, and most of all, weddings were what filled our days. It was perfect, I could meet families at a park with my children, and I could take photos while they played. I got my first computer and learned how to make beautiful storybooks for everyone. My wedding business took off rapidly. Taking pictures for someone's most sacred day touched my heart deeply. It was like a date night. Mom would come out and watch the children one day of the week, and we were together snapping memories for others.

To our surprise, we were making a living doing wedding photos. My husband started to work on the video camera, and later I would edit the videos. People loved our work and lined up to book us years in advance. The beauty of this job was that during the week, I could be mothering, baking, sewing, and going on walks with my children, and one half-day a week, I would go with my husband to photograph a wedding. Many times as I was taking photos of the bride and groom exchanging vows, I would cry tears of joy for them. I wasn't just an ordinary photographer. I didn't want to force them to pose a hundred rigid ways. It was photojournalism, capturing the moment and the spirit of the people was what I did. It became like breathing for me, so natural. I enjoyed touching people's lives with a God-given gift to share.

That summer was filled with outdoor play and adventure. It was a hot summer day, just a typical day in the country where you could hear the high-pitched hum of the locusts. I was out on the deck, holding the baby, and the girls played in the sand. I wondered where that mischievous five-year-old boy of mine was. "Molly, have you seen Miles?" I asked with my eyebrow furled.

"No, but I think he might be helping Daddy because he said so," Molly said patiently as she poured a little bit more sand into Megan's cup. Miles was always running around the farm, looking for adventure and, of course, what could be more adventurous than helping Daddy dig a foundation for the neighbor? Daddy was a carpenter, and he was so good at building houses. By this time, I worried that little Miles would get hurt by the big backhoe, and because Daddy was so busy, he might not see him. Up I went with Michael on my hip. "Come along, girls, we have to find Miles!"

Molly and Megan picked themselves out of the sandbox, setting down their sandy tea party with sandy little teacakes, and brushed themselves off. The best of friends, Molly held out her hand for Megan. Off they went walking across the field to where they could see Daddy lifting dirt with his backhoe. So far, they didn't indicate that they saw Miles. My heart dropped as I examined the horizon for my lost boy. Surely, I thought, he couldn't be in that hole! My walk turned into a run, and six-month-old Mikey was along for the ride. His little fat body just jiggled on my hip as he enjoyed this new excitement. The little girls' walk turned into a happy, giggling skip. Not so for me, because I was sick with worry. As we climbed the big pile of clay and dirt that was about ten feet high, all I could do was to pray the Lord would help me find that boy alive.

Finally, atop the mound of dirt, as we looked down into the pit, there was Miles! He was snatching every snake in sight. There were snakes all over the place slithering into holes. Miles was stepping on their tails and grabbing them one by one. His face had a look of utter determination and complete thrill. After a few minutes, I said, "Miles, get up out of that pit right now!" I left out that he should leave the snakes there, so up he came with a half-dozen two-foot snakes! I hadn't the heart to tell him to let them go when I saw the unusually large smile that stretched across the boy's face. The snakes were curling around his neck and desperately trying to escape. At times the tails would braid themselves together and find their way around his arm like a cuff to his sleeve. We lived in Wisconsin, so I was not so worried about the snakes. They were garter snakes, which are not poisonous. Snakes were a regular find on the homestead for little boys like Miles. As he proudly marched to the house, he spotted a frog. Miles frequently put out frog traps, but since this was not in the trap, he moved quickly. With snakes wrapped all around, he bent down to capture the tiny creature. All that catching practice earlier paid off, because that frog was caught in one swipe.

  We all walked into the house with extreme excitement. The girls' eyes were full of amazement that their big brother could catch so many snakes in one day! I was rushing to set Michael in the swing so that I could grab my camera. I wanted to take a picture of Miles's catch of the day. As I turned on the camera to film this momentous time, Miles proceeded to pass out the snakes to each of his siblings.

  "Here's one for you," as he passed a big one to Molly as she happily wrapped it around her neck. "One for you, Megan," as she very carefully held it between her hands, not knowing what to do from there. "And....one for you!" He handed one to Michael in the swing, and no sooner did he grab its little head than he tried to put the snake into his mouth. I screamed and lunged to the rescue. Six-month-old babies put everything into their mouths, and a snake was no exception. I lovingly passed that snake back to Miles. Poor Mikey started to fuss because he was very excited to have his snake too.

  I had about enough of the snakes in my clean house because they gave off a terrible odor when trying to protect themselves. So, our snake-handling group went to the front yard. Well, Molly and Megan were not as slick with snake capturing as Miles, so the snakes were slithering off the back of their shoulders to the ground. "Girls, why are you letting those snakes get away?" yelled Miles. "You know how hard I worked to catch those?"

  The girls were screaming and crying for their loss of snake. Miles zipped over and snatched them up again and said, "This time, hang on to them!" In the corner of his eye, he spotted a bird. It was not just any bird; it was a Kestrel. Kestrels are a falcon-type bird of prey. They soar across the country sky, swooping down for meals consisting of lizards, snakes, frogs, or mice. Miles didn't want to pass up this opportunity to catch that bird! He looked at Molly for silent approval. And yes, Miles piled all the snakes and the frog on Molly as he dashed off to catch that Kestrel. To all of their amazement, Miles caught that Kestrel in one swoop, for it must've been a young one or perhaps it had been injured. All the same, Miles was proud of his newfound friend. He raced back to where we all sat in the grass and pleaded for us to go into the house where he could count his spoils. I wasn't in the least bit offended, for I thought it was a great thing that Miles brought this Kestrel to me. I loved seeing the bird up close, so off we went back into the house where Miles could count his animal collection in safety.

"One, two, three, four, five, six...snakes," Miles counted, "One Kestrel, makes seven," he paused as he pulled the frog out of his pocket. "One..." and as he was ready to make that final count, up came another frog out of the mouth of one snake! "Two frogs! That makes nine animals!" He said with excitement as the rest of the bunch looked on in disgust. After all, this frog was dead awhile. The interesting thing was that Miles had the whole food chain in one animal collection. He had the Kestrel that preys on snakes, and the snakes that prey on frogs.

After a long day of examining and exploring these fantastic creatures, the four little children washed their hands and talked of that adventure until the cricket's song replaced the locust hum.

Life was settling into such a beautiful, peaceful mode. All the peace and forgiveness I had burst out of my heart was raging to spill over to every lost friend; every relationship that had ever been broken. I knew all the mistakes I had made and the ways I focused on the negative things. Those who were in my life –like family – became family again since we were shut out from the community I had clung to; family became our community. Nana and Bumpa started having adventures with us. We would take the children on hikes all over the place, spend time up at their beautiful cabin in the Northwoods where they would bring them swimming, playing in the sand, and take them on boat rides. All those years when I didn't appreciate the adventurous nature of my parents, I got to relive through my children. We had the time of our

The New Beginning

lives.

Bumpa took Miles everywhere with him and under his wing, taught him how to hunt game and shoot guns.

Nana would laugh loudly as she would watch their fun. They were always the most amazing grandparents. The way they were with my children was perfect in every way. Making all the mistakes, I did while my children were even smaller and all the crazy addictions I had that nearly destroyed me gave me a way to see what I never saw before. It was grace. I had grace for all those things that might not have been good for me; God gave grace and mercy when I did something that was not so good for my family. I could see it full circle, and that was a mighty redemption. I started to see all the good things my parents did to shape me into who I was and not just the bad. God is good.

I could see the good even with Mark's mom. I embraced her with all my heart and looked to all the sweetness that she had within her. "Come live with us!" I told her. I wanted to take care of her and have her right in my home. Loving her was easy, and I knew she had a hard life, now was the time for her to feel wanted again. She gladly accepted, and we built on an addition to our home for her. She moved in, and we were all a big, happy family. That is true redemption when you can go from full rejection and bitterness to complete restoration of a relationship like we did. Her happiness was something I prayed for. She enjoyed the children. Watching her bounce the girls on her lap giggling and seeing her read to them warmed my heart.

It was all going smoothly until she started to notice that her son was not the type to sit and do devotions with his family each day. He had this strong feeling that he didn't want to cram Jesus and the Bible down his children's throats. Doing so might have the opposite effect. If he could teach them about Jesus along the way when we would go on our evening walks as a family, out in the garden, sitting around the table for a meal, or just whenever topics would come up, that was a more natural way to commune with God in his mind. One day I saw her gently set the children in a row on the couch for a Bible study. "If he can't, maybe I am here to be the one to teach them," she said with conviction. I could see this was going to come with resistance. Mark didn't want to do things this way, and by doing it, her way would only bring strife into our home.

When you live with someone, it's easy to see their flaws,

and those little things become more significant as time goes on. The honeymoon of happy family days had become silent battles between my mother-in-law and her son. Her extreme love for our family drove her crazy because she could see the things we were missing. She wanted to help change everything to be more glorifying to our God. Striving for perfection was just the thing we had run from when we closed the door to the Plain People and their rules. First, it was the Bible reading, which is understandable. I wanted that too, but I didn't want to be the spiritual leader. I had just fallen in love again with my husband, and the last thing I wanted to do was try to tear him down. She noticed the Mountain Dew bottles in his truck one day, and she cried. It broke her heart that he was poisoning himself, not to mention leaving a poor example of health and wellness for our family. I had long since given up that battle, but it was hard for me to even think about trying to change him. It reminded me of the times I looked at him the same way.

One day after reading a couple of self-help books on the wife's role in marriage, which were books I was interested in reading more than anything else besides the Bible, I stood guilty. She was not alone; I had pushed the health thing until I became the "Health Nut," too. Early in my marriage, I was like a tyrant in my kitchen, rationing, and commanding. I became controlling and downright angry when Mark didn't like my healthy food. I would force my family to eat strange things that just didn't taste good. It pushed my husband to have a secret stash of goodies that he could eat when I wasn't looking. And I would cry buckets of tears over the caffeinated soda, the boxed cereals, and the sweets in his glove box of the work truck. That was an unfortunate mistake. I wasn't being a loving wife. I was being a brutish woman, treating him as a child. That wasn't okay. It wasn't okay to cry over simple things like food.

It was a miracle he stuck with me when I was such a difficult woman, to begin with. I knew that I had ruled over my husband for years and all the ugly things I did were things I did in rebellion. There was no glory in putting myself and my needs above his. We were co-heirs. I went to my dear husband, apologizing, "I am sorry for being so crazy all those years and dragging you around for all of my dreams. I am sorry for making you feel like you were stupid for eating junk food, too. Since you are the leader of this home, I want you to know that you are free. You are free to buy and eat whatever food you want. I will no longer nag you and make you feel less of a man to the point you have to hide and sneak around to drink soda."

Little things like the constant noise of playing children caused my poor mother-in-law to place her hands over her ears for quiet started to ebb at our budding relationship living together. Soon we all decided that it would be better for her to find a place of her own. I didn't want her to feel like she couldn't escape the noise or the thoughts of her son consuming bad foods on occasion. That was no way for anyone to feel relaxed nor at peace. I soon found out I was expecting another baby, our fifth child. Even though we felt bad when we asked her to leave, I still wanted her to be close by and even invited her to be at the birth. She was precious to me, and having her there would make both of us feel God's healing redemption.

Memoirs of a Keeper: Angels & Demons

Chapter Seventeen
THE EULOGY & THE CULT

The neighbors down the road who gave us our first chickens invited us down one evening, and it was there that I met the infamous Jessie Bell. This hot-headed Sicilian firecracker came in my direction, smiling and talking a million miles a minute. Until that day, I had never met someone who could talk more than I could nor who was as crazy as I was. She instantly became like a sister to me. She wasn't much taller than I except much thinner with jet-black hair and dark eyes; she bounced from one side of the room, captivating the attention of all. I had met my match.

We were sisters in the Lord, which is the best kind of all. Hours of conversations on the phone and many more visits back and forth, both with our children, we were fast becoming like family. She told me her whole life story, and I told her mine when I could fit a word in edgewise. Strangely, we had similar faith stories. This lady didn't even graduate the eighth grade, yet she knew her Bible inside and out like a theologian. Her grammar was generally messed up when she talked, but it went along with her sense of humor.

No matter where we were if there was another breathing soul, she had to tell them about Jesus. She would first ask if they were Christians. If they said yes, the next question was always, what kind? Then, if that did not satisfy her, she would ask them if they were born again. She would talk so fast that I seldom could follow her myself and wondered if these people were left with a good understanding of Jesus or just were completely confused. I still admired her for it. Her passion for lost people was commendable and reminded me of a rescue fire-fighter running into the house as it nearly falls under the flames that consume them to carry out that one person who was trapped in there somewhere. She would find them. At times I would feel a bit embarrassed when she would interrupt people eating at fast-food restaurants and pull them into her usual evangelistic conversation starters.

    I would sit there trying to act like I was into it while still making sure to care for all of our children at the same time out of the corner of my eye. If I didn't contribute, I must not be as committed. It was that feeling you got when someone was so dedicated and passionate about something that you felt if you did not share in it, then you aren't one of them. I always wanted to be one of whomever I was around. It was my adaptability. I could blend in with anyone, but at times I didn't want to be one of her. She seemed to make people feel uncomfortable, and I hated that. I left that feeling alone because I knew that the gospel was supposed to make people feel uncomfortable.

    Our husbands got along great! Jayhab was a nice guy who had dark hair and a mustache; he worked in masonry. He and Mark would talk for hours while Jesse Bell and I would talk, and more often than not, we were getting wild. We would laugh and drink tea, and then we would talk more about the things that Jesus was doing in our lives. I tried to keep up with it all. We all started having church meetings in our homes with the other Amish people who came out of their church. They were all by now driving cars and having electricity. We would meet at Allen's trailer after selling the Amish farm with all his horses and cows. The trailer was situated straight behind Melvin's Bulk Food store since Elsie was his daughter. Melvin, Katie, Rosie, Jessie, Jayhab, Mark, and I would all huddle around on her old couches on the old, dark-brown carpets. It was very different now that they were not Amish.

    Rosie started to come to my home more often because she wanted more of Jesus and less of the Amish ways. She loved playing with the children, helping me out, taking photos together, or just talking for hours about anything and everything. She was with me the night I went to see Chief Shoe-foot and helped me during those times I had to have round-the-clock care. We had become very close and found out that we had many things in common. She was an artist, and being Amish; you can't fully use your talents because doing so would make you more worldly. Music was another thing she and I would enjoy doing together. She would sing harmony, and hearing her sing was like listening to an angel. Such talent and she used to have to sneak around to use it. It seemed sad, and I realized why God helped me out of the Amish because I honestly never would've been able to be myself. With the Amish, a person can never be an individual because they are a part of a collective. To be individual was to be against the core of what community is. Their society was a cycle of unchanging and eternal formalities, ideals, and the repetition of daily life together.

One day she called and wanted desperately to run away from the Amish, so I picked her up and helped her on her journey. Our house always seemed to be open to those who were on a journey of some kind. After she went on her way to her new life, she found a nice godly young fellow to marry, and they started a family of their own.

Sometime later, I found out that my cousin Pete was supposed to be put in jail again, and I appeared in the courtroom that day. "Your honor!" I called out of turn. I was not a witness scheduled to be there, just a random lady in a dress out in the audience. Pete was standing there dressed in bright orange with shackles around his hands and feet.

"You are not supposed to talk out of turn," the judged glared in my direction.

I begged. "Please, Please, my cousin is around bad people all the time, which causes him to continue in his bad behavior." I paused, worried that they would silence me, yet they motioned me to continue. "I propose an offer. Instead of putting him in jail, which costs taxpayers to care for him there, I ask that he be placed in our home for us to rehabilitate him. We are Christians, and we can teach him about Jesus and how to give up your life of addiction and sin to live with freedom and integrity to the law." To my astonishment, they agreed to let me take Pete home.

After hearing this news, I went to his father, Harvey, who was my very favorite uncle. When I was just a kid, he had his little farmette that we all helped with. He had pigs, chickens, and cows. There was no other place I ever wanted to be than Uncle Harvey's and Auntie Fran's farm to play. I loved the animals, and it was partly why I wanted to have animals when I had a family. They were not a perfect family, but they did love each other very much. Pete and his younger brother Clyde stayed in their parents' basement for most of their lives; it seemed. That day that I told my uncle about picking up Pete, he was drinking. Uncle Harvey wasn't so happy that day. It was't like him. When I was little, he and I were Booger Buddies. We would both put both our fingers straight up our own noses and flick them straight back toward each other. It was a secret hands shake so to speak. He was always the life of the party and most days a party animal. I learned to adapt to his party animal kind of spirit and became one myself.

Years before, after I found the Lord, I had begged him to give his life to Jesus, and he told me, with words I will never forget as long as I live, "I am too bad for heaven. I don't need your F-ing Jesus!" I told him that none of us was good enough but that we all need Jesus and that Jesus died to save him from hell. He returned, "I'm going to hell." It was then that I promised I would be there on his death bed one day, and I would still try to rescue him from hell and hoped that he would trust Jesus. He laughed his smoker's laugh that sounded more like a jovial cackle. That was a moment I knew that the gospel was something that could bring the best or the worst out of people, making them sometimes feel judged or uncomfortable. Later, I found better ways to share that would create curiousity and a desire to learn more.

As I stared at him that day, telling him about taking his son into my home, he looked at me and fumed, "You're pregnant again? Holy sh*t, you're trying to repopulate the world! You're taking our tax-paying dollars to feed more mouths. Get out of here!" He didn't even care that I was taking his son out of jail. I picked Pete up the next day at the back of the jailhouse and took him home with us. He slept on our couch, and I bought him a Bible. We brought him to our home church meetings, and he started to listen and learn of God's love for him. Most days, he would have to take breaks for a cigarette. Miles said, "You shouldn't smoke, Uncle Pete!" He called him uncle because we called everyone who was saved our brothers and sisters in Christ, which was like a family and thicker than human blood. It's the binding of souls in the blood of Christ, which is eternal.

Pete enjoyed being a part of our family. One day his dad rolled into our driveway and said from the window, "If you can save Pete, I will trust Jesus too!" I could hardly believe what I was hearing as I watched Uncle Harvey walk back to his car and leave as fast as he came. Saving Pete was what I wanted more than anything in my heart, but sadly, just like anything, things fade. The honeymoon of living with us instead of in jail wore off. Slowly, Pete's enthusiasm drifted away like the smoke that puffed out of his nostrils. He started to see our faults like everyone who lives under the same roof will. It didn't take long for him to start picking us apart, and everything started to seem hopeless. He wanted to go home, and all the things we talked about began to shift to him defending his habits and lifestyle. We let him go, and he soon ended up back in jail, and his dad kept his promise. Because Pete didn't convert fully, his dad didn't either.

The phone rang. It was Mom. She said with a sigh, "Erin, Grandma is dying. She wants to see you." Only a month before, I was telling her about Jesus, too. She was a stringent Catholic, and I could sense that she was scared to die. She told me she was afraid because she probably wasn't good enough. I explained the entire Bible from front to back, God's story of redemption, my testimony of how God saved me when I was at my wit's end. I told her of all the miracles. I told her how God was real, and she could go to Him in her death with all her works, all the good she did, and hope that was enough, or she could go to Jesus with nothing but her faith that He would finish what she could not. She could go to God covered in the shed blood of the cross, trusting in what Christ did to pay for her sins, going to Him with His righteousness, or depend on her own form of righteousness. I could see that made her nervous. It was that simple, and somehow, she had a hard time accepting it. After much explaining and hours of holding her hand, she finally started to break down. She could see it. She accepted Jesus, and she felt free. Crying tears of joy, knowing that she was a child of God herself, Grandma knew that she could inherit heaven one day. The smile she had at that point replaced the anxious look from when I first arrived.

"Hey, Erin," she said the next time I came to see her. "I prayed to Jesus for the first time, and I know He listened to me. I could feel it." It was a silent understanding her and I had from that moment on knowing she didn't have to pray to saints or to Mary, who was unable to hear her. I told her that the Bible teaches there is only one intercessor between God and man, and it was Jesus Christ.

That day as I drove to her nursing home, I knew it would be the last time I saw her. She was my mentor in my early days as a wife, and I was so thankful God kept her for me when I needed her the most. Grandma was a good woman, now a saint by her faith in God. As I walked past my mom in the small room, I could see Grandma was agitated. She had this pensive look. Mom said she was unable to talk, but I could tell she was waiting for me. That kindred spirit in Christ gave me access to her heart of hearts.

I knew what she longed for. She wanted me to assure her of something that only I could do. As the others left us alone in that room, I looked in her searching eyes and asked, "Grandma, are you holding on because you are worried that no one will pray for your family to also come to Jesus?" Her eyes became certain as she nodded yes. I stroked her head and kissed her forehead like a mother to a child, "I will carry on the torch for you. I will tell them your story about your great faith in Jesus. I will pray for them." She clenched my hands ever so tightly as she nodded her head. I cupped her lovely face into my hands and said, "It's okay. You can go now; I will not fail you. I will always love this family and pray for them." I could see the peace of God fall on her face that instant as her eyes settled. This woman spent her whole life on her knees, praying for her family. She rubbed her beads and said a thousand novenas. Having someone to pray was her last dying wish. I could see that she was truly happy and did not fear death. She knew where she was going. Within that hour, Grandma passed on, and I cried tears of joy for her. She could be with our savior in his glory.

The family asked me to give her eulogy at her hometown Catholic Church. I spent hours writing it all out and painted a picture of her dancing with Grandpa with the words, "Today, thou shalt be with me in paradise." I sprinkled the painting of them dancing in the clouds with subtle glitter, and it hung there in the front of the church for all to see. She was granted paradise like the thief on the cross beside Jesus, in her last hour, God telling her she would be with Him.

As I got up to sing a song for her at her funeral and then shared her story, I looked out to the crowd. Hundreds of faithful friends and all her family looked up at me as I shared how she put her faith in Christ. I gave them the gospel as they'd never heard it before. The priest leaned over with his mouth wide open in disbelief that I got away with telling the congregation that my grandmother took her faith in what she could do to save herself with religion and traded it in for the real faith in the blood of Christ to forgive her sins. I explained how she was afraid to die because deep down, she knew that she would never do enough to please God.

The Eulogy & The Cult

I have always been a bit of a renegade. I bet that was the first and the last time someone was allowed to speak against the Church in the Church building. I learned that most people don't even know what they believe or why, but I know that God is not in a box. There is no one true Church. We are all people, and if we put our faith in Christ, we are his body, his arms, his mouth, his hands, and his feet. It doesn't matter what building we worship in as long as we trust in Him. That manmade religion of rules and regulations is something that did not give Grandma peace nor Rosie nor the other Amish people who also felt they could never be good enough. She needed to own it for herself and not just go through empty motions.

Soon we were meeting every Sunday in Allen's old garage. All of us women would bring crockpots full of food to eat after church. Hot food always tasted better on a cold day. There came a frigid winter day that Allen invited this church group called the Church of God. There were a lot of them, and they all looked the same. Each member was dressed in black from neck to toe. The men were buttoned up tight to the neck, tight, with white shirts, and no neckties, but black vests covered in black jackets over black pants. Some men were clean-shaven, but most had a full beard, which was trimmed. If I didn't know any better, I would think they were Amish men. The women had their hair pulled tight into buns on top of their heads with the same white shirt buttoned tight up the neck, the same type of black vest over the top with a black jacket over a long black skirt that nearly touched the floor. They indeed were not Amish women because Amish women always wore the white caps to cover their heads.

All at once, they started in our direction and put out their hands to shake, "Hello, my name is Sister Margaret, and this is Brother Dan. Glory to God!" What was this? Who was the man she came in with? Her husband? Why on earth was she calling him brother? That was a bit strange. What became stranger was that they all greeted us in that same manner. They looked the same and talked the same, and when they started to sing, I was blown out of the water. There were black men and white men all lined up in front of us singing in a soulful, swinging, perfect harmony. I wanted to sit there for all eternity at that moment. That singing had me fixed in a state of toe-tapping wonder.
How could they all look so cultish but then have this rhythm and blues, and crazy, fantastic singing? It was something I wanted to understand

237

fully. Maybe they weren't a cult. Mark and Jayhab saw some red flags, but Jessie Bell and I wanted to quiz them. We started asking cult-type questions like, "Do you have to dress like that?" They answered, "No, not at all, we want to dress in a way that pleases the Lord. Praise you, Jesus!" The phrases always ended with a 'thank the Lord,' 'bless his holy name,' or 'glory to God.'

The following weekend I invited the Church of God over to my parent's empty rental home for a revival meeting. They had about forty of their people dressed in black marching into the back door. My parents and I could see my mom's eyes widening, wondering what on earth I had gotten them into. Here we were with Allen's family, Jayhab and Jessie Bell, all of us and even my brother, Ian, with his family from Chicago. It's almost laughable how they all went along with these three-hour meetings all stacked in rows. When praying, they were thanking God for being sin-free for fifteen years, or that they have been perfect for several years. I had never heard of anything like this.

"What on earth, Erin? That is a cult if I ever saw one!" Mom blurted out after the meeting was over, and they all packed up and headed to wherever they came from. Mom always told it like it was. No filter. That is something I've always loved about her. Michelle was laughing about it over in the corner; her eyebrows pulled up as she shook her head, wondering how crazy we continued to be all the time going from one thing to the next. The family had the unique privilege to be there for all my whims. Not only were they completely weirded out by the cult meeting, but Jessie Bell was also getting under their skin as she dug into each of them one by one.

I started to have my suspicions about this group and also wondered if they were a cult. We went online and looked them up, and, sure enough, they were classified as a cult. I found pages and pages of stories of people who got out of the cult and how they were controlled. They weren't allowed to do anything without getting permission from this leader called Denny Light.

More and more, it seemed they had stricter rules than even the Amish. I wondered why Allen and Elsie would go for it when they ran from rules and regulations for freedom in Christ. We went to a meeting at a school where we met a widow. She told me that her husband died, and came to find out that they prayed for him and refused to bring him to a doctor saying, "The Lord is our physician, hallelujah!" Mark was a bit put-off by that story. Like him, I wondered why they would control life and death like that and not bring a man in who fell from a roof, had a whole bunch of children, and who died a week later from slow, internal bleeding. That seemed very selfish and ridiculous. We trust the Lord, and we also know He can heal, but there comes the point where you can cross that line and play God. When the man prayed that night, I opened my eyes for the first time and peered around at all the people saying, "Thank you, Jesus, praise you, God!" They shout these phrases out while the man was praying. I watched him. He was creepy as he squinted his eyes and looked to make sure they were all doing as they should. He looked like the devil, and I felt a shard of evil pierce my soul looking at him. His name was Patty O'Sham, an old and gray-bearded man dressed in the black of evil.

    I went to my computer and started printing off the papers of these stories about this cult. I grabbed my stack of documents and brought them to Allen's garage meeting. I prayed that none of the cult would be there that day so I could warn our friends. There was a spy there; one young man who was watching me with my papers. He went out and then walked past as I was trying to tell Elsie. She swallowed hard as she said, "Patty keeps calling and asking what we are doing." Just then, the phone rang, and we just about jumped out of our seats with fright. I said, "I bet that's him, and I bet his spy told on me." She picked up the phone, and her eyes became as wide as saucers, and she said very little because it appeared that he was scolding her. Slowly she hung up the phone, and with her head looking back and forth for the man who was spying on us and who gave our cover away, she said, "You're right. It was him. He knows about your papers." A shiver went up my spine thinking they may have convinced Allen, and I wondered if there was any hope to get him alone to tell him. There sure would not be a chance so long as their spy was there.

    After we left and stopped to fuel up at the nearest gas station, our cell phone rang. Mark was in the building, paying, so I answered, "Hello?" And the low, gruff voice replied, "Hello, this is Brother Patty, is your husband there?" My heart started to pound, and I froze saying, "He's in the gas station, can I have him call you back?" I was trying to get out of it, yet I knew he had found me out. He continued with his evil return, "No, actually, I wanted to speak to you!" His voice got louder and gruffer, "YOU, the wolf in sheep's clothing! I know you brought papers to show. I know everything. You can't hide from God!" The chills ran down the back of my neck, and the fear paralyzed me as Mark approached the vehicle. The look on my face told him that I was on the phone with the devil himself. Brother Patrick continued, "YOU, the thief trying to deceive, trying to steal from our flock. YOU will not get away with this; God will get you!" Slowly I pulled the phone from my ear and shut it, praying that everything he said was a lie and that he didn't have any power to unleash God's wrath upon us. Mark quickly managed to get me to repeat what was said, and he confirmed immediately that this man was evil, that he was a wolf in sheep's clothing. In a flash, I knew I was okay, and that God would keep us safe.

As soon as we got home, I got out a pen and paper and began to write them a letter, my last attempt to warn them. God's words poured out of me through the flick of my pen. Tears ran down my cheeks and dripped onto the paper below. The Letter of Galatians came to mind, and as I looked up the exact verses to support every ounce of my God-given inspiration toward them, I saw clearly that they were walking right back into that which God had brought them out of but even worse. When everything was delivered upon that tear-stained paper, I folded it up and placed it into an envelope to be mailed out the next morning. That night I was hard-pressed to sleep. I could only think of that evil man and how he was manipulating our dearest friends.

When Allen got the letter, he called me, and he said in a very mocking tone, "That letter is a joke, laughable!" As I continued to talk to him with a quivering voice, I could soon tell there was no hope that he had given himself over to the devil. The mocking spirit was not of the Lord. The Allen I knew would have wept reading that letter, and he would've come in humility. All I heard on the other side of that phone was another version of THEM, the Church of God. Allen was gone. I mourned them spiritually. Our friends were gone, and it would never be the same.

They began to lure other Amish into their cult. I was in the midst of a war for their souls. Now that we were onto that cult, the Amish were quick to allow me access again because I was there to help educate them. It felt a bit weird at first to come dressed in my everyday skirt and shirt attire with no head covering when I drove to the Amish, but they didn't mind. In fact, Martha said, "Erin, we're so glad you're finally honoring your husband." They were glad we were on one accord and still loved our family dearly. But this Church of God was pressing in on the Amish, coming to their quilt sales to evangelize them, to their weddings and funerals. They took advantage of any chance they could prey on the Amish who might have doubts or feel dissatisfied with their lifestyle.

The Church of God would entice them with something holier. Those Amish that indeed had a hole in their heart to please God with their lives were easy prey. That's how they got them. They didn't get the Amish by telling them they could be free; they got them by giving them a higher standard. More rules. More singleness of dress. More dedication to God. One by one, sadly, they convinced a number of their people to join in. Of Ezra and Rosa's 13 children, only Harry, Milo, Orpha, Martha, Elvesta, and Maybel did not jump on that bandwagon, and it grieved their hearts beyond any consolation. When they have to excommunicate their loved ones, they may never eat with them, and they have to treat them as a sinner on their way to hell. They loved me for warning them and appreciated my diligence to try to stand in the gap where they could not. By that time, though, I was marked as a wolf in sheep's clothing, so if Allen already convinced them, they also were convinced I was of the devil, too.

When I went to Elvesta's wedding at Ezra's farm, the growing Church of God group was there. They all had the same clothes on and that same mocking spirit. Pride oozed out of their mouths as they boasted of their holiness in comparison to the Amish. They didn't even care that they were making a scene at their little sister's wedding and breaking their parents' hearts all the while they spewed out heresies. It was my opinion at the time that they had all sold their souls to the devil, believing a dangerous and false doctrine. It strengthened my faith because I wasn't going to be moved by their crafty words about the fact that they thought their church was the only way to heaven. If you aren't in their fold, you were a sure goner, and I just wept as I brushed the dust off my feet, for there was no convincing them.

This caused me to see people as people, not with what they wore or what church they were in. All people want to belong and feel safe. I could see that the Amish who left their culture just wanted to belong and to feel loved. The community life was all they knew and without it, they must have felt like fish out of the water, no matter how small their pond was that they were confined to. They found community in that group, and I didn't want to take that away from them either. If they could be happy with a mountain of manmade rules dressing in black and feeling closer to God that way, I figured that they should be allowed that freedom. I stopped trying to convince them or anyone who didn't want to hear. You can't force your ideas on anyone. I learned that God's Spirit would draw people who are searching, and if they come willingly, sharing the love of Christ will open their hearts to what they need. Only God can adequately fill everyone's needs.

Chapter Eighteen
The Visit & the Siren

That spring, we went down to visit the Cane Creek Community down in Tennessee because I wanted to personally thank Miss Donna for writing to me and her book that touched my life. I felt God used their ministry to impact my healing, deliverance, and my marriage. It was hard to find them. We had some of their materials, and when we arrived in the general area, no one knew who David Glee was. Mark drove around for hours on winding back roads through creeks and up dirt paths. One person at a little junk store in Pleasantville had heard of him, and while he puffed his cigarette, he pointed us in the direction of this small church house, yet we still got lost. All at once, we saw a street sign that said Glee Rd. As we winded down over a crooked, wooden bridge and beyond the creek, we could see this strange building. It was a very plain-looking, red-painted shed that was hoisted about eight feet above the ground to keep the floodwaters out.

Some man passing in a truck told us that it started at ten a.m. Sunday morning. A little sign was posted above a volleyball court that said something to the effect of wearing modest apparel if you are on his property. The first time we attended their little church on the creek was unique. There were chairs, odd chairs of all sorts, set around in a big circle. The families came in one by one and sat there on the chairs, which all had a blue hymnal on each. Dave and Miss Donna came in last, and they sat there on one end while the families were setting their little ones in perfect order in their row. We were all staring straight at each other and wondered what their stories were. The songs were sung, and the women were quiet, which meant they were not allowed to speak or even call out a specific song. They were not permitted to ask for prayer or share any sort of story. Most of the women had long skirts on and button-down shirts with long hair cascading down their backs. All the little girls had pigtails or braids, and they wore flowery dresses. Some of the women wore pants, but they seemed in the minority at that small church.

Dave announced each song and then asked for the men to share. A few men got up from their seats and rushed to the front to convey some sort of truth they learned from reading the Bible, or they shared a testimony of something great God did in their lives. After several men shared, Dave took his turn, and he would expound about a specific chapter of the Bible, going into great detail each verse and what it meant. He seemed brilliant with his dissection of the Bible. When it ended, the people left in a hurry, but I wanted to meet Miss Donna to thank her. I walked in her direction, and she was in such a hurry that she only had enough time to hear me say thank you, and she said, "Your husband is so handsome." She smiled and winked at me and dashed out the door. Most of the people seemed unfriendly. They didn't stand and make you feel welcome like a typical Baptist church. There were no greeters. I got the feeling right away that we may have been intruding, which didn't influence me in the least.

The only family at the church that Sunday that approached us was the Jansen Family, Stan, Miss Tilly, and their five children. They invited us to their little home on the other side of the hills for lunch. Miss Tilly quickly prepared some vegetable soup out of a glass jar, and we had a great time getting to know one another while our children were off running around outside playing in the little brook beside their home. Miles was out there catching crawdads and trying to pinch the other little boys with the poor creature's pinchers while he would wildly laugh. Their children were all homeschooled and so intelligent. Their oldest boy was brilliant. He had invented all kinds of things around the home outside and talked more like a professor than a ten-year-old boy. I took in a lot that day observing what she was doing, so when my children were old enough, I could homeschool them as well. When we said our goodbyes, we took off down the road for the twelve-hour journey back home.

My due date was soon approaching, and I was getting around great. Because the Lord had fully healed my pelvis and my bulging varicose veins, I had entered my last trimester in good health. There was no lingering pain or issues, yet I still planned to be induced for some odd reason. I figured with my last delivery and all the trauma that surrounded the birth of Michael; we didn't want to take any chances that something would be missed again. God caught what the doctors missed, so we had to have more faith at that moment. I had my choice of the day, and I chose to give birth on our wedding anniversary, May 23. Our son was going to be our anniversary present.

Mark was there with me as they put all the drugs into me, and I began the labor pains unnaturally. I quickly asked, "How soon can I get the epidural?" Having felt real labor with my last baby, I wanted to avoid that altogether.

"The soonest you could get the epidural is when you are three centimeters dilated," the nurse reported. I frequently had them check, and as soon as it was about two and a half, I called them in to do my epidural. The rest of the labor was so relaxing. Mark's mother came in just before I was ready to push. In two pushes, our fifth child was birthed into the world. As he gasped for his first breath, he let out a scream that I have never since heard. It was loud like a siren and so loud that it seemed it could crack the glass. We all looked at each other, wondering if he was hurt somehow. What baby screams at that decibel? Most first cries are so precious and sweet like a little whimper of lungs' first use. My baby's cry was blood-curdling, and the sound of horror.

His little head was covered in black hair like his daddy. Mark quickly said, "I am putting my name on him. He's the only one born with hair like mine." He smiled as he grabbed the screaming baby into his arms, "His name will be Mark Junior." I was glad the screaming did not stop him from naming him. I figured I would get blamed for the loud part, but because all the other babies looked so much like me, this was a proud daddy moment. His baby boy looked just like him. Mark's mom couldn't wait to meet her newest grandson, and she was so thankful to be there at his birth. She held him squalling and wailing, rocking him back and forth to comfort him. We all had to agree silently not to allow the noise of this little one to spoil the moment. He was precious and perfect in every way.

Memoirs of a Keeper: Angels & Demons

    I brought him home to a team of little children running in my direction to see this new treasure. When they heard him scream, they all shook, and Miles asked, "What's wrong with him?" We had to explain that it was just how he cried. There I sat on the sofa with a pile of little children, all five and under, bumping and shoving in to have their turn holding their new brother. The nights were long. He would jolt us from deep sleep to wide awake in a second when his siren went off. There was no warning, no build up to the scream; it was instantly. Sleep-deprived and frazzled on every edge of nerve, one night, I stood wide awake with the screaming baby. I held him in my husband's direction, and I said, "Take him! Take him! I can't do it any longer!" Each time he woke like this, I looked to see if an animal was biting him or a pin poking him or if he had all his arms and legs. There was no reason for it. Mark carried the basinet to another room and closed him in there with a blanket to dampen the noise. That old farmhouse with wooden floors and old doors offered no noise reduction of itself. Soon I was putting him in the swing downstairs to see if that would keep him asleep. We survived it, and the little night owl often slept during the day, which gave me enough energy to care for the other little ones who were wild with play.

    At my six-week checkup, I had brought my five little ones because I didn't have any other option. Mark was out working with the Amish about thirty miles away. The doctor had been trying to convince me to get this IUD placed into my uterus to prevent pregnancy. It had been clear to her that we never used birth control, and we were getting pregnant within months after each baby was born. Mark didn't want me on the pill or having that device placed into my uterus because he felt these methods could mess with my hormones or kill any future children the Lord might give us. Staring at my group of children sitting on the floor and when our little loud siren went off again, I said, "I am ready. I'll get that IUD." I knew I shouldn't do it, but I felt like I could barely handle the children I had, and I couldn't bear to be pregnant again, so she sent me off to the bathroom to get ready. I was worried that Mark would find out and that God watched me dishonor my husband's wishes.

    She told me to lay down on the medical table right there above the floor, where all the children were sitting quietly; by that time, the nurse had given them all a lollipop except the new baby. The doctor told me that she had to measure my uterus with this long metal-poker-looking thing. She pushed it into my uterus, and then I heard a thud, and it seemed like my whole insides had been stabbed. The look on her face told me that that was just what had happened. The blood started to trickle out, and she was frantically grabbing a gun of some kind to burn my uterus with. The children were crying as they saw me panicking and blood dripping to the floor. She dilated my cervix more to allow space to get in there to stop the bleeding. My uterus was then cauterized, and I was stuffed with cotton to stop the bleeding. There was no IUD that day, and I went home with a wounded womb.

If I had listened to my husband, I wouldn't have gotten into that mess, nor would I have had the issues with my uterus that I had from that moment on. I know it may sound foreign, but when I read in my Bible that the husband was the head of the woman and that there was protection in that order, I could see it full circle. I could see that I had slipped under that covering. It was a spiritual covering, not an oppressive force of a man subduing a woman; it was a loving, protective layer. It never should be misused in that way.

That summer, we were invited to Mark's brother's wedding. While he was dating Michelle, I pleaded with Mark's mother to make sure that she was supportive. The rejection I had received was something I didn't want to be repeated. We packed up and drove down to Illinois to attend the wedding. I offered my photography services as a gift to them, so I was busy trying to juggle nursing my newborn in between shooting the photos. They had the most beautiful time celebrating their love, and it was perfect in every way. The children enjoyed playing and dressing up. Seeing all of Mark's family, there was so special.

Soon after, we had been hired to do another wedding for one of Mark's cousins who lived in Tennessee. We contacted the Jansen family in Tennessee to see if we could haul our camper down to stay at their property. By this time, Stan had built them a good home. This new home was off the grid. He had solar panels on the roof, collecting the rays of the hot Tennessee sun all day long. They had running water but not a running toilet. Instead, they had a wooden box in their bathroom with a toilet seat over the top. Stan began to instruct us, "When you go, you take this plastic cup and dip it into the sawdust to gather up enough to cover what you left. That keeps the smell down." It worked so well; I was utterly shocked. The pail under the wood box had to be emptied a couple of times a day, which he designated that job to one of his little boys. They would dump the waste and sawdust into these composting bins out behind the house.

They had gardens built on the terraces around the house with sheep grazing on little pastures. The lights were all solar-powered, and they didn't have any air-conditioning. That was rough. We were not used to the Tennessee heat and humidity. I took several showers a day to cool off since there was no escaping the heat. Sitting there with the sun beating down on the tin roof, we baked. We parked our little pop-up camper on the only flat spot they had on their rocky hillside. Tilly cooked meals for us; she was a lovely cook. She had fresh-baked loaves of bread and soups. I loved her organization with her schooling, with the children's chores. Everyone had a list of what they were required to do during the day. They ran a tight ship there. The children were not allowed to disobey. If they did, they got the switch. That's one of the things the Glees were famous for teaching people how to train their children. The children were often busy creating things outside all day. It was pretty amazing. Calvin made a big potato launcher and was showing everyone how far he could shoot the potatoes. Miles was captivated by his new friends.

While we stayed and when we left for the wedding, we took the children. I spent the day in the most glorious cathedral taking his cousin's wedding photos in downtown Nashville. I have never seen such a beautiful place in my life. It was like a castle, so elegant, so regal. Her brother had played his violin during the service, and it was breathtaking. He could make that instrument sing with a master's touch. The reception was even more beautiful, and we dined like kings and queens as I took photographs of everything.

In the next few days, as we stayed at Jansen's home, we learned more about each other. One evening as the children played quietly upstairs; we started to share our testimonies on how we believed in Jesus. When it came time for me to share, I began to tell about how worthless I had felt and suicidal when I was only fifteen years old. However, when I started to get into all the details of my abuse, the look of disgust came over their faces, and they asked me to stop talking. Mark and I gathered up our little ones and headed out into the dark of the night, walking down the hill to our small camper. I wasn't sure at that time if they were asking me to stop talking because they were upset or if they were tired. It was abrupt, so I was left wondering.

The next morning after we had a hearty breakfast and all the children, as well as our husbands, scattered, I began to help Miss Tilly clean up the kitchen. She walked into my direction with a very sober look as she declared, "Erin, never speak of such vial things in our home again!" My heart started pounding as I felt I was being punished for some sort of crime as she continued to rant, "You caused me to envision these perversions, and now I am defiled in my mind. Your husband should have run the other way when he met you. I can't imagine how you could deserve such a decent man." I dropped the broom, as the tears welled up in my eyes, and I dashed her back door. When I went outside, I saw my husband off in the distance. I could barely see through my tears as I ran to him, and I was hyperventilating by that time. My chest was pressing in, and I found it hard to breathe, hard to open my mouth and speak, for her words just destroyed me.

It was all I could do to say with complete defeat, "I don't deserve you. You should have run the other way!"

He stopped my stammering words with his soft voice, caressing my pain, "Erin, none of us deserves anything good!" He grabbed my face into his loving hands, and he pointed my face so that it looked up to his while he proclaimed, "I am so thankful for you and all that God has done in your life."

With sadness, I returned, "But she said I defiled her. I didn't ask for those things to happen to me, yet now I'm the pervert, I'm the one who's hurting her."

He wiped away my tears and said, "No. No. If she's going to say something like that, she has a problem. You did nothing wrong. What she said was wrong." His words fell on me like the peace of God, and I was healed at that moment, reminded of God's love and healing in my life. God used my husband to remind me when the devil tried to weasel in there with another accusation. The love of God rushed over me, and my tears turned back into joy. Mark packed up the family, and we waved goodbye to our friends. I learned a lot from Miss Tilly that day. I learned that you couldn't tell certain things. Not everyone will be able to handle something like that. She was right; the details were too much. I never again told another soul the details of what happened to me. I could not bear knowing that I may have defiled someone and I knew that two wrongs never made a right.

Memoirs of a Keeper: Angels & Demons

Chapter Nineteen
THE MILK COW & THE RUN AWAY PONY

That winter, we got our very first milk cow. The day had finally come, and my dream of having the farm was a full-fledged reality. She was a Jersey, and we named her Clover. I remember the icy morning she came on the trailer. Mark was busy readying the barn. The children were all bundled up as we watched our Clover bolt into the big red barn in the backyard. It was the first time we used our big barn for animals. That barn was about a hundred years old, and it used to be a dairy farm back in the day. The pregnant cow ran back and forth as Mark and the man who hauled her tried to corral her into the pen designated for her, which was covered in soft straw for her bedding.

Every day we went out there several times a day to make sure she had enough water and hay to eat as we all waited for her to give birth to her calf. Having a calf meant MILK for us all. Mark would rush out to the barn about four times a night to see any signs of labor. Since this was her first calf and our first milk cow, we didn't want to miss anything. One especially cold morning before the first crow of the rooster, Mark told me that the calf had just been born. I woke Miles because our little farmer boy would not want to miss that moment for all the world. His eyes sprung open like never before as he could barely put his boots or coat on, for he just wanted to get out there straight away.

Miles ran ahead, making footprints across the sparkling moonlit snow until he ran under the shade of the barn, and I could only see the dim light of the window that was deep into the rock foundation. I made my way carefully to the barn. Miles climbed up the fence, trying to go over, and my husband pulled him back by the collar of his jacket, "Miles, you have to be careful." Mark continued to scold, "This is her first calf, and she might be protective of it. Never go into the pen unless I say so. We don't want you to get hurt!" As I got closer, I could see the calf steaming in the cold. It was wet all over, and the mother cow was licking her.

"This is the most beautiful sight," I said as I moved near my husband for warmth and put my arm around Miles, who was staring intently at them. The quiet of that snowy morning and the gift of life was something I would never forget nor ever tire of. Time stood still for that moment while seeing that tiny creature with a quivering mouth and big brown eyes looking toward us. Soon the calf stood to its feet, and we realized it was a girl, a little golden heifer. She was spritely as she sprung around on her new legs that seemed clumsy at first. All at once, she made her way to that full udder under her mother and began to suck. Her little head popped up onto the udder.

"Look, Mamma, she's eating!" Miles said with excitement. Soon we all made our way back into the house to tell the others, and for a moment, there were coats and boots, mittens, and hats flying around in a flurry to get outside as fast as they all could. "Kids! Kids! You have to see the heifer; she is eating right now!" Molly, Megan, and Mikey were all tromping out the barn with Miles, and by now, the little snow prints of the early morning was a widened path from all the boots that drug the snow away from my herd of rowdy children.

The cow looked a bit concerned as our little ones were ooohing and ahhing over her new prize wrapped in fur. That little calf was leaping from one end of the pen to the other, and the children giggled with joy. We had to start milking her but didn't even know how to begin. This new mama was not happy to have anyone handle her, much less her calf. She wanted to be left alone, but we didn't get her so we could look at her. We got this milk cow so we could get her milk. The trick was to figure out how to contain her, but the first step was to separate her from her baby. It wasn't an easy thing, I must say. Mark made a stanchion for her that would hold her for her milking. We called in some people from our church who had milked a family cow, and they came over to assist. It was all we could do to get about two pinches of milk out when she whipped my poor husband in the face with her tail that

The Milk Cow & The Runaway Pony

was full of cow poop. After getting the technique down, we hoped she would let her milk down, but it suddenly occurred to us that she may be holding it back for her calf, so we put the calf's face to her face, and then the milk began to flow.

The hot pail of milk had little crusty pieces of poop and fur floating in it, and the romance of it all started to fade. Mark plopped the bucket at my feet, and I had to figure out how to make it clean. How on earth do you purify milk? My first thought was a coffee filter. I wanted to make sure it was ultra, ultra, filtered if I would feed this to my children. That took a lot longer than it was worth as it would just drip one drop per second, which seemed like an eternity. The children would count the drops to entertain themselves while waiting for a glass of this fresh milk. But it tasted as the cow smelled, so it was almost unbearable to drink.

The thought of the Amish barns flooded my mind at that moment. I remembered that they had a big bulk tank that made the milk ice cold very fast, so I applied that concept to our milking. I knew I needed to cool it as quickly as possible, so the straining had to be done through something not so light as the coffee filter. The linen tea towel would do. I sent it through that, and I could see it was catching all the debris, and then I could place it into the refrigerator fast. Now the cream settled on the top, which was about 1/4 of the whole lot. It was amazing. I soon started whipping the cream for butter, yogurt and making kefir with some fermenting grains. We indeed were in the land of milk and honey until one morning.

One frosty morning, Mark came into the house so frustrated. It took him a very long time to get the cow in her stanchion, and he needed to leave for work. There was no time for him to milk. In his aggravation, he challenged, "You wanted that cow. You go and milk her yourself!" I jolted to my feet, and without hesitation, I grabbed my winter boots and coat, then headed out to the barn with my crew. It was still dark, and I could see my breath. There Clover was, looking a bit mad as she stood there.

There was a dream that I had once. It was a dream from the days before I began a homestead. I saw myself with a long-draped skirt being swept in the wind, my hair in a long braid with a scarf pulling back the stray hairs that wanted the freedom to follow the path of the breeze wherever it listed. In this dream, I saw the paintings of the milkmaids.

Memoirs of a Keeper: Angels & Demons

I used to envision myself holding the milk bucket and making my way out to the barn. I would find the sweet old cow out in the pasture, and I would call her. With romantic hope, I would await the clang of her bell with each step toward me. As I continued on my dream, I would gently lead to her soft stall bedded with the straw of the richest golden color.

I would find my milk stool and set it beside her udder. The light of the morning sun would come through the window of the barn set in the fieldstone so eloquently. My braid was long, and it fell over my shoulder, and the sleeves of my dress were rolled to my elbows. When I would pet her, she would let down her milk for me. I would yodel and sing to her as if she was my best friend. I could hear the birds singing as the milk filled my pail, and the rhythm of each stream hitting the side of the bucket would ring in my ears like a sweet song. I would look down at my pail with the milk foaming to the top, and it was done with such ease. That was a dream.

But this was not the reality of that cold morning. The romance of owning a milk cow faded quickly as that udder got tighter and begged to be relieved, and there was no one to relieve her except me. I had a slew of babies in tow. My oldest was five years old while my youngest was not even six months old.

I walked up to the cow in the stall, and it probably looked like I was heading in her direction to murder her the way she protested. She started having a meltdown while my babies were sitting in the cold beside me in the barn. They all joined me out of excitement, but the reality was that I had gotten myself in a pickle with this angry cow. So, by the time I finally got her feed put into her trough, they all started crying because it had taken too long. The baby was still asleep in the house. I sat on my great-grandfather's old milk stool from a hundred years ago. I petted her on her side and got a big fat sidekick to my arm. No braid. Was there time for braiding my hair? Nope. It was too cold to roll up the sleeves. And forget about the birds. They were still sleeping. Do you think I was singing to the cow? Not a chance. The crying kids were hungry and cold, and I was staring at an udder as hard as a rock at this point, and I had no idea what I was doing.

I pinched the teat and hoped for that significant swelling stream. I got a few drops. Now it was not just the kids crying—I started crying. That cow thought it would be cute to try to wipe away my tears with her hairy tail that was full of poop. It was not cute! At that point, I

The Milk Cow & The Runnaway Pony

started to have a meltdown. And I was staring down into my pail that contained about two squirts. It seemed to go on like this for an hour, and I wondered how on earth I ever thought this was romantic. I got out of there, let the beast go back to her calf and rounded up the screaming kids, and felt like a failure. Yes, that was my first experience milking a cow.

Why would I keep pursuing homesteading after such an experience? I guess it was in my blood. I just figured it could be figured out somehow. I ended up getting some farmers out to show me the ropes, and after some practice, I improved. I never liked milking. I never was the picture of the milkmaid. My husband had to learn to enjoy milking the cow that I had to have! And eventually, he did. That was the fantastic thing about my husband: he just did what had to be done, figured it out, and humbly gave himself over to the greater good of the family. I just became good at making butter and cheese from that milk.

With snow all around the ground, the children and I wanted to make the most of it. We bundled up in our snow gear and made a huge snowman for Daddy. The snow-packed nice, so we rolled and rolled until the snow formed huge boulders. Miles and Molly had to help me lift the massive snowball up and onto the next one until we had it the height we wanted. This tall man of snow was right outside the kitchen window. Miles found pieces of coal for the eyes, and Molly went inside for the carrot nose. Megan had the hat and scarf for our snowman. We all snuck around waiting for Daddy to come home, planning to pretend we didn't make the snowman. Miles warned the others, "Don't give it away. Shhhhhh. We'll tell him a man is looking in the window." Mikey and the girls huddled in a little pack by the door. It was dark by the time he rolled into the driveway, so when he came to the door, the children jumped up and down, screaming, "Daddy! Daddy! A tall man is looking in the kitchen window. Hurry!" I winked at him as he passed, making their plot all the more mysterious.

"Where is he?" He said as he followed the mob. "Oh, no! He must be a burglar!" I better get my gun. Miles was laughing and bursting with excitement that we fooled Daddy. He got his gun and flashlight and went outside to check this man out as we all clung to the window. "It's a snowman, guys! No need to worry!" The little ones climbed all over Daddy, screaming with delight as he wrestled them and gave piggyback rides. I had a shepherd's pie baking in the oven, and we all sat around the table that evening, glancing ever so often to the snowman peeking into our kitchen window. Those were some of the cozy family memories we love to reminisce, and the only thing missing was a pony to make the homestead complete.

Jessie Bell had a friend who lived near her, and they had a pony that they were giving away to a good home. I believed with all my heart; we were that 'good home.' He was a black pony about as tall as I was, which wasn't saying much. Mark called him Tony the Pony. Instead of hauling the pony to our farm, I asked if he could be transported to our Amish friends, Lee and Orpha's place. Lee's boys trained ponies and horses of all sizes to pull carts. They were so excited to teach us about driving pony carts that they went to an auction and found the perfect size for our little family. It was red with two benches in the back so that I could drive, and all my little ones could ride along.

The pony trained quickly, they said, but training me would be the hard part. I had to learn how to hook in all these harnesses and clip these belts up correctly for the gear to work correctly. Many days I would take the children up to Orpha's for the day to take my lessons. I would always dress pretty plainly when we went up. Those old Amish dresses were all in storage, and whenever we went up, we all dressed Amish. I had gotten into the habit of doing that out of respect for their children and not wanting them to feel uncomfortable. The other reason is that my children could play with their children if they all looked the same. When another child looked different, at that age, their children just stared, and staring was not going to be fun for my children all day.

One of Lee's boys, Merlin, took me out each day for my lesson. Each day he talked as he hitched up each strap and what they were all for. We would then ride up and down their long gravel driveway, and I would take the reins after a space of time to see if I could steer the cart where I wanted it to go. It was exhilarating. My children were always lining up to take their turns with Orpha's little ones as well. Our little Mikey never wanted to get off. He would just sit there with his little hat and coat in perfect stillness. I could always tell when he was the happiest. He had this little smirk and a twinkle in his eyes. I would always say, "Don't smile, Mikey!" And then he would giggle when he couldn't hold the smile any longer. His personality was more controlled, like his father.

The Milk Cow & The Runnaway Pony

I heard a scream coming from their shed. It was Megan. Lee and Orpha had a litter of Dachshund puppies in the shed, and, of course, my little ones wanted to play with the puppies. The mother Dachshund got angry and bit part of my daughters' lip straight off and ate it. She had a little hole the size of a pea where her lip was. We whisked her into the house, where we tried to stop the bleeding and calm her down. It was evident that we needed to bring her right into the ER. I called Mom and told her what happened, and she commanded, "Demand to have a plastic surgeon fix her lip." Mom worked in surgery, and she knew that they might mess it up if they weren't used to cosmetic-type surgeries. No general ER doctor could do it right, she asserted. That was just what I did, and the plastic surgeon did an outstanding job! You would never know that part of her lip was bitten off when she was a little girl of only three years old. After she recovered, we continued to go there to learn more about our pony cart riding so we could haul him back home to our homestead.

Finally came the moment of truth. I said, "Let me test my memory and see if I can do this on my own. If I always have you do it, I'll never learn. You won't be at my home, so I better just see if I can do it." I was a bit nervous, but thankfully, I have a pretty good memory. When I felt I hooked it all correctly, I grabbed the reins and sat up onto the cart, and with a holler, I said, "Get up!" The pony took off with a dash, and I was driving for the first time all by myself.

I drove past and waved at a smiling Orpha at the window. My children chased me down so they could hop in with me. In a low voice, I said, "Stop." Tony stood there like a statue, and the children boarded the cart. Mikey, smiling, sat right beside me and the other three sat on the back seat. Away we all went up and down the lane until I could see the pony getting tired. It was a proud moment when I knew I could do it all by myself. We soon hauled the pony and the cart down to our farm, and I was out there in the cold of that winter, hitching him up day in and day out. Mark used his backhoe to carve us a track around our farm in the snow. Every morning Mikey would wake me up saying, "Mama, pony ride, pony ride?" How can a mama say no to that? Impossible. Those baby blue eyes got me every time. We would all bundle up and make our way out to the barn in the sparkling light of the sun over the snow. Mark would be out there with Miles milking Clover and bottle feeding her healthy-looking, energetic calf. I would hitch up Tony the pony, and we would all pile on the cart and go around and around the house singing "Jingle Bells" as our heads bounced from all the bumps of the snow-covered yard.

That early spring, we had a little get together at our homestead. Jesse Bell and Jayhab came, as well as my parents and other friends. Mom and I were in the kitchen preparing food when Mark came in the back door, saying he was going to take all the children on a pony cart ride. He knew how to drive the pony cart, yet he never hooked it up before. Many times he would unhook everything, so he figured he could manage to hook it up. With my hands full of flour mixing a cake, I asked, "Are you sure you know how to hitch him up?" He replied, "It doesn't take a rocket scientist to figure that out. I'll be fine." I was glad I could rely on him to do it because I wanted to get dinner on for all these precious people. In a short time, we heard all the children screaming outside, and my heart nearly came out of my chest with worry. I knew something had to have gotten hitched up wrong. We all ran out the back door to see what had happened. There Mark was holding the pony by the bridle, and the cart was left on the other side of the road.

In vexation, Mark announced, "I forgot to hook up the reins to the bit, so the pony went nuts and took off out of here like a bat out of hell." Breathing fast, he continued, "We went down into the ditch and then up out of the ditch, over the road, down the other ditch, up the field, and into a fence. Kids were falling out the back, and when I pulled the reins, they came into my hands like clips and all!" I was worried he would tell me that I could never use the pony cart again at that point. "By the way," he proceeded, "next week when you invited those people over for a day on the farm…you aren't giving pony cart rides, and that's final! That pony is all messed up now." I was right. My pony cart days were now over. When he says that is final; it meant there was no bargaining.

The next week came, and I had not the heart to cancel the day on the farm. These were some of my dearest photography clients and their little ones. They came because their children wanted to ride on the pony cart. Mark was off to work, so I figured I could test Tony out. I would know if the pony would go nuts or not. Was this traumatic event the week before going to spoil the fun we had planned that day? I wasn't one to give in that easy. After hitching Tony up properly, I saw Mikey standing there saying, "Pony ride, Mamma! Pony ride!" I

The Milk Cow & The Runnaway Pony

couldn't say no, so I pulled him up beside me on the cart with his thick one-piece snowsuit. Off we went in a jolt while the customers sat by watching with excitement for their turn. Once around the house and it all seemed like clockwork, Tony was going at a steady pace, and with each tug of the rein, he would go just as I had wanted him to go. On the next pass around, something happened to Tony; he must've had a flashback because he went completely insane. His head bolted down in defiance as his hoofs bucked up in our direction. He bolted at a full canter of perhaps twenty-five miles per hour by that time, blazing past the onlookers, whose eyes were bulging from their sockets. There was no stopping Tony. I pulled the reins with all my might as I stood to my feet and sawed him at the bit.

I was not an expert with horses by any means, so I didn't know what to do when a horse, or pony for that matter, went crazy. My maternal survival instincts kicked in as I saw my beautiful boy Mikey sitting there like he had no idea what was going on, enjoying the journey. The road was just ahead, and we were pointed in that direction full speed with no intention by the pony to stop for anything, not even a truck if it happened to come whizzing by. I did what any good mother would do—I grabbed my son and threw him off the raging cart. Mind you; I threw him in a way that I thought would be safest at those speeds, rolling him sideways so that his suit would buffer the fall, and he would roll off on his side. As the cart kept racing toward the road, I looked back to see if Mikey was okay. He was screaming, and I knew I needed to bale. I jumped, tucked, and rolled off from that runaway pony. I hit the ground so hard that I could only see snow and sky and snow and sky until the roll ended. As soon as I stopped rolling, I limped over to my child, who was walking toward me, scared and wondering why his mamma threw him off like that.

I picked him up to make sure he didn't have any injuries, and by the thickness of his snowsuit, he was kept safe and sound. The customers came running to see what had happened, and we all watched as the pony and the cart raced off into the distance. No pony cart rides for that day. Mark was right again, and I felt a surge of conviction in my mind that I should've listened to my husband. Final meant final, but I was a bit rebellious at times. I learned a good lesson that day, never to tempt sound reason. Just then, I remembered that the pony was heading right for the busy highway where someone could be in danger to hit him.

Memoirs of a Keeper: Angels & Demons

The memory of our Amish friend Allen telling us how his horse and buggy caused the death of a couple of drivers smashing into it, came flooding back. I grabbed for a cell phone and flipped it open to dial 911. The lady on the line was confused as I exclaimed with panic, "The pony is running away! It is headed for the highway with the cart! You have to come!" The lady replied, "Ma'am, why don't you find someone nearby to help you find your pony?" She didn't understand the severity of that situation, so I hung up, and they never did come to help. I never told her about how I threw my son off and how it all happened because I was too worried about what would happen next. It probably gave them a laugh that day that someone lost their poor pony and called, not at all sounding like an emergency. I had to run myself down to see if the pony had caused an accident. There was no carnage on the highway, so I kept following the tracks in the snow and the pieces of the cart that ripped off along the way. In no time, I found the pony violently panting and shaking of fear hooked into someone's fence trying to escape. For a long time, I had to calm him enough to get him untangled and walk him back home. He was skipping around in his mad state of mind.

Ezra and Rosa came down for dinner one evening with Willis and Mary, and they said they could tame that pony. We went out that afternoon just before dinner, and I took one step into the cart and found out it was not only the pony that was messed up. I was messed up too. My fear was also great at that stage. They made me sit on there, but the entire time I sat there breathing hard as my heart raced, thinking the pony would bolt at any moment, which would make me jump for my life again. It took me years before I could ride in a cart. I didn't trust myself. There were no more pony cart rides.

A lady down the road from us had a goat-milking farm, and one early spring day, I visited her farm with the children. They loved seeing the little bottle-fed goats. The joy I saw in my children that day made me want to bring home one baby goat for each. The goat lady was glad to lighten her load as she loaded the four baby goat kids into the van with my five little children. There was giggling and goat calls going on in the van the whole way home. I came home and surprised my husband. He could barely understand why we would need four more goats, especially these that needed a lot of extra care with bottle feedings. "I couldn't pass them up. The goat lady down the road gave them to us for free," I said as if that would make it better.

The Milk Cow & The Runnaway Pony

"Nothing in life is free, my darling," he said as he went to find some old wire fencing to make a pen for them out in the barn beside the cow, her calf, and Tony the pony. He concluded with a smile, "You pay for it somehow." Molly had the smallest little, pure, white goat. It was half the size of the others, and it looked more like a perfect, spotless lamb. These little goats would prance and bounce behind the running children across the barnyard. It was so beautiful. Nothing in life can be as precious as children playing with baby animals. Miles had a job to do the first feeding in the early morning. He would march off to the barn with his dad, fill the warm fresh milk into the plastic baby bottles, and feed the little goats. One morning we asked Miles how the babies were doing, and he stood there dumbfounded.

"What happened, Miles?" I inquired. Something didn't seem right. I knew my son to be bubbly and cheerful, and his silence meant something.

"It wouldn't eat! I told it to eat!" He continued, "So I popped it on the head with a stick, and it laid down. Now it won't get up!" With horror, we all ran to the barn to find the lifeless creature. It was Molly's little white goat. We all gasped as we looked upon this tiny precious animal. I'm not sure how it all happened, but Molly was crying, "Mama, Miles killed my baby goat!" I couldn't take the pain away. I couldn't make my boy feel less guilt for he didn't hit the goat because he wanted to kill it; he just thought tapping on the head would make it listen better somehow. Molly was the only one of them now without a goat, and she had cherished it so much. All I could do was wait until Mark came out to help assess the situation.

Mark said, "Molly, stuff like this happens on the farm. Animals die all the time," but the fact remained that Miles caused it, so he proceeded, "Miles, you'll have to dig a hole and bury this animal since you killed it. Even though you didn't mean to, hitting a little animal on the head wasn't the right way to handle it. The little goat maybe was sick, and that's why she didn't take the bottle." Miles grabbed for the shovel with tears in his eyes. I could hear him praying for God to raise it from the dead before he placed it into the hole and covered it with dirt. Every day he would check to see if God raised it from the dead, and every day he came in disappointed.

Soon I went down to the same goat farm and asked for another white goat. The lady had a cocked head that needed to be bottle-fed and would not make a good milker on her farm, so she gave it to Molly. This goat always walked around a little lame, and its head always looked up like it had a question. It was a bit weaker than the others, and they seemed to like trampling on the poor thing, so we had to eventually separate her from the little herd and try to nurse her to health. Molly always had a way with the animals. She could nurse anything back to health.

The sun started to warm the cold spring air, and we all decided one day to sit on the front porch and just enjoy the beautiful breeze. Mark had Junior sitting on his knee as the other children were off running through the grass frolicking. All at once, we heard Molly's cat screaming and moaning. A male cat pinned her down, and it looked like they were fighting. Molly cried out, "That cat is going to kill my kitty! Hurry, Miles, get that cat off her!"

Miles rushed to Molly and yelled, "No, Molly. They're mating! Let them mate!"

Molly was not about to trust the boy who killed her goat a few weeks before, so she yelled back, "No! He will kill her!"

Miles shouted in return, "Do you like kittens? Do you want Spunky to have some kittens?"

"Kittens?" she asked, confused.

With confidence, Miles declared, "Yes, kittens, Molly! If they mate, she will have kittens!"

Molly started to jump up and down for joy as she replied, "Oh, yes! I want kittens. Lots of kittens." Miles made his way back in our direction as we laughed to ourselves after hearing their hilarious argument. Miles stared at each of us. He had this look of a pondering spirit wondering, and you knew that he was in deep thought as he scanned each of our faces down to the face of our littlest one sitting on his daddy's lap. He then posed this question, "Do you mate?"

Mark was shocked at the question but returned, "Yes!"

Miles then asked, "Can I watch?"

I was horrified at that question, but Mark, with his quick wit, returned, "No. No. That's a private thing, Miles. People are different than animals!" That seemed to satisfy our son's curiosity, and he bounded off to play with the others in the warm rays of the sun.

Mark and I just sat there giggling in disbelief, and we chalked it up to another day in the life of the Harrisons.

Chapter Twenty
THE KILLER DOG & THE MINISTRY

That summer, we found out that Mark got a job to build a log home in Tennessee, which would take him far from our family. However, he came up with an idea. He said, with as much enthusiasm as a guy like him can muster up, "How about we rent a place in Tennessee so we can all be together?" It seemed like a great idea. The only problem was that we had all these animals. It took my entire life until that point to finally get my farm and to follow his dreams; we had to sell the animals. Willis bought all the animals from us, and one day he showed up with a driver and an extended animal-hauling trailer. I wept as I sat behind that kitchen window facing the barn. I saw the cow and calf just peeking out the slits in the side of the trailer as they bumped past with the pony and the goats. My heart broke in that instant, wondering if I would ever have another milk cow in my lifetime. It all seemed so hard to start the homestead just to have it all taken away in a trailer. Mark assured me that we could always get more animals.

We packed up the things we would need on the journey along with our chickens, the cat and her newborn kittens, and Jibity, our hairy Airedale. We contacted the Jansens, and they secured the house for us down the road from them. It was the same place they rented while they built their off-grid homestead. Old Miss Hassling trusted their judgment and let us rent that little house on the hillside. We unpacked almost everything since the small house was fully furnished; all we needed were dishes, clothes, and bedding. There were two loft bedrooms upstairs, one for the boys and one for the girls. The children were quite happy to be in a new place. Mark had to start his job the next day, about an hour away. We were in the wild of Tennessee, and all I had was that little flip phone in an area that barely got a signal.

Outside we heard growling and hissing and banging. Miles started to scream, "It's a stray dog, and he's trying to kill our cat!" We had our cat in the little plastic pet cage with her brand new kittens just to keep them warm and safe. I ran out to find this coondog trying to rip the pen apart. He snarled and dug his claws into the door of the cage, trying to rip it off with his teeth. We were all terrified, standing on the wraparound porch, not knowing what to do. I grabbed the phone, and I couldn't get Mark. I didn't know if we had a gun. But we had to do something, so I called Stan Jansen next door on the phone. I said frantically, "Stan, there's a rabid killer dog out here trying to rip apart the cat cage, and it won't stop. We're so afraid."

He replied in a very low, peaceful, southern accent, "Miss Harrison, it'll be okay; I'll be down in a minute." Well, it wasn't a minute; it was a long time that I could hear the cat hissing and the savage beast trying to break in to eat them all. I stared at the driveway looking for Stan. The girls were crying and shaking, worried about the kittens. All at once, the dog managed to roll the cage out from under the porch, and he rolled it down the hill to the creek, ravaging the outside shell until it burst open and he stuck half of his body into the cage and pulled out Molly's cat and shook her violently. I was screaming by that time, "Nooooooooo!" I ran down after Miles, who was trying to hit the dog with a shovel as the beast grabbed the kittens one by one shaking each one to death. My adrenaline was soaring high, and I started throwing rocks at him and screaming at the top of my voice with the other children on the porch screaming as well. Finally, Stan rolled in the driveway with his gun, which seemed an eternity to me. The saying that southern people take it slow seemed a logical assumption at that point.

Calmly and collectedly, he asserted, "Now, ya'll just get back into the house." We turned around and went in as he marched off toward the wild dog. And then we all jumped with every loud BANG, BANG, and a Yelp! The dog was dead, but Stan wasn't done. He came into the kitchen and asked me for a sharp knife. What did he need that for? To cut off the head! After shooting this dog, he had to cut its head off, and he walked out with that knife and came back in with the head looking for a bag to put it into. I was in a state of shock, and the girls were still crying. Stan walked back toward us on the porch and proclaimed, "Welcome to Tennessee!" He had such a mischievous grin on his face; it seemed like he was trying to tell us that this was just how Tennessee was and that we'd better get used it. I didn't like that. He calmly and peacefully left with the head to bring it to be tested for rabies. The rest of the carcass laid out there in that humid afternoon filled with flies. We found the cage, and of the six kittens, only two had survived. They were the only two in the pen that the dog didn't grab with his ferocious jaws. We looked everywhere for the mother and figured she would go away to die. We thought we would need to get milk, a heating pad, and a little bottle to feed the poor orphans.

  I just sat on the edge of the porch staring blankly ahead, wondering why we moved from our homestead for this. Mark pulled in the driveway, and I'm sure he could tell we had been through a type of war by the looks on our blank, worn-out expressions. I told him everything I remembered, and anything I missed, Miles filled in. Mark blinked his eyes a few times and said, "Let's go to the Sonic! That will make it better!" That got a smile out of me because I was so distraught, the thought of cooking a meal after seeing that headless dog revolted me. The Sonic is a drive-in fast food place that was only ten minutes from where we stayed, and fast food sounded good. Or maybe I just wanted to get out of that place so bad that fast food was a great excuse. When we returned much after the sun went down, our mama cat was waiting by the door to go in to feed her kittens. That was a miracle. We were so glad that she came back. She had been injured pretty severely, so we made sure to make her as comfortable as we could so she and her little ones could be nursed back to health.

  The next night, we heard some rustling near the chicken coop out back, and Mark ran out there in his underwear with a flashlight and gun. BANG! One-shot and he killed the opossum that killed one of our chickens in the night. I was beginning to think this part of Tennessee was wilder and wilder, and it certainly felt like we were in the boonies. There were poisonous rattlesnakes found near our place, and I was terrified to go out there, not to mention getting bit by those dreadful no-see-ums. I hated mosquitos, and these gave the same punch, yet we couldn't see them at all. They just land, bite, and go on their merry way with a belly full of your blood. I hated Tennessee. I just wanted to go back to Wisconsin to our beautiful homestead that was entirely remodeled and just sitting there empty.

The next morning was Sunday, and made our way to that same little red shed, David Glee's church house on the Cane Creek. We sat in the big circle, and it was much the same as it had been before. The exact order of operations, the same coldness, and I felt even more lonely. When I heard that some people would come back several hours after church to play volleyball on the sand court, I wanted to go. Mark was so athletic; I felt he would enjoy playing volleyball, and maybe that would be a way we could meet other people and make some friends. There was a tall, bald guy with a tank top playing ball named Ned. He was Dave's oldest son, and he looked a bit like him. Ned had the same professional camera I had, so I walked up and said, "Hey, that's the same camera I have!"

Just then, he looked down at me and said, "I thought you were Amish! Why would you have a camera like this?"

I couldn't believe he thought I was Amish, because I didn't have anything Amish on. I was simply wearing a skirt and a t-shirt at that time, and my hair was in a ponytail. I returned with a smile, "I am a professional photographer. I photograph weddings, graduation photos, and anything in between." By the time we had our photo talk, he had asked many questions about why we were there and what Mark did. Mark told him he was working on a log home an hour away when Ned told him that he should work construction with him. He asked me if I wanted to help film his dad doing a teaching video on knife throwing. It was perfect, and just what we needed to fit in a bit more.

Soon I was over at the same place near that old church house on stilts beside the creek to film Dave with Ned. Dave was over six feet tall with a long gray beard and white hair on top of his head. He was rough and gruff, and his piercing eyes could penetrate your soul. He didn't meddle around. Everything had to be organized, or he would become quite restless. I filmed him making the targets and then painting them. He would throw big, sharp, metal knives with precision as he would talk right into the camera I was holding, teaching others to do the same technique that would provide the same results. My children were playing around in the background. I'm not sure why I never worried about them getting stuck with a knife, but I figured he was careful enough. On another day, Ned's beautiful blond wife, Shelly, was there with their baby girl. She offered to take all of our children on a little walk around the property to concentrate on work. After a couple of hours of intense filming with even more intense characters who were twice my size, I started to look for my little ones. I walked back to the ministry office and entered the staff kitchen door to be met by an outraged lady. It was Miss Donna, yet I'd never seen this side of her. She scolded in her southern drawl, "This is not a public building. Get off this property right now!"

The tears started welling in my eyes as I was looking for my children, not knowing what to do. I replied with a quivering voice, "Shelly has my children, and I was just filming Dave's knife throwing…"

She interrupted, "Dave's knife throwing is not a part of this ministry. We aren't responsible for finding your children! You need to leave!" I ran back down to Dave and Ned in tears and told them what happened, and they started to laugh.

"Her bark is worse than her bite!" Dave chuckled. He didn't entertain another moment of my situation, so I was just stuck hoping Shelly would come back with the children at some point since I wasn't allowed to ask.

"My mom probably thought you were a lesbian spy," Ned smiled. I was thinking, what on earth? How could I be confused with a lesbian? Or a spy for that matter? They had some negative publicity with their methods of child training, and the media was sending certain people there to check things out.

I didn't want to bring my children there again for the filming, so I asked the Jansens if they could watch them one day. After a long day of filming, I came to pick them up, and Mikey was standing there at the edge of the living room, crying so hard, he was taking jerking breaths. Stan told me that Mikey would not obey, so he kept giving him little switches on his backside, and he wouldn't move. He said it like he did the right thing, and I wondered why he thought he could whip my child for hours. I was thanking God that my little boy survived it even with a weakened heart. I was so livid that I whisked Mikey up into my arms and never took him there again. Mikey was scared to have me out of his sight for a long time after this traumatic episode. I cuddled him and helped him recover and told him I was so sorry and that I would never leave him. I decided that my children would just stay close behind me when I was filming, and we even had some of them in the video trying to throw knives. Miles was nearly seven years old by then and was getting quite good at the knife-throwing. Dave had Miles featured on the video sticking about six knives into the target using his methods.

Soon the video was in the editing phase. I asked Dave and Ned to come by to see the format of my intro. Dave came in the back door, tucked his pants into his boots, and plopped them down on top of our kitchen table. In disbelief, I asked him, "Why are you tucking your pants into your boots and putting them all over my table?"

He quickly replied, "Ticks. Your dog has ticks." I could see he didn't like my dog, but when I showed him my bearded dog smile, he laughed. There was a part in the video that I super-imposed my dog's bearded smile bearing all her pearly-white teeth over a spot where Dave smiled. That made the video a bit humorous for the sake of entertainment. Dave liked it that way, so we had put some stunts and outtakes to polish it off. Ned started a company called Glee's Outfitters, and he planned to sell the video in that store one day. At the point, I began to enjoy working with those two big oafs, learned to take their sarcastic humor, and gave it right back to them. Our project had reached its end, and I was about to travel up to Wisconsin some weekends to have weddings booked.

Mark decided that we would make Tennessee our new home. We had to travel up to make our Wisconsin home ready to sell. It sold fast because it was so adorable. The weekend we traveled up to gather up our entire belongings from our house was so sad. I got there, and everything was so beautiful. All the memories we had there made my eyes well up as the tears poured forth. Mom cried with me. She hated to see us move away. We were taking her grand-babies away from her. I hated it too. I didn't want to say goodbye to them or my beautiful homestead. I remember walking through the kitchen into the dining room that looked like a fancy bed-and-breakfast place, and everyone wanted to start taking it all down to pack it all up. I sat there, weeping, and said, "Stop. Please let me have a moment." I just wanted to look at it, remember it, and frame it all in my mind one last time. I wanted to sit on the porch one more time to hear the rustle of the leaves and see the clouds pass by as they did in that broad country sky as vast as the eye could see.

Little by little, I was able to dry up my tears and begin to fill the boxes. Jesse Bell was there helping, along with her family and Mark's mom. They asked me if I wanted to save this thing or if I needed that other thing. She asked if she could have those things back that she bought for the kids to play with it at her place. I didn't care because we had too many toys. With all the people ready to load up their treasures from my piles of stuff, I just wanted to give it all away. What was the use of keeping anything since we didn't have a place to put any of it? Mark ordered a small storage unit in Tennessee, but how much could we even fit on the trailer? It was all just stuff anyway.

We said our goodbyes as we headed south and to our new life there. I was so sad to leave everything I knew, all those who loved me, for a place that seemed so cold and unfriendly at the time. Leaving my children's grandparents, who cherished every moment with them for a community saturated with children where no one cared or noticed mine was difficult. I even resorted to going door to door in the Plain community trying to recruit a grandmother. I went to a little old lady who had a little Bakery in front of her home. She said, "I simply do not have time for more grandchildren, I have plenty already." Two doors down was the old midwife. She was as plain as plain could be. She rather looked a bit like a female version of Joe Pesci without the humor. Her voice strangely sounded like his voice but instead of a thick New York accent, it was Pennsylvania Dutch. She was advising in matters of dress and morality with a little dash of pride covered by humilty which I found to be the way of most plain people I knew. Many days I would come sit on her porch in the hot summer with her wood stove making it even more sweaty and hot but it reminded me of home. The old fashioned look of this bent over heavy set Grandmother was all I needed to make me feel like I had family again.

The phone rang. This lovely voice on the other end said, "This is Mindy Oldes from church. I know you are new here, but I wanted to see if you needed clothing for the children. Come on by to my trailer on the creek, and you can choose from many things. We had a garage sale the other day, and we are about to haul off the things that we could not sell to the Goodwill. I figure since you have little ones, you could come and have your pick before we take the leftovers in." We loaded up in the van and headed to her place on the creek. I was so excited to finally hear a friendly voice who was so concerned about my children. It wasn't like I needed the clothing, but we needed friends, so if apparel would be the ticket in, I was on it.

It was a bit difficult to find that trailer because it was set so far up on the hillside behind rows of trees, but she gave me a house number, so I just followed the long driveway up the hill. There it was, an extended, white trailer with black shutters. It was nothing fancy. When we came out of the van, we could hear the voices of children playing, so we followed the voices that led us to a deck off the backside of that trailer. I fastened Junior to my hip as the others marched toward the children on the trampoline. They all started to jump together, and I fixed my eyes toward the glass doors that slowly opened. Mindy and her teenage daughter walked out from the trailer and to the deck to greet me with smiles and sweetness. Mindy was short but a little taller than I, and she had blond hair and very tan skin. Her daughter had dark hair and they were both pretty. They wore long knit skirts and t-shirts of a different color. I felt at that moment that I had a new friend.

She started to pick up little handmade dresses and said, "Oh, this would be so perfect for your little girls!" I smiled and nodded, seeing these dresses that she had made. Little pants and shorts, t-shirts, and bathing suits she gathered with her daughter and placed them into a lovely pile. I couldn't believe her generosity. That was indeed a way to welcome the new members of the church by sharing what you're not using. Her daughter started punching numbers into her calculator, and I was wondering what was happening at this point. When she peeked at the calculator, she announced, "That will be $30." I had no idea that she wasn't giving the clothing to me. I thought these were the things going to the Goodwill. There was not a dime to my name after we just spent the money moving all of our things down to Tennessee. $30 was more than I could afford. I never bought clothing because we could never afford it. Relying on hand-me-downs or what I could make on my sewing machine was what I had been accustomed to. Mark would never allow me to spend money on used clothing like that. I had a dilemma. I could see she was set on pushing off the old clothing on us, and if I refused them, I would seem ungrateful to my new friend.

I came up with an idea. With a smile on my face, I said, "Thank you so much, but I don't have the money to pay. However, I can offer you a service." She looked interested in my offer as I continued, "I am a professional photographer. That's what I do, and I can take your family pictures in exchange for this bag of clothing." Mindy was ecstatic. She accepted the offer, and we became fast friends. Most summer days, she would call us and invite us to her creek to play. It was gloriously beautiful. The water in that creek was so clear you could see six feet down to the rocks below. Fresh and flowing, the water would rush over our bodies as we would bask in the hot Tennessee sun. Being at the creek all day made the heat bearable. Miles would jump off logs into the water below, splashing and playing with his new buddy William while Molly and Megan swam with her daughter Nelly. Everything seemed so perfect.

After Mark came home from work, I asked if we could all go to the town park for the children to play. While we were there, I noticed a lady sitting on a bench with long brown hair nearly touching her waist. She looked familiar, but I couldn't put my finger on it. She started staring at me with the same look. I walked to her and said, "Don't I know you from somewhere?" She answered, "Yeah, I was thinking the same thing. How weird!" Finally, it came to me. I knew her from Fort Wilderness in Wisconsin the same summer I met Mark. "I'm Stacy, by the way."

I stammered with excitement, "You were that newly married couple serving at Fort in 1996!"

She added, "Yes, Tom and I had just gotten married, and we served that first summer together!" I could see we had children all the same ages, and she had the most beautiful smile. It was great to have someone from Wisconsin to befriend. She lived here on Candle Creek her whole life, and Tom had met her at the same church we had been visiting. Tom was from the same area that Mark was from, which was in the suburbs near Milwaukee. He had just served at Fort like the rest of us. Stacy invited me over for the day, and while the children went out back to play, we sat at her long, shiny, wooden table to have a cup of tea and talk. Stacy and I had so much in common, and we laughed and shared our whole life stories. I told her about my new best friend, Mindy, and she hung her head down low. She confided, "Please be careful. Stay away from her. She will hurt you. She doesn't mean to, but she has emotional issues." I could barely believe it. When someone tells me things like that, I just take it with a grain of salt and give them the benefit of the doubt. Mindy was no exception.

Months passed, and Mindy and I spent most of our days

together. Mark and I moved right next door to her in a beautiful farmhouse on the creek. It had a barn, pastures, and 1500 feet of the beautiful Candle Creek. Our new home was unique, and I woke up each morning thinking I was in a dream. There were pecan trees, cherry trees, plums, apples, and peach trees. The barn was ready for animals. That fall, we bought a cow from a neighbor and began to milk her. Her name was Beauty. She was a blond Jersey, and she gave the creamiest milk. The Jansens went in on a milking machine with us and half of the milking to get half of her milk. It was a great bargain for us. We only had to be responsible for half of the week, which helped Mark out to be off working most of the time and making ends meet. We had our chickens and got a free black draft horse from one of the Plain People down the road. His name was Prince, and Miles loved riding him bareback all over the pasture. I praised God for giving us back every bit of our homestead life.

We only lived down the road from the sand volleyball court beside the church house. Mark would go in the evenings to play volleyball, and I would go along to watch them all play. Mindy was one of the team captains. She picked the teams and always posted in the middle of the sand, doing most of the sets for the spiker or bumper. Volleyball was a serious competitive sport for these people. If they allowed me to play, Ned would take his barefoot and scrape a big circle around me in the sand showing me my boundaries. I was not allowed out of my circle to get any balls. I soon figured out that I was not cut out for this game, and instead sat on the benches watching the children running around wild. Junior cried or screamed most of the time, and the volleyball players asked me to make him be quiet. Often, Megan cried, chasing the other children around, and Mindy told me not to give in to her whining, that she was too sensitive. Other adults started to tell me to watch out for Mindy's children because they lie and often are very naughty, yet their mother sticks up for them every time. I wanted to be liked, and I wanted to be her friend, so I tried my best to listen to her and deal with my whining child or screaming baby even if it happened to be her kids who caused the problem.

It finally came time to even the trade. I scheduled Mindy's beautiful family for their photoshoot, and we went all over. I took photos of them walking hand in hand up the hill behind their brand-new, beautiful home. We took pictures beside the creek and in the fields. After the photos were taken, I sat with her, editing the images. I finally handed her a CD with the photos for her to print. In a state of confusion, she said, "So this is all I get for $30? No prints?" Suddenly I felt like she was accusing me of taking advantage of her.

Typically, I charged my customers $250 for a session as elaborate as we did. For weeks after that, she pretended that she didn't even know me. Every time we went to church, she walked past me quickly as if she didn't even see me. My only friend was gone because I somehow, without intention, didn't treat her fairly. It was beyond my comprehension. I thought it was more than fair, but she didn't value my service as much as she valued her used clothing, so I figured out how to make her feel better. I took the photos and blew them up to give to her as a peace offering. One of the pictures of her and her husband in a loving embrace, I painted it by hand on canvas. The other photo I toned in sepia of them all walking hand in hand. The silence between us was more than I could bear, so I called her and invited her over to collect her gifts. She came and nearly cried when she saw the beautiful pictures and the painting. It seemed to mean so much to her that she made my girls some matching dresses to bless me in return. Not long after this, she sent me a card. In the card, she wrote how I was like a sister to her. Many moments she would cry to me about her shaky faith, and I would hold her in my arms to bring her hope. She was raised in a Plain Church, and because she had been under so many rules, she had a hard time accepting God's love for her. Our hearts intertwined once again, and most days, her children came down the hill to play at our house or swim in our creek.

That spring, as Mark was tilling the place where we would start our first garden, I saw a vision. I saw us around a table in a film, eating all the food we just grew on our homestead. I ran toward Mark, jumping up and down with joy, as I exclaimed, "Mark! We have to make a DVD for teaching people how to homestead!"

He wrinkled his forehead in disgust as he replied, "That's the dumbest idea I've ever heard. We don't even know what we're doing, much less teach others!"

His negativism didn't hold my tongue back with excitement as I proclaimed with all my heart, "That's the beauty of it! We're not experts! If we can do it, anyone can!" I saw it all. The whole video playing in my mind right then and there, and I knew it was a call from God and that this homesteading video would bring people from all over the world back to Him, back to creation, back to the land, families working together for the greater good, and people enjoying the simple joys of life. He shook his head as he always did when I had one of my hair-brained ideas and went back to what he was doing. I ran into the house to grab my professional video camera and started filming him working with the children in the dirt, getting all the rocks out of the way so they could make rows. It was the beginning of something extraordinary. My neighbor Sarah was working in her raised-bed garden, and when she found out I was filming, she offered to help teach about her method. It was such a good idea for building up the soil that I thought I better have our garden like that too. We were all learning while I filmed. What I figured was that I could film it and the worst thing that could happen is that it was a flop, and then I could film it all again. I had the garden plan drawn up, and all the seeds started on the old front porch. Molly and Megan helped me plant the seeds in the little pots, and each day we would run out there to check to see if they sprouted. Megan would carefully water each plant with her little headful of tight curls.

Molly caught a cold, and it lasted unusually long that early spring. Her fevers were ongoing, and all I could do was give her lots of fluids and sit by her side. When the fever finally left about two weeks later, she started to look thinner each day. Her spark left, and she was tired most of the time. Molly was six years old at the time, and I noticed she was frequently urinating, so I just figured it was a bladder infection. I knew that bladder infections were common, and since I had done my research, I knew what to do to help my daughter naturally. There was no pain, and she didn't seem very sick, so that I could help her. I thought I had figured it all out, and I went out and bought cranberry pills and offered her lots of water.

Days passed, and she was urinating steadily, which I thought was normal because of the amount of water she had been drinking, and her thirst was encouraging to me. The only troubling thing was that she was steadily losing weight, which I overlooked at first. When I felt her back one evening, it was sharp with her bones, and I began to wonder. I knew that something might be wrong at that point. We lived out in the middle of nowhere, and I debated whether or not it was something that could wait until the morning. It didn't seem at the time that she was having pain or that she was in an emergency, but I knew that I needed to take her to the doctor the next morning. I went to Mark and said, "Darling, I think we better bring Molly to the doctor."

He looked at me with his rolling eyes, "She's fine. It will pass. It's just probably a little infection. There's no need to go to the doctor." I made that call. I shudder today that I did not bring her in sooner and that God kept her alive because He knows more than we know. I had no idea what was wrong, only that I had a feeling that something wasn't right. That night became the longest night of my life. Something came over me. I went to her bed, and she was sleeping, but I still felt petrified. I pulled her body into my arms and cradled her all night long, just praying and asking God for mercy. I trembled with fear. I knew, somehow, that her life was in the balance, and I kept thinking about calling 911, but I thought, what if I am overreacting? And if they came and it was nothing…well, it was hard not to call.

She was asleep, and it didn't appear that she was in danger—it was just a feeling I had. At first light, I helped her get dressed, and she walked with me to the car, and I drove down to the doctor's office, where he immediately tested her blood sugar after hearing about her symptoms. "Your daughter has Type 1 Diabetes," The Doctor said as he showed me a blood sugar tester. He continued, "She needs emergency care. You'll need to turn around and take her to Vanderbilt Hospital in Nashville." That's just what I did. I raced down the highway with my sick little girl, and no sooner did I bring her to the ER than they put her into PICU (Pediatric Intensive Care Unit). Molly had encephalitis from the Diabetic Ketoacidosis (DKA), which can be a fatal complication to that disease. Her brain had already been swelling because of it, and they kept her very closely monitored in the ICU for nearly five days.

I was scared. I had no idea what I was dealing with. For the first couple of nights, they had to keep her quiet and allow her brain swelling to come down. I was only allowed to be near her at certain times of the day so she could rest and they could get her stabilized. They soon tried to teach me how to stick her finger with this thing to test for her blood sugars and then poke her with this needle to give her a precise amount of insulin. There were two different types of insulin and a whole lot of math. We had to measure her food, read labels, count carbs, and try to balance that with the readings on her meter. It was a mathematical equation every time she went to sleep at night, every time she ate, and each time she would play outside. It was overwhelming!

After a week of intensive training, I still felt utterly inadequate to figure out medication doses. And imagine this, I had to hold my daughter down while she was screaming to give her painful shots. And the doctor said I had to because, without her injections, she would surely die.

They needed Mark to come in for some training, and as he walked into the room, something seemed off with him. All at once, he dropped over and was lying there flat on his face on the floor. We had no idea why he passed out at the time, nor did we have the time to figure it out because Molly needed us to be strong for her. Mom came down while we were at the hospital to help care for the children. Her and Auntie Maude made it fun for them, but when we came home, we were so ill-equipped. Mom took some of the pressure off since she was a nurse, and she could help me figure out the doses. Soon she had to go back home, and I was left there to be my daughter's nurse with only one week of training. Some days I would walk outside, and I would just bawl. My precious child's life was in my hands. If I gave too much, I could kill her, and if I did not provide enough, she could go into a coma. It was a very humbling situation because I couldn't fix her. I couldn't make her better. I just had to pray each day that she would make it another day. And God was my hope. I felt I had nothing else to lean on. I felt helpless.

Mark was slowly but surely getting worse each day. He started to act very tiredly all the time and not himself. Most days he was spending in bed, and he could not work. I had to try to figure out how to juggle it all. Every day was another battle of mathematics, figuring out how to make ends meet with my photography, and being a full-time nurse to my little girl and husband. I just wanted my mom. I wanted to fall into her arms and let her fix everything like she always could when I was sick. It was then that I really could understand what it was to be my mom. She could care for people so much better than I could, but doing it day in and day out caused me to appreciate who she was. There's no one like her on this earth. A person who could just drop everything, set her needs aside to care for the sick, was who she always was. I just never saw it until I had to be like her, and it didn't come to me as naturally as it ever was for her. It was who she was. I had to think about it. She didn't.

I cried out for reinforcements, which I mentioned to Mindy because she had a husband who also was a Type 1 Diabetic. She understood and had compassion for us. She sent her oldest daughter,

The Killer Dog & The Ministry

Henrietta, to come to my aid. She made meals for us and helped care for the children. All that care came with a price. I had to pay her by the hour, and I could barely pay the bills, so I had to stop having her come and help.

There was no one else who could help. I was working part-time for Ned's business, Glee's Outfitters, and Missy's Greenhouse, as well as for Dave and Miss Donna's ministry, taking photos, doing layouts, book covers, and video work, but it was not enough to keep me busy full-time to support the family. Without my husband working, we were sunk. All my weddings were up in Wisconsin, and Mark couldn't drive because he was so sick. Nashville was two hours from our homestead, and the thought of leaving home to drive in the night for weddings just about killed me.

What I could do was continue filming our Homesteading Videos. As the garden started producing, I would film every stage of it to the butchering of the chickens we raised. I figured it wouldn't hurt to finish that project and see if I could make the video available that year. It was a lot of work, and Mark usually was in no condition for wanting to be filmed, but I tried to pose as a fly on the wall and get what I could get without bothering him very much. If he were having a good day, he would say a few things on the video, but when he was having a bad day, I had to hide around corners to film and not aggravate him. This sickness made him very aggressive and temperamental toward me. It was certainly out of character.

We had Uncle Smiley come down for a visit, which helped take our minds off of all the medical issues we were facing each day. William and Nellie usually came over every day, and they loved Uncle Smiley too. He became everyone's uncle. When all of us girls were dressing up for a tea party, Uncle Smiley put on a big hat and a British accent. I brewed a kettle of chamomile tea that was once brewed before, and then he went around filling our cups one by one. Like an old British woman, he said, "Ooooh, darling, here is a spot of tea for you! And a spot for you! Would you like one cube or two? Oh, heavens! My, you all are so lovely!" We just giggled as he put on this act with his falsetto voice. Then as we started to drink, Nellie curled up her face in disgust. She said, "This tea tastes terrible!" We all started to sip it, and it did taste terrible. It tasted rotten. I remembered that the tea leaves we reused were in there a long time, and yes, they were rancid and completely rotten. Then Uncle Smiley, still in character, said, "Would you like some rotten tea?" We all burst out laughing because he made it so fun for us all.

After Smiley left and we were left back at the homestead with so little help, the Oldes kids would still come down to play, and some days I had all I could do just to survive. I was not in the mood for any sort of little kid fights. The game they called, "Keep Away from Megan' was not a game I wanted them to play. Megan always came in crying because they would deliberately leave her out. Nellie just liked Molly. She was a one-friend type of girl and could make up stories about almost anything and make them so believable. She had a talent in acting and storytelling, for sure.

Megan came into my office, crying and telling me that they were singing a song about her underpants and making fun of her. I was in one of my "I am not in the mood for this" moods. As I held her close, I started to instruct, "Megan, it's okay. I will sneak outside on the porch, and I will hide from everyone. You go back out there and start swinging. I will see what they do and catch them in the act." Her tears turned into a smile for our little secret plan. I followed her out the back door and slid behind the porch, waiting. I could see Megan climb into the swing that her daddy hung from our carport rafters.

She began to swing, and then the other kids chanted, "I see Germany, I see France, I see Megan's underpants. They might be purple, they might be pink, they might be pretty, but they sure do stink!" Then they laughed louder and louder.

When they tried to start their teasing again, I called out, "Nellie! William! Come over here!" I thought I would see if I could catch them in an outright lie. I inquired, "So, Nellie, were you teasing Megan and singing that underpants song?"

She looked me square in the eyes and said, "Oh, no, I would NEVER do that! Megan is my best friend; I love her so much."

I returned, "You little liar! I was here the whole time, and you just sat there and lied right to my face. Didn't you know lying is a sin?" She and William both just turned the other way and ran back up the hill.

Just minutes later, I got a call from their mama. "Don't you ever dare scold my children and have deep spiritual conversations with them. Send them home when they do something bad. Just send them home. I

The Killer Dog & The Ministry

don't want you talking to my children about lying." There was nothing I could say. She was not happy with me, and I knew our friendship would never be the same. There are certain people that you just don't cross. They hold on to it. I had to do what I did. I had to know. Everyone told me they lied. They warned me. Megan was always getting into trouble because of the things they would lie about, and I never could go against their mom. I would take their side every time, and it was dead wrong. I finally had to take Megan's side and validate her heart. She was viciously teased and left out by them, and it was not good. It was just as well that they didn't come too often anymore because I genuinely had my hands full with figuring out my daughter's blood sugar issues along with my sick husband.

Dave came by each day and knocked on the back door. He would quickly say, "Is Mark okay?" I would say, "He is okay, still pretty…" I could not even finish my sentence to him as he would turn around and walk away fast. It was his way. He wasn't the type to just chit chat. He came for an answer, and then he went on his way. He was worried, though. I could see that. Dave never did just drop in on people. He usually had to have a purpose because he was a private man who kept mostly to himself most of the time.

One Sunday, when my husband was too weak to go to church, I had asked the man next to me if he could request prayer for my husband. I tapped him on the shoulder and whispered into his ear, trying to do this, so no one noticed. He raised his hand and asked, "Can we pray for Mark Harrison? He's still pretty sick in bed."

Dave returned, "Did his wife just put you up to that?" He said yes, and then Dave finished with a cold, sharp answer, "Let the sick call for prayer. Not the wife. If Mark wants us to pray, he will need to ask us." I gathered up my flock in a flood of tears and sat in the truck weeping. I couldn't believe the coldness of these people, and I was desperate for help. I brought Mark in for tests and CT scans, trying to determine why he was deteriorating so quickly. He lost a lot of weight by this time, and my thought was that maybe his tumor on his pancreas came back. I told Mark we had to move back to Wisconsin. I needed help. I had to work, and I knew I could get weddings in Wisconsin lined up for the next year quickly. He could not argue with me because he knew that was true.

Dave came to our home again. This time he said, "I like your family. I wish you would stay. Many families come here because they want to move into our community, and they get disillusioned, disappointed that it is not what they were looking for, and I can say that I am not sad to see them go." He looked down at the ground and pushed the dirt forward with his shoe as he continued, "I would be sad for ya'll to go. You fit in here. You can get weddings, get more work because you're good. You just need to dress more modern, maybe that would get you more work." He chuckled as he looked into my eyes with a sincere love for our family. I knew they loved us, even though they didn't have the warmest way of showing it at the time. He walked away saddened, probably because he knew he couldn't keep us there.

The community wasn't what we thought it would be from all their articles. It was very independent. People came to church, it was so founded on truth, but the love was different. It was not a warm and cozy love, but it was dutiful. When someone was in genuine need, they would do what they could within their abilities. Families who were involved in the volleyball scene were very much on their own. There weren't a lot of get-togethers aside from church meetings nor ways to connect with others. It felt cold. I thought when I moved there, there would be a bunch of homeschooling, homesteading people who wanted to get together for working bees like the Amish while the children would play out in the pastures. It was a dream that I had, and it faded like a lot of other things. Besides, my heart was no longer in Tennessee. My heart was longing for family, longing for grandparents who love my children, and want to spend time with them.

That summer was dry. Bone dry. Tennessee was experiencing a terrible drought. All the animals had to be sold or given away because we had to move. We left Beauty with the Jansens along with the milker. I hated to leave our homestead life again, but there was no getting around it. I couldn't tend to a farm and work full-time. They were planning to take her, but the day we were packing up, she became ill. Somehow, the cow came down with a bad case of mastitis, and we had asked Stan to get a vet, but he wanted to do his research and fix her naturally. For days he plugged her utter, and it only made it worse as he would do apple cider vinegar flushing. We watched her wither away, and there was nothing we could do to help her. It broke my heart, watching that cow suffer. She was about the sweetest creature I've ever met, and the day I walked out there to find her lifeless with her beautiful eyes frozen open and staring ahead, I broke down in a flood of tears. I hated that our last day in Tennessee was that memory.

    My parents were so happy to welcome us back home, and they even invited us to rent the home they owned next door. It was in town, but living in town was just what I needed to get more business and be closer to my work. We made the long journey home with our moving trucks loaded. I had to help drive since he was not feeling so good. We stopped a few times and stayed at a motel so that he could handle the drive. It was the start of another chapter in our life. The city life again, something we both did not like deep down, but you have to do what you have to do when trying to survive it all. I was just thankful that I could be by my parents again. God was so good to provide us with family and loving hands to help in our greatest need.

Chapter Twenty-one
The School & the Hollywood Man

We moved into the little gray house next to my parents' kennel in Little Chute. It was a cute small house with hardwood floors and a lot of character. I decorated it with old-fashioned flare. This house was situated smack dab on a busy road with traffic zooming past all hours of the day and a train that went through on the hour at the very edge of the property. I had to get used to the noise of it all and adjust to a different lifestyle quickly. We never know where life will bring us, and we have to make the most of it, or we would never be happy. It's the thing I hated—the noise of the city and the rat race of society. It was the very thing I ran from years before, but I had to swallow my urge to resist it and be thankful for the little things. I learned to bloom where I was planted. I brought my children to parks for play, walks on the sidewalks, hikes at the nearby nature centers, and visits to our Amish friends on occasion. The children adjusted well to the new life in the city. We had a television with cable so we could watch programs in the evening. We were used to a whole list of chores every morning and evening, all the homesteading and making all of our meals from scratch, and we had to learn to rely more on the grocery store again for the majority of our food.

Because I was now the breadwinner of the family, I became very focused on making money. Mark was still very ill with whatever he had and wasn't able to work, so he would often sit in the recliner watching television while I thought up of a hundred more ways to earn our family living.

That year, I made over a hundred thousand just in weddings alone. I did every wedding show I could to display my work and get my name out there. In the evenings, I would have my children walk next door to my parents' home so that I could have appointments with brides. I would have the entire house clean as a whistle, and the candles lit with all my photography displayed around the room as if I didn't even have a family living there with me. As they would page through my storybooks, they would catch a vision of their day. They could see that I genuinely loved what I did and cared for each couple I worked with to make their day more memorable. Soon I had my entire spring, summer, and fall booked at weddings. The word spread, and many more would call even two years in advance to find out when I was available because they wanted me to be their photographer so badly that they would plan their wedding around my schedule. It was so humbling. I couldn't believe they wanted my services that much, and for the first time in my life, I felt like people appreciated my care for them.

I would have done it all for free because I enjoyed working with these precious people. I had to have an exclusive contract and a whole list of packages, or else I would have given it all away. The part of the business that always was hard for me was believing I was worthy of hire. If I could hand them a paper and they could make a decision, hand me a down payment, I could separate the two in my mind. If I didn't have it all written out, I would never have survived. My entire family always would get frustrated with me because they wanted me to understand it was okay to charge people money and that we needed money to survive. I made sure there was a cheap package that was a bottom-dollar budget for anyone who wanted care without the cost, yet they all signed up for the one package that had all the frills and bells and whistles. On average, these brides wanted it all, and they were willing to pay top dollar. It was astonishing to me at the time, but I was just thankful that God was providing a very comfortable living for our family when my husband was unable to work.

On a pleasant afternoon, our family visited Mark's mother, who lived in a beautiful home in the country on the other side of town. That day Mark was feeling incredibly sick and tired, so he made his way to the recliner in her expansive, open living room, which had the most glorious view of the trees. While sitting there, we could see birds cheerfully flitting past the window or land on a feeder to eat a bit. Her home was always so serene, so peaceful, like a haven of rest for the soul. She didn't care for any sort of technology or television, so when we went there, we would talk or watch nature from the window.

The children had a whole play area in her basement to build things out of train-tracks or blocks. Often, she would just sit on the sofa and read them a good book. We had been talking, and I had told her all about the move and the photography business at the kitchen table when I saw her friend Mildred walk past the window and make her way to the front door. I didn't know she was expecting a visitor, but I was always so happy to see Mildred. Mildred was a middle-aged woman who had an extensive family. She had ten children or more. They were all talented somehow, and some years before, when she was living with us, I met her. There was a day that Grandma Kathy asked me to inquire at my alma mater about music lessons for the children.

I called my friend Doris who worked in the art department, and she told us they didn't have classes for such young children, but that Mildred and her family would be a good connection. Doris was good friends with Mildred, and she had invited us those years back when we lived in Black Creek over to her country home and performed some lovely Christian songs as a family band. I was quite impressed and knew that they were my kind of people. Doris and Kathy were the best of friends, and they had decided to live together there at this beautiful home I was so blessed to sit in that day. Doris was the sweetest, most gentle woman with a hearty smile on her face that pushed up her cheeks with wisps of short golden hair around her face. Her eyes were kind, and I always felt warm and loved in her presence. I was quite glad that Kathy found Doris and that they could keep each other company in that big house in the country. They had similar interests, so it made sense that they could share in the care of the home and other related expenses. As I sat there waiting for Mildred to walk in, I could hear the indistinct chatter of small children emanating from the basement and the greeting of close friends at the door.

Mildred walked into the room and sat across from me at that little wooden kitchen table, and we began to catch up for the lost time. I told her all about our adventures in Tennessee and how glad we were to be back near the family so the children could have their loving grandparents close by. I spilled all the beans about my thriving, new photography business. I never could stop telling people all my endeavors in life. She smiled, but I got the idea in my spirit that she had a purpose for coming that day. It almost seemed like they had something planned.

Mildred opened her mouth to give me some counsel with the most loving intentions. "Did you know that a husband who does not provide for his own family is worse than an infidel?" I sat there in a state of shock, wondering what that was supposed to mean. Was she referring to my husband? I got it just then, yes, she was. She must have been informed that my husband was not working, and I was the sole income earner. I started to feel a bit agitated as our lovely conversation took such a negative direction from that point. She continued in a lowered voice, "Erin, did you know that this is in Scripture? You know that the will of God for you as a woman is to be a keeper of the home, not a working woman."

Still, in a shock with the lack of mercy she had upon my sick husband and our situation, I returned, "Didn't you know that my husband is very sick? He would work if he could." Just like all humans do when they have someone attack them and accuse them of something, they start to throw the stones back, and I did. I wasn't right, but I began to pick apart her situation right then and there, and I tried to find some faults with her, and I did. I mean, who did she think she was to tell me my husband was worse than an infidel? The audacity. I wasn't too friendly with her from then on. A true friend will show love and mercy. They seek to know your situation and refrain from judgment. The serenity of that home quickly left my soul, and I just prayed for her to go. All I wanted was peace in the sea of my life that seemed always to be turning upside down around every corner. Just trying to survive it all, I had to have my windows of peace and hope. The last place I needed to be was on the stand, receiving my condemnation when things were beyond my control.

It was evident that I was too busy to homeschool my three older children. I hated the idea of not having my children near me all day, and teaching them school was such a joy to me. The first day I decided to send Miles to the public school was one of the most challenging days of my life. It was like I traded time for money. I felt like a failure as a mother. How could I march my children off to an institution each day? I had no choice. If I was to be the sole income earner in the home, I had to make sure my children had all they needed to learn. I walked Miles to school since it was only about a block away from home, and he seemed excited to start. It was free to send him there, and I had been used to paying a lot of money for books when I homeschooled. After a few days, I wondered if I should send the little girls. They were scared to go, so I held back, but yet I wasn't sure I could offer them the time needed to teach them sufficiently. The day I walked my little girls down with me to pick him up, I will never forget. A mother was cussing her little boy out, a little boy that happened to be in Miles' class at the time, and then she had a big cigarette hanging out of her mouth while she raged. I thought at that moment, NO. I can't. I can't send my children to a place where parents act like they don't even love their children. When it's free, you get all the people from every walk of life, and I remembered those kids in school who had parents like that. They often got into the same trouble as their parents did before them, and the cycle just continued. I didn't want that life for my children. I spent half my life trying to redefine myself and break those molds and strongholds of disfunction.

There was a private Catholic school down the road, and I walked right there that afternoon with all three of my little ones. As the principal sat us down in her office, I felt a sense of security there. I started in with the full disclosure, "We don't agree with the Catholic religion...with all the rituals, and prayers to the saints..." I took a deep breath thinking I dug myself into a hole, "We are not just religious people, but we do believe in Jesus and love the Bible. I'm not sure you will accept us here if we're not practicing Catholics."

She started to chuckle and returned, "Ah, it's perfectly okay, Mrs. Harrison. We accept everyone, no matter what their background is." She leaned over with a smile and pointed to the man in the hall as she exclaimed, "Our guidance counselor is a Jewish Rabbi!" I breathed a sigh of relief as I could feel that she wanted us to feel accepted. I was so used to religion and cults who have their barriers and walls and feel they are the only ones going to heaven, so I figured they would be the same. It was so refreshing. I asked if our children could be left out of the morning rosary prayer to Mary and the Friday morning Mass. I didn't want them to be learning how to be a Catholic. I just wanted them to learn academics, and she wholeheartedly agreed. With that handshake, I signed up Miles, Molly, and Megan for school, and they started the very next morning.

    The first morning I brought Miles to his class, and he jumped right in like he knew the whole bunch his entire life. I walked out, knowing that he would manage just fine. Molly was a complicated situation due to all of her diabetic needs. I had to spend half the day training their school nurse all the different things that could happen and what to do in each scenario. She had a granddaughter with type one, so she had some experience already, which left me feeling more secure. Megan was a whole other matter. I dropped her off for the afternoon kindergarten class, and she clutched onto me with all her might. When I tried to distract her and walk out ever so quietly, she came running and screaming down the hall after me.

    For the next few weeks, I had to be there full-time to sit in class with Megan while my mother would take turns sitting in class with Molly making sure the staff understood her diabetes. I couldn't abandon my children like that. I wanted to make sure they felt safe, and when they felt safe, I did too. The time eventually came where I could leave them, and the girls wouldn't cry. They started to make friends and enjoyed learning. Whenever there was a field trip, I always came along and sat with my girls. I needed to make sure I was looking after Molly on the bus. So many things could happen with a person with diabetes. She could have high blood sugar one minute and then the next minute, she could be nearly passing out from low blood sugar. It was tough to manage her condition. No matter how hard I tried, there was always the element of surprise. Miles never seemed to need me as he would rush off to play with his classmates.

    I could see right then and there that I did not fit in. The children had their cute little uniforms, but I looked like a sore thumb at that school. Each day when I would drop the children off, the other ladies would turn up their noses as they scanned me up and down with their eyes examining my long drab skirts with button-up cotton shirts printed with flowers. My hair would be slicked back in a bun, and with no make-up on, well, I looked more Amish than I thought. In their minds, I probably was Amish. People don't know the difference. If you wear your hair in a bun and you have a skirt on, you're Amish. Forget about Mennonites; they hadn't even learned about them yet. In stark contrast, all the moms had perfectly curled hair, make-up, and the latest trends in clothing. When they walked past with their boots clicking and their hair flowing in the wind, it went by in slow motion as if I was watching a commercial. They were all so put-together. You could tell they had money, the fanciest cars, and probably fancy houses to go along with everything else. Now that I was making money, I thought I could afford a new wardrobe as well. It didn't take long to figure out what would be socially acceptable in my new city lifestyle, tight jeans, and pretty tops with long sweaters. I wasn't dumb. I knew how to dress to kill. For my new hairstyle, I consulted my sister-in-law, Michelle. She brought me to a hairstylist who took about ten inches off my hair, layered it, put some highlights, low lights, and gave me some strict instructions on how to style my hair each day with a blow dryer. Those days of just frumping up my hair in a ball were over. I started curling my hair, painting my nails, and putting on the trendiest outfits. When Mark first saw me, he just about had a heart attack from shock.

Somehow, I could transform myself and look completely different. It was dramatic, especially from Amish to City Slicker. Like I had always been my whole life, I could change my appearance and look a new part. Every morning I would wake hours before the children and go to the health club to work-out as to tighten up my figure. Dad would walk up to the back door to let me know he was ready, and we would race out the door at about four a.m. while the dark of night was still pervasive, yet the orange glow of the streetlights brightened the way to the car. Dad always found it imperative to take care of himself. When I was in high school, we would wake at four a.m. even then and lift weights every morning before school. That routine was engrained because when I got back into it, it became second nature again. After a couple of hours of weightlifting and swimming laps in the pool, I would race back home to curl my hair. When I finished every last detail in front of that wide mirror of the gray bathroom, I would make breakfast and wake the children. The girls needed hair done, and uniforms ironed. The dirty barefoot, farm-kid look was replaced with a clean and classy counterpart.

Megan was in half-day kindergarten, so I felt like I was running back and forth all the time. Now that I think about it, I really could have just homeschooled them, for the number of hours it took me to doll up to make the grand entrance, paint the nails, drive back and forth several times each day, packing lunches, talking to the teachers and mingling with the other moms. Who was I kidding? I think I made my life a veritable sea of chaos and vanity all in one shot. I had to keep up with those dreadful, shiny, French-manicured nails by painting the pink part and then the white over the top, every other day. It was the bed I had made, and I had to live in that new part of the act I created now that I was getting more and more clients in the area. Mark stayed home during those days with Mikey and Junior sitting in his chair watching the television. It wasn't my idea of a good life.

  I didn't like sending the children off, nor did I appreciate a husband who watched T.V. all day. I signed up for it. When I married this man, I promised to love him in sickness and in health, for better or for worse. Most days, he would just sit there all day in the chair and not talk. I didn't want to talk to him or agitate him at all because I would regret it. He was a time bomb waiting to go off. If I asked him anything, he would yell back, "Don't act stupid! You know the answer to that!" I could barely believe he had become such a jerk, but I knew it was beyond his control. Whatever his disease or sickness was, it was taking his mind. I had to be careful not to cross him, or he would start yelling or shaking me with his strong hands. I got in the habit of making sure I looked after everything and never asked him anything. He couldn't remember anything anyhow. If he set his keys on the dresser, he would yell that someone stole them a few hours later because he would look in his pocket, and they were not there. He would forget that he took them out of the pocket and set them on the dresser.

  I had to be very mindful of every move he made so that when he was aggravated, I could calm him down. Most days, I was scared. I thought he had lost his mind. It was like I was married to a stranger. Finally, I sent him off to the doctor to be tested for Lyme disease because they couldn't find any other condition to point his symptoms. I figured it was a long shot, but it was something they never tested for. They kept saying he was just depressed. The tests came back positive, and we were somewhat relieved to have something to fight finally. We knew it was something. Lyme disease was not very treatable if you didn't catch it in the first month. It had been over a year, so the rounds of antibiotics did nothing for him. He continued having brain fog, agitation, memory loss, and blackouts.

  "Hello, Mrs. Harrison," I could tell it was the principal from the school. She continued, "Can you please come to my office to discuss an issue we are having with one of your children?" What, now? I had a feeling it had to be Miles. I agreed and immediately drove down the road to the school and marched into her office to see what the problem was. "Have a seat." This must be serious, I thought. I have to sit down for this one. As her voice lowered, I could tell that she wasn't too happy, "Miles is telling the other children that the Virgin Mary is dead and that she can't hear their prayers, that the only one who can answer their prayers is Jesus, not the priest." I almost had to hold myself back from being happy that my son was so passionate about his beliefs.

I wanted to say Amen to Miles, but I knew that it would've only made things worse for all of us. I know my son. He won't stand for lies. It didn't surprise me that he would open his big mouth and say such things. She took a deep breath, exhaled as if she was not finished, "Furthermore; he is telling them that their parents lie to them about Santa." She leaned into the desk with all her weight, for she was not a small woman. Resting her forearms over the top and folding her hands, she concluded, "Mrs. Harrison, I understand that you do not share in our religious beliefs, but the other parents are becoming upset that your son is spoiling their Christmas and causing such confusion. This has to stop."

That was that. I had to say the only thing that I knew at the time was right, "So sorry, ma'am. I will talk with Miles, and this won't happen again." I had to make it work. We were on their turf, their rules. I did it before, where I lived by the motto, 'When in Rome, do as the Romans do.' Being all things to all people and playing the part was an easy thing for me in my life. I knew I could not convince the children without a good lie. My husband was sick and off in the chair. He didn't pay much attention to what we were doing. I decided to gather the children around me and play up the idea of Santa. I felt it was all I could do at the time to keep them at that school.

After they all huddled around in the other room, I started, "Did you know that there was this man so long ago that was a Christian? He loved Jesus so much, and the little children so much that he went around giving gifts to them." Their eyes widened. I whispered, "His name was Saint Nicholas. Santa for short. Do you see? That's where you get that story from. If you try to be like the other children at school and play along with their game, he will give you lots of presents, too." I hated to lie to them, and I felt pretty guilty, but I didn't want them to get kicked out of school. I knew that even if I told Miles not to tell the other children, he would feel so desperate to warn them about the lies, he would tell them the secret because little did the principal know, I had already told him not to tell them. He was telling them secretly, in their ears, or else on the playground when the teacher wasn't looking. Miles was scrunching up his face with skepticism.

I winked at him, leaned over, and said, "Miles, you never know unless you try. Let's just try and have some fun like the other children at school. If we can stop telling them that Santa is not real and play along with the fun game, maybe we'll be surprised with lots of presents this year." I knew Mark would cringe if he had been in his right mind and would put a stop to it all. We all decided to just play along with the fun Santa game that year. I went out and bought presents since I was making a lot of money that year. We all trimmed a tree and listened to Christmas music. All my childhood memories of Christmas flooded over me like a trance. I was lost in the realm of warm family tradition. All the presents were hidden, just like my parents hid ours when we were kids. I wrapped them all in secret and stuffed them in the rafters. The excitement of it all overwhelmed me.

They all sat the night before Christmas wide-eyed and full of anticipation. The white snow had fallen and laid its blanket across the dirty city streets, and it was glorious. As the moon and stars lit the snow, it sparkled, and we were lost in the splendor of it all. We never did Christmas like this until that day, and it was the only time we ever did it in our whole married life. It was the one thing Mark would never allow, but it was one of my good memories as a child. I remembered being a little girl, the night before Christmas, looking out on the snow and wondering how high the sleigh would be and if Santa would be faithful to remember me. He was my God when I didn't have one. I would stare out in hope. The next morning I would see the gifts stacked under the tree, and it seemed magical, mysterious, and like a dream come true in my world with so much sadness, it was the one thing I clung to.

After the children went to bed, and I knew they were fast asleep, I tiptoed through the house with each wrapped gift. I felt a bit like a sneak or a naughty elf doing this while I knew it was not what my husband would want. I have since learned when women make more money than their husbands, frequently, they make their own rules as they go. A woman making all the money in the house might feel entitled. I know I did. I made that money; I can have my form of fun, was a thought that

The School & The Hollywood Man

crossed my mind. It was the first step in my rebellion. This was pure fun for me to wake up the next morning and see my children race down to the tree and know that they had so many presents to open. They started to find the ones that were theirs as their piles were wrapped in different paper. You could hear giggling, ripping paper, and the sounds of thankful hearts.

Everything they dreamed of was wrapped in pretty paper. The girls ran off with their new dolls to dress them up in all their new doll clothes while Miles dumped the Lego castle box out and started to build it piece by piece. Mikey and Junior were making zooming noises as they scooted their dump trucks and pirate ships across the old hardwood floors in the dimly-lit morning. Mark came out of his slumber, and he sat there smiling. Even though I did this all in secret, there was the child within him that found it magical too. He smiled for the first time in months, and he seemed happy. I could see hope again for us in our little made up Santa game for Christmas morning.

"Let us take him," Miss Donna had said over the phone. She did hundreds of hours of research to find herbal remedies to help my poor husband with the Lyme. After telling her his erratic behavior, she thought it would be best for someone to drive 700 miles to our place and bring him back to Tennessee to be cared for. But Mark would not go. He is big enough that no one could make him go against his will, so instead, she sent up Suzy, her niece, to lend a hand with the work and the children. She came bearing the herbal remedies that would soon help my husband get on top of his symptoms. Suzy came up and stayed several weeks with my mother-in-law by night, and by day she would help with the cleaning, cooking, and weddings. I had taught her how to shoot weddings with me, so she would help me haul the equipment around and take photos of different angles. Having her there and having my parents right next door made it all doable for me. I couldn't have done it without the extra love and support I received from our friends and family.

Little by little, Mark started to feel better. Suzy flew back to Tennessee, and all seemed to be getting back to our new level of normal. He began to act more himself but never quite felt a hundred percent. It was enough that I could finally talk with him and relate to him again. When he started to feel well enough to think again, he decided to take the money we had from selling our Tennessee farm and buy another homestead in the country. He found a very secluded farmhouse on thirteen acres with a big barn and a shop. We all went out there to take a peek at our new home and found it to be just what we needed for the right price. We even had money left over after the down payment to fix that old house up. It was seriously out of date with flame-orange shag carpets throughout, paisley linoleum, and dark brown, fake wood paneling. Just what we hated.

It was like taking a trip back to the '70s when you walked through the door, but I knew what Mark could do with it, so I just smiled in excitement. The children ran up the steps looking into all the bedrooms upstairs and which ones they would claim for their own. Being the dreamers we were, we could see a future there, and the transformation of what it would look like was nothing short of miraculous. When there is a will, there is always a way. While I was busy running my photography business and running the children back and forth to their school, Mark was out at the farm, busting out walls, chimneys, paneling, and rolling up carpets. Soon enough, he was putting up the new drywall and refinishing all the beautiful old hardwood floors that stretched from the dining room into the kitchen.

I started to write music on the piano when the children were off to school, and our other little boys were sleeping upstairs to that small gray house. Writing songs came pretty fast for me, and my brother helped me record them. Some of my brides would ask me to perform the songs at their weddings. I had a love song and a father and daughter song that they wanted to play when the bride and father had their first dance. The wedding shows were underway, and I was meeting other wedding professionals. This beautiful blond-haired lady came up to my booth one evening in the heart of the wedding show, telling me that I had done good work. She was also a wedding photographer, and a good one. I went to her booth and saw what I believed to be stunning displays of real art.

Holly and I became close friends and started sharing all the stories of things we had to deal with to make an ironclad contract at the end of it. The contract had to be such that it would protect me from being treated like a piece of meat. I had it set up so that if someone did hassle me that way, I would go to the bride and groom, notify them that if that behavior did not stop immediately, I would leave, and they would not get a refund. I've been to weddings where guys will grab me in the nether regions or try to solicit favors from me when on the job. The way I had dressed may have had a bit to do with it. I wore black pants, heeled boots, with my styled hair, makeup, and the way I paid attention to people was a sure message to them that I was for sale, somehow. To the men, I looked available, and I knew they were interested because they would ask for my number. I had lots of offers. I didn't realize how serious my conduct was.

My husband said, "Why are you trying to look like a teenager? You are thirty-two years old with a family. Why do you want other men to desire you?" I've made many foolish choices, but I thank God that He is patient with me. Maybe deep down, I liked the attention, even just a little. A woman loves being told she is beautiful and looks ten years younger than she is. Whatever the reason, I kept up the charade.

One weekend I traveled down to Chicago to record my songs with my dad and my little girls. We worked on a handful of songs, and I even had Molly and Megan sing a small part in the father-daughter song that I wrote. It was so adorable with their little girl voices. On the way home, Dad was driving, and all of a sudden, I started to cramp up. Blood started rushing out of my bottom, and my pants were wet with blood. He pulled over to a gas station where I made my way to the dirty bathroom, and an enormous clot came out the size of an egg. Shaking, I pulled dozens of paper towels out to clean up the blood that was still streaming down my legs. I fastened my pants on and carefully walked myself back to the car and sat down. "Dad," I said, breathy and fearfully. "Something's wrong. I'm losing a lot of blood."

He never said a word as he looked forward and put the car into drive. We merged back onto the highway, and I started to feel faint and weak. Under my breath, I said, "Pull over now!" The thoughts of dying came flooding into my brain, and my daughters were crying in the back, wondering what was happening to their mother. I didn't want to call 911, but I felt that it would be better than my dad trying to save my life while caring for my two little girls who would be crying and scared, not to mention a daughter who has diabetes needs special care. He had no idea about this because he was never trained. I flipped open my cell phone and dialed 911. I told them I was bleeding and where the blood was coming from. To the best of my knowledge, I told them where I thought I was on the highway and between what two exits as we were a couple of hundred miles away from home. It was embarrassing that I called myself an ambulance, but it was before the invention of the GPS, and we were in the middle of nowhere, and I couldn't bear to have my dad stuck with an emergency. I had no idea how serious my situation was; the only thing I knew was that I was feeling weak, and the bleeding had not stopped. They stuck me in the back of the ambulance, and Dad followed behind until we made it to the nearest hospital. They put an IV in and ran some tests.

I was pregnant and was having a miscarriage. I didn't even know I was pregnant. The blob I found in the bathroom, they said, was more than likely my baby, and I just flushed it down, not knowing what it was at the time. It wasn't life-threatening and felt like a real loser to call an ambulance. "Don't feel bad, Mrs. Harrison," the ER nurse told me. "I would've done the same." I sopped up the rest of the blood and got back into the car, and we all drove back home. If I had been at home, I would've been okay. I would've figured it out. Losing another child through a miscarriage was hard. Since my uterus had been so damaged from the IUD mishap, I suffered another miscarriage after that. It seemed as though when they cauterized my uterus, it may have damaged the lining so that it could not keep a pregnancy.

That summer, we moved into the new home, a bit unfinished. There was no trim up, and the bottom step and railing for the staircase were missing, so Mark placed a big cinder block there on the end of the steps, so we had something to step onto to get to the stairs. We always tended to live in our homes, half-finished and undone. Making it work was a part of the fun, yet I still yearned for the trim. The new windows had fluffy plastic insulation stuff foaming around each one. It was ruddy and yellow, but I also got used to that. Curtains hid a portion of it.

The kitchen had no countertop yet, so we just slid boards over it until we could fix that. We just made things work. It was the homesteader in us. For the first several days, we did not have running toilets, so we set up a commode in the shop that was about fifty yards from the back door. We had to make a fifty-yard dash anytime we had to go to the bathroom. When the toilets were in, we all cheered. The children were getting dirty again, running barefoot, and not combing their hair. It was freedom from keeping up with the Joneses. The school was out, and I was happy to be back in the country. We all were.

Weddings were in full tilt, so we were off capturing their special days one right after the other. By this time, Mark was coming along, and I was glad he was there. He was acting more and more himself, and life felt amazing. We were a team. He would take the video while I shot the photos, and we even had a five-course meal at the reception while we were working. My mom or his would be there at the home front watching the children, and often it seemed like we were on a date once or twice a week.

It bonded us so closely to work together. He had everything charged, every battery and every detail was looked after with precision, and I didn't have to worry about anything. He carried all the equipment, dropped me off at the doors, held all my lenses, and even had our silent way to communicate. It was sort of like sign language. He kept an eye out for me and I for him, waiting to see if there was anything needed. If I needed a different lens, I would look at him and point my finger to the lens, and he would know that I needed the other one. I would walk to him like in one fluid motion while all was completely silent in the church and without a peep, and I would switch that lens and freshen up my batteries and, in a flash, be out taking hundreds of more photos.

In the evenings when the beer started flowing, the crazy drunken men would try to come for me, and I would point toward my very handsome man on the other side of the room and say, "You see that gorgeous man over there? That's my husband." We had it all planned out, I would point to him, and he would nod his head with a very sober look while folding his arms like a bouncer, and then I would continue, "He is bigger and stronger than you and way better looking than you. If you so much as look at me like that again, he might just come over and bust your face in." I would say this with a wink and a smile. That took care of the drunks at the wedding.

There was always something about Mark. Take one look at him, and people know not to mess with him. He wasn't a fool in any way, shape, or form. His presence commanded respect and anyone who messed with me ultimately had to mess with him. It was sort of fun. I loved seeing their scared expressions. Who did they think they were? They could never compete with Mr. Manly Gorgeous, who I call my husband. One smash of his fist would finish them, and they knew it.

Soon came the fall, and I had signed up our children for an online homeschool curriculum. It was fantastic. We had all the course work there waiting for us each day with a click of a button. And it was free. All the books, the computers, everything, was sent in the mail. They even paid a percent of the internet. Every lesson was beautifully written with photos and graphics that made the learning fun. It was a classical style of education, which is my favorite. For their physical education, I took them to the gym for martial art classes that I instructed. They hired me to teach alongside another teacher for mixed martial arts. We spent our days together in every way, and I was so delighted with all they were learning.

I kept a detailed schedule. I woke up each morning at three a.m., and I would work on the storybooks from all the weddings, editing, and creating beautiful layouts until about seven a.m. when I would make a big breakfast for the family. We would sit down to a warm meal and then start our homeschooling. I had a big schoolroom set up in the upstairs of the farmhouse where I had all little wooden desks in a row. We finished most of our schooling by lunchtime, and for lunch, we would often pack a picnic, if the weather was nice, and go on a hike somewhere. I would bring them to all the beautiful places my parents would take me as a child. Instead of my mom packing the lunches, I was the mom packing the lunches, and we were on forgotten railways, climbing to the tops of Mosquito Hill. They were the children with wonder holding their arms outstretched, feeling they were on top of the world and singing their trill as they ran down the big hill. I relived my most incredible memories as a child through my children, and we were living the greatest story together. Every day was a memory etched into my heart.

Nana and Bumpa would ride along for many of these adventures, and I could see them reliving their childhood, my childhood, and another form of youth as the same breeze would push our hair from our face, and the gentle touch of the sun on our foreheads. It was all like a frozen period in a capsule of something precious we all shared. In silent wonder, we all stared at each other as we would bite our sandwich in the same place we ate Mom's sandwiches. Dad's eyes were older, and his knees were getting tired. His little walking stick helped him manage, and the giggles of small children, both young and old, could be heard among the trees and over the fields of that happy place. That's the wondrous thing about life. With each new generation, you're allowed the simple joy of reliving your childhood through their eyes.

When I wasn't teaching or adventuring, in the afternoons, I would write songs and play the piano. After attending so many weddings, I met other wedding professionals who offered many other services. One such man was a DJ. He was a middle-aged man, with freckled, dark skin. His name was Hal. A songwriter and performer, he had a studio and took a fond interest in my music. Soon I was working with him on jingles and other projects. He had an idea to work on a concert dinner that would help married couples. He had asked me to perform one of my songs at the concert, and I agreed.

Many evenings I would drive out to his place and work with him on music. There were times that he would start getting a bit more personal and would start sharing about the struggles he and his wife were having. I tried to help him by telling him some of my many miraculous stories, how Jesus saved me and my marriage, how much in love my husband and I had become through the years of our struggles. Somehow, in my transparent way, I had revealed a bit more of my soul than I should have, and I could tell he wanted what I had. He wanted the idea of a happy life in his struggle. I'm sure the light and love of Jesus shone over my face each time I would share the story, yet I think he confused it with a feeling of love for me or the idea of a love that I possessed. Jesus was what he needed.

I knew something was wrong when one late evening as we worked on music, he leaned toward me and touched his hand to my leg and said he was in love with me. I shrunk back in disbelief, removed his hand, and made my way to the door, knowing I could never go back there again. I had no idea that I gave him the wrong idea. When I arrived home that evening, I told Mark, and he was also saddened. He was sorry that I could not go there again. Feelings of guilt spread over my mind like a fog, and I sat all night, wondering if I could have done something to prevent this attachment. The very next morning, the phone rang. It was his wife. She asked, "What were you and Hal doing last night so late?" My heart pounded. Could she think that I had done some immoral thing? I couldn't bear it. After I told her that we were working on the jingle until late, leaving out the long talk we had, I called him, and I told him that I couldn't be around him anymore because I worried for his wife, who had become suspicious.

As I made my way into the living room, the children came running to me, "Mom, something's wrong with Mikey!" I saw my little, blond-headed boy standing at the top of the steps with tears streaming down his face, holding his belly.

"Mikey, are you okay?" I asked as I motioned for him to come to me. He could not move or talk. My heart began to race as I leaped over the cinderblock and up the steps to find out what was wrong. There was a check-in my spirit right then and there. I knew it was life-threatening. Somehow, I knew it was his appendix. I carefully pulled him up into my arms and gently walked down the steps. Every step I took, he winced in pain. He was groaning and still holding his belly. I laid him flat on his back and pressed my hands into his abdomen, where I knew the appendix was, and pulled my hands away quickly when he screamed out in utter agony. That was what it was. I carried him out to the van and raced to the emergency room, where they immediately found that his appendix had ruptured. Because of his heart issues, they had to send him to a much larger city hospital, the same hospital where he had his heart surgery, which was about two hours away, in a helicopter.

Mark was still at home with the other children, and when they asked me if I got motion sickness in helicopters, I said no, even though I did. I had to deny my motion sickness because Mikey was so scared, and I didn't want to be separated from him. Tears were still streaming down the sides of his little face, and as we started flying through the air, I had to grab the puke bags and out I hurled for the entire trip. When we arrived, they immediately prepped him for surgery, and I ended up in a waiting room where I paced the floors, wondering if he was going to make it. Finally, the doctor came out to tell me that they successfully removed the appendix and that I could see my son in recovery. Mikey was lying there in the hospital bed, barely awake, and I was so glad I could be the first thing he saw. I knew he felt safe with me being there.

They had brought him all kinds of toys. They allowed me to sleep on a chair beside him, so I did not leave his side. One day they told me he would have to go down for some tests, and my sister-in-law drove up from Chicago to pick me up and bring me out for an hour. I hated to leave, but she thought the fresh air would do me good. After I came back, the room phone rang and it was Mark's step mom, "Hello Erin, this is Kelly. You can come and stay with us at night if you like." There was no way I could leave for that long, so I declined the very kind invitation, yet she returned in frustration, "Oh, I see how it is. You don't want to come here because we don't have as much money as your brother!" Where did that come from? Why would she say such a thing? I was dumbfounded and bewildered by that accusation in such a crisis as I was going through with my little boy. As my heart raced nearly out of my chest, I could not find a corner deep enough to crawl into. I just wanted to run into a corner and cry like a dog that had just been kicked.

I quivered in return, "That's not how it is. I just don't want to leave my son's side. He would be so scared if I was gone, not to mention if something would go wrong and I would not be here."

She didn't entirely listen to my reasoning as she continued to jab at my heart, "All you care about is money, and that is the truth, don't try to deny it." She quickly said she had to go. In that small moment, I felt defenseless and in utter fear.

When people would come at me with a stick to prod me with one accusation or another over a misunderstanding, I never felt like I could fight back. I felt like I deserved it somehow, and I somehow reverted to feeling like a little girl again. The victim in me cried out for mercy and found none. Money never was something I cared about, so being accused of loving money like that, I was broken. Part of me was so angry, wondering how a person could do that to a young mother caring for her very sick child. Who does that? I had to wipe the tears off my face and move forward with my son in his recovery, trying to forget the drama and getting into better spirits. Each day Mikey became stronger and stronger, and soon he was able to walk around, eat, and smile. Mom drove down to pick us up and drive us back home. She always dropped anything to come to our aid.

Life went back to normal soon enough, and we were doing school and going back to the gym for martial art lessons. Mikey was jumping around like a little bean on the trampoline, and we knew he was about to feel like himself again. I would often get on the trampoline with the children and jump. We would laugh, and I would bounce them higher and higher until I started noticing I would leak the higher I bounced. I brushed it off for a while until the urine began running down my legs at the gym. I went to several specialists and found out that I needed a routine bladder lift, which seemed to be something that many women need. My obstetrician recommended that I have my uterus removed due to the scar tissue and issues I had been having and referred me to her colleague, Dr. Blynd, to perform the bladder lift. She told me that he was the best.

The day I went to his office, he showed me photos of older women over fifty who had a similar issue after examining me. I had a herniated pelvic wall so severe that my bladder was coming outside of my body, which explained the leaking and the pressure I had been feeling. He told me that if I didn't have this fixed, it could cause even more issues. The catch was that I had to accept the fact that I could never again have pregnancies.

This was something I had to pray about. It felt so final to me, and I wanted more children. Mark said, "You have so many issues with pregnancy. Maybe it would be for the best." He pulled me close to his chest and held me in his arms, "Besides, we can always adopt. So many children out there need a family." I stood there, hoping he would save me, say something to make the inevitable decision not come true. I knew I had to honor his wishes. He had so much to deal with whenever I became pregnant. It was sometimes a full-time job looking after the little ones and me when certain uncomfortable issues came up. We started to forget all the miracles at that moment and chose to trust in the medical. I knew I had to trust my husband, and I found out the hard way when I went against his better judgment. One of the choices I made got me in that predicament because I tried to get that IUD and my uterus became injured. I hoped I would become pregnant to have more time to pray and think and know that this was from God. The thought of never again having a baby haunted my nights.

Feelings of selfishness started to braze over my mind to the point I figured if he doesn't let me have more children, I will do my own thing. I began to focus on my music. Holly came by to film my music videos, and I made the covers of my future albums. Hal, whom I vowed never to work with again, called to tell me that his friend from Hollywood was in town and wanted to meet with me. I agreed to meet with this man and met Hal in the parking lot, so I would not be alone with him. The man was a producer and flew in to meet this woman he was told could be a star. I walked into this office where the man was seated. He was a larger man dressed in a suit, and when I approached him at the desk, he was just using that day, he pulled himself off his seat to meet me halfway. We shook hands and introduced ourselves.

He said, "So I heard some of your music, and I could land you a job singing for Disney, but I also heard you do comedy, do you?" Right then and there, I stood to my feet, and I started to give him a show I'm sure he would never forget. I had him laughing, hunched over in his chair, and as he composed himself, he said, "I could see you auditioning for Saturday Night Live! You have a memorable face. People could like you very much."

He became very serious as he leaned in a bit closer, "You could make it, Erin. You could have it all. But they will have you in return. They will own you. It's a crazy place, Hollywood is. And when you entertain them once, you have to keep that door open, or you'll lose your footing." I kept searching his face for more as he stopped, paused, and then looked at Hal, "They will eat her alive. She would have to have protection. It's not a safe place, Hal. She is so innocent." We all started to lose the flare of the moment as all became still and quiet. He pressed me, "I can take you to the top, but do you want that, Erin? Let me know. Hal, you know where to find me!" I left the office as I had been on a roller coaster ride. Since I was a little girl, people told me I would be famous. I was created for something bigger than I ever knew, yet for a moment, I was lost in a flood of stars mixed with fear. Was this my calling? Could I remain faithful?

I raced back home as fast as I could, the entire way talking to God and feeling more and more that it was my calling. I could be famous for Him. When I would do this show or that, I would have a platform. When I would be interviewed by this show or that, I would tell the world about my stories, about Jesus, and there would be this great revival. I could see it all in my mind, and my mind was made up. As I zipped down the gravel drive to our home that hid behind the great big pines, I flung open the door and hurdled over a tricycle that was tipped off to the side of the walkway that went to the back door and made that fifty-yard dash to the deck that went off the back of the house. I leaped up the steps and flung open the door to look for my husband, who was in the kitchen, wondering why I was breathing so hard. With a thrill, I proclaimed, "I am going to Hollywood!" His eyes were wide. There was always something, some grand story that seemed almost too hard to believe, so he just sat there waiting for me to continue. "You see, I can be a beacon for God. He is opening the door to Hollywood right now for me to get in, and then I can tell the world about His great love!"

Mark, in all his sobriety and steadfastness, returned, "I don't think that's a good idea! Move us to the city, and we will all surely get caught up in that rat race!" I didn't even hear his words; I was lost in a new world with stages, people clapping, and God shining His glory around me. I was bound and determined to make it work. Just then, a vivid memory bolted into my mind. As I saw my memory pass through,

Memoirs of a Keeper: Angels & Demons

I could see that I was sixteen at the time. I met a man named Bill. He was the high school student that Dad helped run away from home so many years ago before I was even born, probably. He went to chase his dream in Hollywood as an artist. Bill made it into the special effects' makeup side of things, creating monsters that people paid to watch on horror movies. Things my nightmares were made of when I was a child.

Back then, I told him I would go to Hollywood, and he told me that it would be the biggest mistake of my life. I remembered him tell me of the evil things he saw behind the scenes, the immorality and the way the higher-up people acted, the ones who controlled everything, the ones who decided which stars performed in which film. They were the big dogs who had all the power and money. He told me things they made him do to get in the industry. It wasn't always who you know; it was who would do the most for the one at the top, almost like selling your soul to the devil, as he put it. Once they intice you with the challice of fame and fortune, they can get you in compromised situations where they have the goods to blackmail you if you ever decide to leave. They own you and your very soul. Chills ran down my spine as I recalled the things he told me when I was a girl.

Why that memory came into my mind at that moment was challenging for me at the time. I wondered if it was a warning from God, but then again, maybe it was there for me to know, yet God would always protect me. Maybe Bill didn't trust in God, and he went to Hollywood without that protection, so perhaps I had that memory so that I could be a voice for these people who are abused in the industry. I could save them all. God could use me that way. I can't believe today as I look back to that moment, why on earth I just kept going in that direction, that godless path that leads to hell? I was so convinced that there was nothing anyone could say to stop me from falling into that trap. I know now that it would've been the ruin of my soul and my precious family.

God loves me so much that He would do whatever He had to do to get my attention. If I would not listen to my husband, or the man behind the desk, or the memory from Bill, He knew by His great love He would have to sweep His dear daughter right off her literal feet. I had to be stopped in my tracks. He would send another messenger. A tiny one.

My youngest child who was only two years old came tiptoeing

in my direction as I started out that cold January morning. He had the look of horror on his face as he directed, "Mamma! They are going to hurt you!" I held him close and said, "No, they are going to help mama." Maybe he was sent by God to warn me. God spoke through burning bushes and donkeys. The Bible says "out of the mouths of babes", afterall. In one way, I was taking it as a funny little thing that a two year old would say, but in another way it was an eery premonition. It didn't stop me, though, I kept marching into the dark frozen cool of the morning to another destiny which awaited me.

Life changes in a blink of an eye and if we are wise we would listen to the still small voices that God sends our way. God loved me so much that He saved me from myself. And that's just what He did one cold January morning.

But that story is for another book.

Made in the USA
Monee, IL
03 December 2020